The Treasury of American Wines

The Treasury of American Wines

by Nathan Chroman

Photography by J. E. Cakebread and
J. Richard Forbes

Designed by David Boss

A Rutledge-Crown Publishers Book
New York

DEDICATION

For four select clones of the world's finest varieties:
Petites Mamselles Lucie, Gina, and Stacie,
whose dowries have been severely depleted by zealous cellar acquisitiveness,
and *Petite Madame* Judie,
the perfect mate for a glass of wine.

Fred R. Sammis, Publisher
John T. Sammis, Associate Publisher
Doris Townsend, Editor-in-Chief
Allan Mogel, Art Director
Jeanne McClow, Managing Editor
Jeremy Friedlander, Associate Editor
Gwen Evrard, Associate Art Director
Arthur Gubernick, Production Consultant
Annemarie Bosch, Production Manager
Margaret Riemer, Editorial Assistant
Sally Andrews, Editorial Assistant

David Boss, Project Director
Steven Escalante, David Johnston, Design Consultants

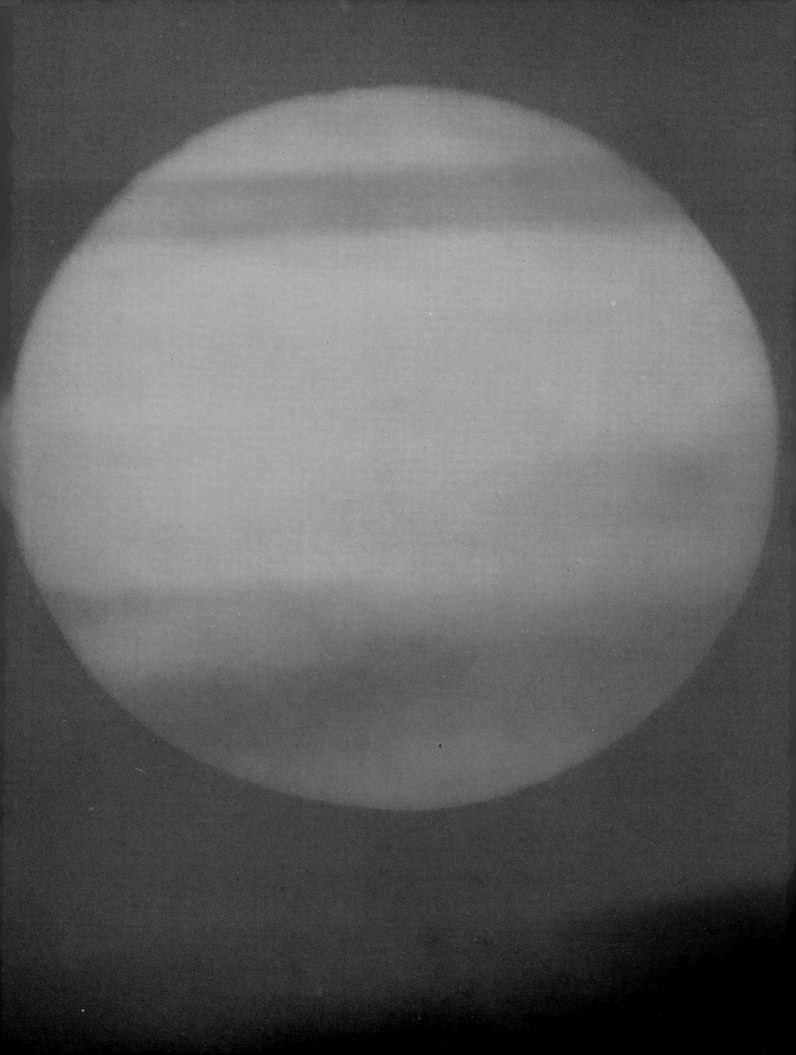

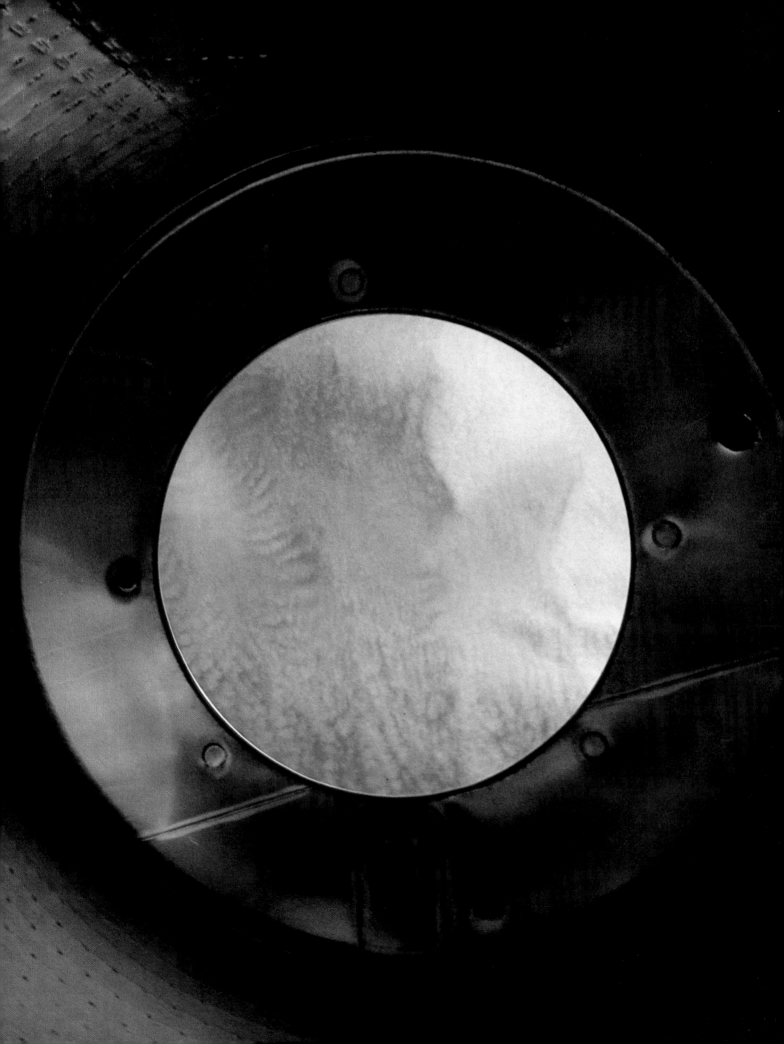

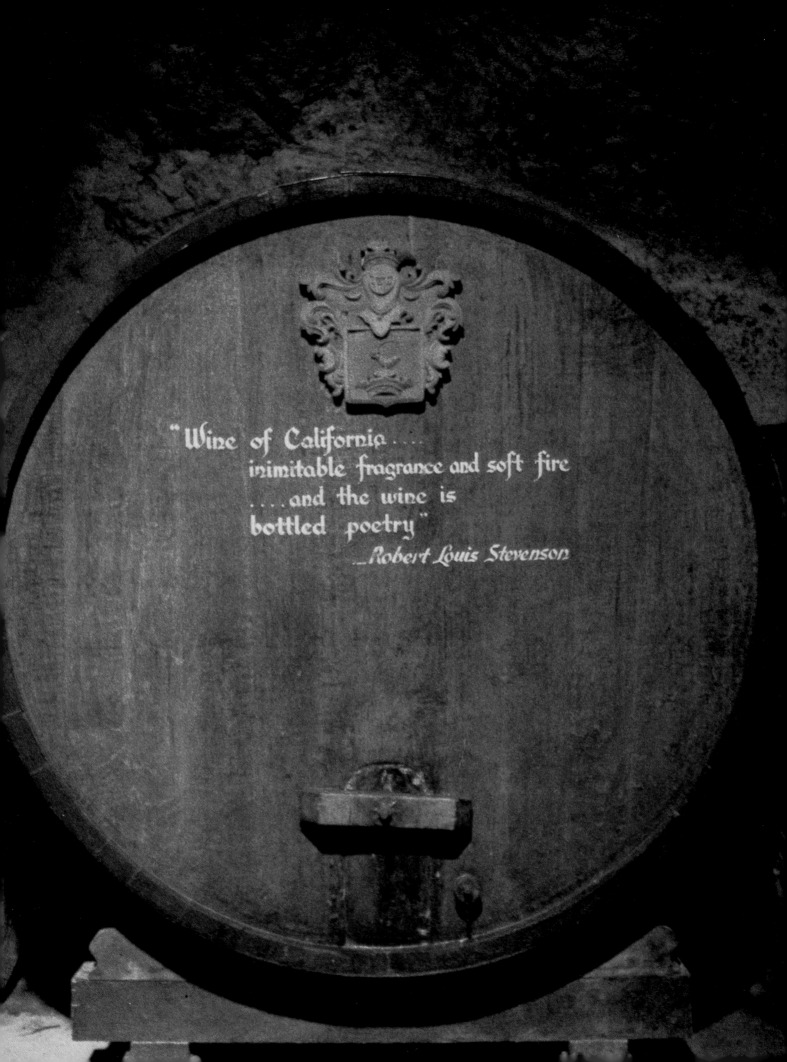

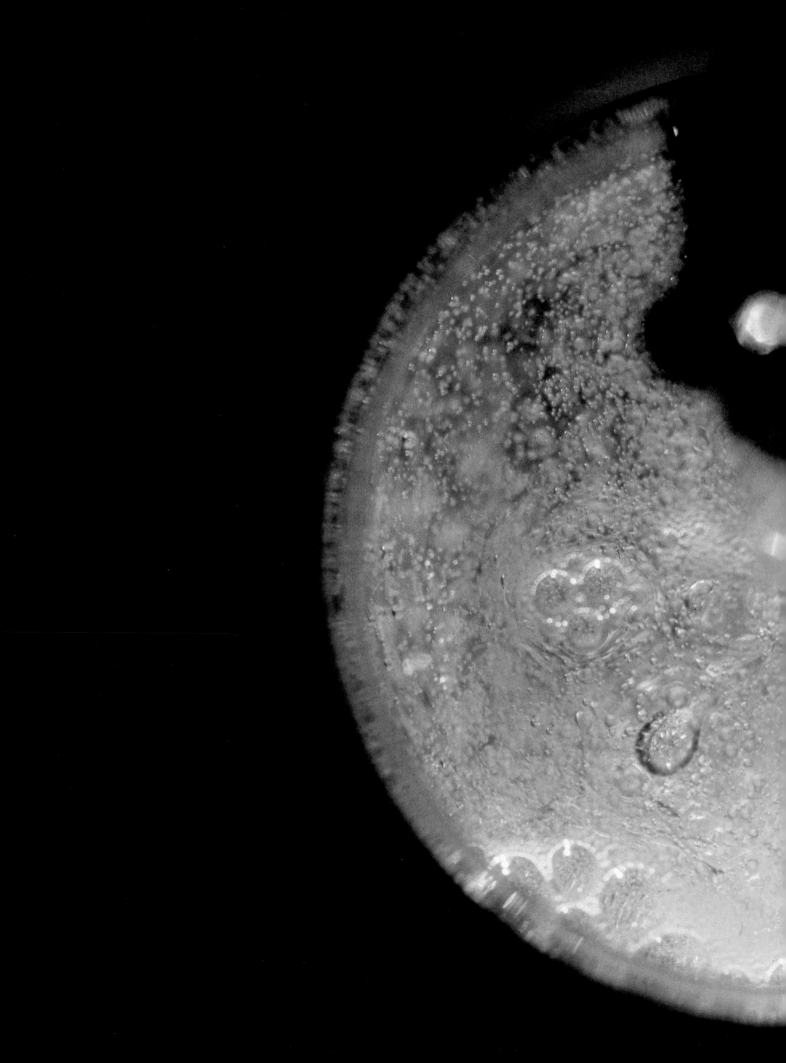

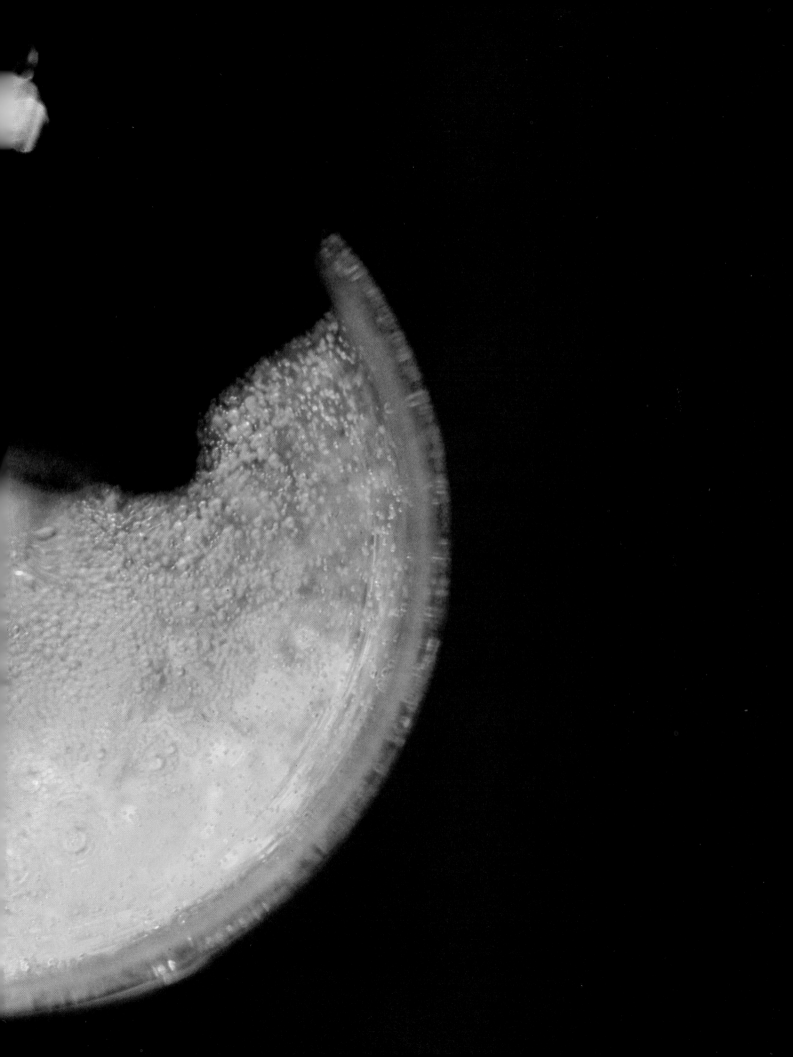

CONTENTS

am a wine drinker. I love wines that have good taste and varietal character, wines that are true to type. I love sound wines, fruity wines, fresh wines, complex wines, wines that have something to say. *In vino veritas*. In wine there is truth. And for me that is it: a wine that is true to type and sound and good to drink.

Principally, I am a wine drinker because I am in love with the soil. When I'm able to relate good taste with the soil, I am drinking wine that has the character of the grape that it purports to represent. Sometimes that is idealism of the highest rank—especially in these days of stainless steel tanks, modernization, blending, bulk production, and rushed marketing.

No words in this book—no words in any book—will give you that ideal. I could spend hours writing about the marvelous virtues of a bottle of, say, Beaulieu's 1947 Private Reserve Cabernet Sauvignon. But all the words and all the descriptions would mean nothing. If you do a book on art, at least you can reproduce a picture on the page. You can say Renoir was a superb artist and show why. But what can you do with wine? Reproduce labels? Declare that the wine was magnificent? I wish there were some way I could transmit at least the smell of the wine onto the page. Then you would have some idea of what I'm talking about.

I teach a class in wine appreciation at UCLA Extension. I tell the students that most wine books are a waste of time. I tell them you can write a wine book but you can't taste one. If you want information about wine growing, about winemaking, there are books that cover those topics very well. But if you are looking for a book about the taste of wine, you won't find very many.

This book doesn't fill that gap. It can only be the roughest sort of guide to what's going on in American wine—past, present, and future. The only way this book can come alive is if you are tasting and testing while you are reading it.

I say this from the reality of my taste experiences. You see, it began for me with a book, too. Once a few years ago when I was studying for the bar, I became restless. I was in the library, and wandering about, I picked up a book about wine. Although it seemed a waste of time, I began to read and …I got hooked. I became infatuated with the grape and I became a wine nut.

I drank a lot of junky wines then. But the experiences, while low level, were not irrelevant. When you learn to drive a car, you don't begin with a Rolls Royce. You start with a jalopy and you work your way up. Then when you get behind the wheel of that Rolls, you'll know that this is a fine car.

The difference in wine is that even when you get to the Rolls Royce—when you taste a bottle of that '47 Beaulieu—you still go back to the jalopy; you still take rides in Fords and Chevies. That is what keeps your spectrum of appreciation alive. I drink a lot of bad wines, a lot of mediocre wines, a lot of average wines. I would get bored drinking the best all the time. And if there's anything I don't like in wine, it's boredom. I like change and excitement.

Every day I learn something more, add some bit of knowledge to my palate. I've been exposed to more wine than most people have, and that serves to give me confidence in my judgment. For the most part I think that if you've done something long enough with interest and enthusiasm, you're going to learn, no matter what it is. The wines are there for the tasting, and there's no reason why you can't become as knowledgeable as I appear to be. The only thing you can't do—unless you are very fortunate—is taste the American wines of the '30s and the '40s. I've been lucky enough to have tasted a range of California wines going back to the 1890s—great thrills indeed, but you'll have to take my word about them.

Spending a great deal of money for a great wine experience is easy—when you've got it. That's not how I like to play the game. For me, the greatest moments are those that do not cost a lot. My goal is to find a superb wine that costs under five dollars a bottle. After I buy the bottle maybe I will put it in my cellar and leave it there for fifteen years. Being a wine drinker requires a lot of patience. One of the great American wine sins is the desire to taste now. A Cabernet Sauvignon may be six years old and of a superb vintage. It is quite good now, but it will be outstanding if it is allowed to age another five years or more. Most Americans don't have the time. We drink it now and never do know what *outstanding* really can mean.

I have not tasted all of the wines in the world, nor have I tasted every wine available in America, although I suspect I may get to that point sometime. What I would like to do in this book is share my tasting meanderings. I do not want to be a critic of wineries but rather of wines. Whether I offer praise or criticism—or a little of both—I want to underline the importance of putting wines in perspective. I have a rating system for wines, not wineries. What you should gain from this book is a working knowledge of what wines wineries are likely to make or

are capable of making. Having gained that knowledge, you will be able to purchase wines that touch greatness.

You are terribly important to the winemaker. You have as much to say about the wine as he does, not only because the winemaker, in the long run, is going to be influenced by us, his critical audience, but because usually the wine is not ready to drink when it is bought. When does it become ready to drink? When you've stored it in the bottle for an adequate period of time. When you've done that, who has completed the wine process? Not the grape grower. Not the winemaker. You have. In that sense you have become the winemaker. It's a special, unique association. You don't finish the painting, you don't finish the movie, you don't finish the book—but you do finish the wine. That day when you sit down with a corkscrew, a glass, and a friend or two, you have a right to be as proud as the winemaker who started the wine process a long time before.

Sharing is important. I wish I could have you here at my table right now so we could open a bottle of wine and discuss it, criticize it, praise it, and search glass by glass for *veritas*. But if you were to sit down with me you would have to want to talk about more than wine. I have always believed that wine should be a part of the human experience and not the experience itself. A bottle is not something to worship but rather something to respect, a launching pad. We have season tickets to the Hollywood Bowl outdoor concerts. We get there at six o'clock and we bring our dinner and our wine. By the time the concert rolls around, we're feeling good and the music's lovely and…well, the evening is perfect.

That's what wine drinking should be. Being a wine snob is just not my style. For me everything turns beautiful with a glass of wine. Maybe it partly has to do with the alcohol, but the sensations and pleasure that come from a really fine bottle of wine are more than that.

It is hard for me to put into words how I feel about wine and its importance to me. It goes back to the soil: it always does. And what other product can do that? Ice cream is manufactured. I never see the baker of the pastries I eat. Kellogg cereals come from a big mill. All Cokes taste alike. I can't easily see anymore where the cattle are raised or where the chickens may come from. Even most of the oranges I eat now come from Arizona or New Mexico or Florida.

With wine it's different. I can know the vintner and I can picture him picking the grape, fermenting the wine, and letting it rest in oak. It's my marriage to him and the soil, and I like that feeling. I know that if you take some grapes from John Doe's winery in the Napa Valley and the same grapes from Jane Doe's winery in Sonoma County, you're going to have two different wines, each reflecting different personalities. These taste differences come glass by glass.

At that point we start sharing. An art lover buys a magnificent painting and puts it in his home, and you may never get to see it. Wine drinkers love to share. I know that when I sit down with a glass of wine there are lots of other people doing that same thing—in the wine country in California, in the wine country in New York, in Bordeaux. A wine lover sitting down at his table after a hard day's work in the vineyards is searching for the same things that I'm looking for —that is, varietal character, body, aroma, flavor, bottle bouquet, and the aftertaste.

When I started getting involved in wines, people thought I was crazy. They told me to stick to law. Wine? Someone who liked wine was a wino, skid-row material. Or a bloody bore. It's different now. Not too long ago I was at a party and the daughter of a friend—a girl about eighteen or nineteen—had just gotten back from Europe. She sat down with me for nearly an hour, and she wanted me to tell her everything I knew about wine.

There are people, too, who come up to me and say, "Why should I drink American wines when I can buy fine European wines?" My answer to them is: Drink whatever you please. I love the fine wines from France and Germany, too. But I tell them why I drink the American wines, why I love them. It's not just because they're good, interesting, artful, made by talented people. It's because they're mine. They are my legacy, my heritage. This is my home, where I grew up, where I live, where I'll die. When they start fooling around with the vineyards in northern California, when they talk about building freeways through the Napa Valley, they're fooling around with me. When an American goes to Europe and does something thoughtless, that reflects on me. When American wines are produced, they're mine. I'm going to enjoy and take pride in them.

Even though I'm writing about wine history and technical aspects of winemaking, what I really am is just a wine consumer. I love food, too, but I don't pretend to be a chef. I'm not sure I want to know how to make bouillabaisse. Oh, I'd like to know some of the constituents of it, but what do I care?

I'm a diner, not a maker. So when it comes to wine, what do I really care about malolactic fermentation? I'm curious about the subject and I get very excited about it when I'm sitting down with the vintner and we're talking wine problems. But what I really care about is the wine, not theoretical enology discussion. One of my big criticisms of some winemakers is that they theorize so much they leave their winemaking in the winery; they never do get it in the glass.

Wine tasting in America is a great thing indeed. This literally is the one place in the world where all wines are offered — French, German, Italian, Portuguese, Spanish, Yugoslavian, Chilean, Australian, South African wines. And our own wines — from the Midwest, Northwest, New York and California.

I am a Californian and the enjoyment of a glass of California wine has instilled in me a chauvinistic attitude of sorts, not necessarily about California but about how the grape performs here. The Cabernet Sauvignon, the Pinot Chardonnay, the Pinot Noir say something in California they do not say anywhere else. And it's not that one country's wines are greater than another's. I don't like comparing wines between regions. The point is that they are deliciously different.

These differences make wine the most interesting and mysterious of beverages. If all wines were to be the same — and this is one of the problems of the bulk wineries — they would offer no taste mystique. But each day of my life I can find wines that offer a different taste, meaning, and origin.

Not all of America's wines are great. Some are great, some are good, some are not. In the lists of best bottles that accompany the wineries in this book, I have attempted to use past performance in a way that may help you in future selection. And since who knows what the future really will bring, it necessarily must serve as a guide, not a classification. The rating goes like this: X is a good, interesting wine; XX is a better quality; XXX is potential greatness; XXXX is greatness (assuming the proper aging process is completed). If I have not rated a bottle even as high as X, it does not mean that the wine is bad. In fact, it may have been good; it's just that others were far better. Time is a precious intangible. I often will say of a wine, "Time and taste will tell." It simply means that I haven't had enough experience with the wine — or, perhaps, the winery — but that after later tastings a perspective will be gained.

Keep in mind that almost any producer can take a particular vintage and, in most cases, produce something superb. It takes the cooperation of nature, but it also takes attitude, skill, time, and sometimes money.

In this book I have tried to give capsule treatment of most of the wineries of America, sketching background, present, and future. Winemaking is at a crossroads today. The wineries can take a number of directions — bulk winemaking with uniform standards, medium-priced winemaking, premium winemaking, and, at the top, the making of wines that are exciting, that have depth and flavor, that can literally bring tears to the wine drinker's eyes. Some day try a California Cabernet Sauvignon that has had the benefit of ten to fifteen years of aging. You will see what I mean.

Nathan Chroman

Nathan Chroman
May 14, 1973

A glass of Ficklin Port displays sturdy "legs" to the contemplative winebibber.

Volente deo post longa itinera ab insula Croenlanda per meridiem ad reliquas extremas partes occidentalis occeani maris iter facientes ad austrum inter glacies biberniam et septiles eustenio socii terram novam uberrimam videlicet vineferam invenerunt quam vinilandia insula appellaverunt henricus Croenlande regionum que finitimarum sede apostolice episcopus legatus in hac terra spaciosa vero et opulentissima in postremo anno pontificatus Pascalis accessit in nomine dei omnipotentis longo tempore mansit estivo et brumali postea versus Croenlandam rediit ad orientem hiemale deinde humillima obediencia superiori voluntate processit.

Groenlada

Vinlanda Insula a Bruno repa et leypho socijs

Mare Occeanum

Magnae Insule Beati Brandani Branzilie dicte

Mare Occeanum

Beata isile fortune

Iardanda Ibernica

Islanda insula
Islannia

Insula terza insula

Desiderate insule

Rex Norucorum

Dacia

Iequa

Bigi

Ipsa

Rex francorum

Vrbo Roma

hispanorum regi

alba

Tunesis reg

Ianora

Bela reg

Rex Ihara

Pha

maiuus

nium

No one is sure where Leif Ericson landed in the summer of the twelfth century. It may have been in New England. It may have been somewhere along the St. Lawrence River. We only know what he found —grapes, in such profusion he called the land he had discovered Vinland. And so the story of America and the vines that were a native part of it began on the same day. The traditions of wines have deep roots in the history of America.

Five centuries later the first colonists found grapes. The vines belonged to the *Vitis labrusca*, a species of grape that still supplies the bulk of winemaking in the East.

The French explorer Champlain discovered more vines and more grapes in the channel of the St. Lawrence. One island was so overrun with vines he named it Bacchus Isle.

In the South, in the Virginia colony, wine was an early commodity. Captain John Smith wrote of the native grapes called muscadines: "They be fatte and the juice thicke. If the vines be well manured they would prove good like our French and British wine."

John Smith may have been speaking for himself with those words, but he did not speak for many of his contemporaries. In truth, the early settlers were unhappy with the quality of wine that they were able to obtain from the native grapes. It might have been different had they been more patient and devoted more attention to the details of what they were doing. Instead, they chose unsuccessfully to attempt to transplant the native vines of Europe, the *Vitis vinifera*.

A detail of the controversial Vinland Map which shows at top, left, the first drawing of North America.

Among the men who tried and failed in this viticultural misdirection were William Penn and Lord Delaware. For the most part, the climate of the Northeast was too rigorous. In one desperate move, the American Captain John Mason actually offered to trade the land that now is the state of New Hampshire for 300 tons of French wine. King Charles II declined.

The American colonial inroads into winemaking were painful and generally unsuccessful, a contrast to the fruition brought to Mexico by the Spanish explorer Cortes. In fact, winemaking in Mexico was so productive it actually had to go underground because the mother country, Spain, feared a serious rival.

Wine was a necessary part of the sacramental ceremony, and as such, the growing of grape and making of wine became the responsibilities of the missionaries and friars. These men obviously knew what they were doing—many years later commercial grape growers planted successfully on the same soils in the same areas.

The heritage brought by the Spanish missionaries was a proud one. Wine came to Spain by way of France in about 600 B.C. The planting was done by the Phoenicians. The Spanish suppressed a commercial explosion in Mexico, but the missions that spread throughout the country brought the vines and grew the grapes.

No one is really sure what happened in Baja California early in the eighteenth century. The first mission there was founded in 1701 by Juan de Ugarte. He grew grapes and made wine, but the origin of the vines

1

CALIFORNIA'S FIRST WINEMAKERS (preceding pages)

The Franciscan missionaries who helped settle California were the state's first winemakers. A sculpture of an early padre creates an occult mood in a shadowy alcove of the Mission San Juan Capistrano.

The missionaries brought more than religion to California; they established a culture that influences Californians even today. Clockwise:

a. An ancient wine press stands in the backyard of Mission San Gabriel, which had the most productive vineyards in the mission chain.
b. The bell tower of Mission San Diego, erected in 1769, was the first of the Alta California missions.
c. Generations of pigeons have made the colorful courtyard at Mission San Juan Capistrano their home.
d. The Mission grape, believed to have been first planted at San Juan Capistrano in 1779, is cultivated even today for many California wines.
e. At Mission Carmel, where Father Serra was buried in 1784, wild California poppies grow in the yard.
f. The signature of Father Junipero Serra, the devoted priest who, at age 56, began the development of the mission chain that eventually extended from San Diego to San Francisco.

remains a riddle. Did Ugarte and the Jesuits bring vine cuttings or seeds with them? Or did they find the vines growing in the Baja, south and west of what today is Ensenada? We do know that wild vines were growing in California then, but it is believed that they were of no appreciable value and not of a type to make good wine.

In any case, from 1701 to 1850, all of the wines made in California came from one grape: the cepa (creola) or Mission grape. It is a grape that is still with us today, although all modern California wines come from the European varieties of *Vitis vinifera*.

The origin of the Mission grape is not as important as its contribution to wine history. It has done very well as a producer of sweet wines, but it has failed as a producer of dry wines. And two centuries ago sweet wine was more practical because of problems of storage, maturation, and bottling.

It was not easy to grow grapes in Baja California. The land was rough and barren, without benefit of much rainfall. Aging cellars were as scarce as rain; the wine frequently oxidized and spoiled.

The missionaries never sold their wine and, according to an eighteenth century Jesuit writer named Clavijero, used it only for Mass, the table, and the sick. The leftovers — if there were any — were used in bartering and as gifts.

Barely fifty years after Father Ugarte's move, there were fifteen missions in the Baja and five of them had vineyards. Most of the grape-growing missions were located in the center of the Baja, near the Gulf of California on the eastern side. In one report of February 12, 1772, five missions had a total wine inventory of just over 1,000 gallons.

The first wine pioneer in Alta California —

the California that was to become a part of the United States—was Father Junipero Serra, a Franciscan who founded a settlement at San Diego in 1769.

Father Serra and his followers moved up and down the California coast, following the El Camino Real (which now is U.S. Highway 101) and establishing missions as far away as Santa Barbara. With the new missions came the vines and the grapes. Although there were no definitive records, it is believed that yearly vintages began in 1784. By 1798, ten missions—Santa Barbara, San Buenaventura, San Gabriel, San Juan Capistrano, and San Diego in southern California; Santa Clara, San Carlos, Soledad, San Antonio, and San Luis Obispo in northern California—were producing wine.

Even though wine culture spread with the missions, there still was dependence on Baja California and Mexico for wine. The vines did not grow as fast in the northern part of California as in the south, not because of the deficiencies of the soil (today's successes prove that) but rather because of a lack of winemaking knowledge. In the early years of the nineteenth century, the dominant wine-producing mission in California was at San Gabriel.

The commercial sale of wine began in 1797, and by 1815 the fixed prices (set by the Spanish governor) were one dollar a quart for brandy and seventy-five cents a bottle for wine in northern California, and seventy-five cents a quart for brandy and fifty cents a bottle for wine in southern California. But the domestic wine industry grew slowly and in 1835 Richard Henry Dana wrote: "The country abounds in grapes yet they buy, at a great price, bad wine made in Boston and brought round by us and retail among themselves at a real [12½ cents] a small wine glass."

Many commercial sources prospered, however. In 1815, a woman named Doña Marcelina Felix Dominguez planted a vine at Montecito near Santa Barbara. That single vine became a national sensation, producing as much as four tons of grapes in favorable seasons. Doña Marcelina lived to be 105. Her vine prospered for 60 years.

The first known wine "critic" was the Santa Barbara mission winemaker, Father Duran, who wrote the following to the California governor in 1833:

The wine at San Luis Rey in my opinion is not the best nor the best suited to place before a friend. I think that there are only two kinds: the red wine and the white wine. The latter, which is used for altar purposes, is rather unpleasant, because it has no sweetness whatever but is very dry. The best wines which I have found in the various missions are those of San Gabriel, where there are two kinds of red wine. One is dry but very good for the table, the other is sweet, resembling the juice pressed from the blackberries and so rather pleasant. There are also two kinds of white wine. One of them is from pure grapes without fermenting. I mean from pure grape juice without fermenting it with the skins of pressed grapes. This produces white wine. The other of the same juice is fermented with a quantity of grape brandy. These two make a most delicious drink for the dessert. The wine from the pure grape juice is for the altar; the other for any use whatever.

In the 1830s, the decline of the mission influence in winemaking and in secular life as well was quite evident. The church's prosperity and influence were in decline. The crushing blow came in 1834, when Mexico, free of Spanish rule, secularized the missions.

As secularization spread, maintenance of the vineyards declined. Some of the vineyards may even have been burned out of anger with the church; others lay in ruin. A period of general decay in California viticulture had begun, and the state looked to commercial interests to take over.

In actuality, large-scale commercial growing in Los Angeles had begun in 1824, when Joseph Chapman planted 4,000 vines. His bid eventually failed, but a while later William Wolfskill created a thriving winery in the Los Angeles area, largely because he relied on the old winemaking methods of the missions. As crude as it sounds, it went like this: Four posts, each 4 feet high, were set in a 2½-foot square. A raw cowhide was fastened over the posts, hair down, with a sag in the middle. The grapes were dumped into the cowhide, and a man would plunge in, feet first, and mash the grapes. The juice from the efforts was then aged two weeks at maximum before being sold as Choice California White. While wine produced by hurry-up methods like that must have been anything but choice, the venture was a commercial success.

A Frenchman from Bordeaux, Jean-Louis Vignes, brought love and caring to California winemaking in the 1830s when he planted a vineyard of 400 acres in Los Angeles called El Aliso. The vineyard was on the site where Union Station stands today.

Vignes had faith in the Mission grape for its brandy potential, but he had more confidence in the grapes of his native land for other wines. Vignes's cuttings from France may have been the first European vines brought into California. Vignes's great experiment worked beyond even his wildest expectations, and his bold moves laid the groundwork for generations to come. When Vignes sold his vineyards in 1851 (he was eighty at the time), he was one of the state's most esteemed wine producers.

With quality up and production high, an expanded market was necessary for the southern California growers. They found that market in the boom town of San Francisco. But as the northern vintners began to produce, the south began to decline in prosperity.

The formidable wine forces in the north were those of John Augustus Sutter (at Sacramento) and Don Mariano Guadalupe Vallejo (at Sonoma). Vallejo, Mexico's military defender of California, had holdings of over 80,000 acres, most in the Sonoma area.

According to the 1850 census, California wine production for the year totaled over 58,000 gallons, with all of it produced in Los Angeles, except for 700 gallons made in Santa Barbara. Those figures, however, are wrong, since it is known that wines were being produced in Sonoma, particularly by General Vallejo, and in Santa Clara and Solano counties.

The mad rush to the gold country beginning in 1849 paralleled a rush to grapes. Wine growers, producers, and opportunists invaded the north of California. It all seemed easy, for there the soil and climate were highly disposed to the grape, and the vines grew easily and well. They called California "the land of the golden grape," and vines

The enigmatic Zinfandel grape, a Vitis vinifera of unknown origins which, apparently, grows only in California.

The Los Angeles winery of Louis Vignes, circa 1835.

were planted helter-skelter up and down the state with much the same fervor as they are being planted today. The motive was usually the same then as it is today—to make the planter rich. The grape boom of the 1850s did just that to a lot of people. In 1857, the California wine industry was grossing $8 million and vineyard land in the Los Angeles area was selling for $1,000 an acre—a substantial figure in those days.

As the wine industry grew, the state began to be classified by particular grape areas. Sweet wines, such as port, came from Los Angeles, while Napa and Sonoma counties produced mostly red and white dry wines, much as they do today. The areas along the Sierra Nevadas and in Sonora and El Dorado counties were known for wines such as sherry and Madeira.

In the 1850s, it was believed that California wines resembled those of Italy. California wines have always been compared to European wines, whether French or Italian, and from many quarters it was suggested—as it is today—that California should strike out and produce its own particular style and type of wine without regard to how it was being made in other places.

By 1860, winemaking was probably the largest industry in Los Angeles, at least rivaling flour. It ranked seventeenth in the state, a remarkable position when you consider the conditions that had existed only twenty-five years earlier. California's vintners were producing wines of quantity but not of exceptional quality. There were dreamers who believed that both were possible, and the outspoken man who led the idealists was a Hungarian named Agoston Haraszthy. He is acknowledged to be the father of modern viticulture in California, and it is, if anything, an understatement. Haraszthy believed that California wines could not only equal European wines but be superior.

Colonel Agoston Haraszthy de Mokesa was born in August, 1812, in Hungary. He supposedly held a number of high political positions in the Austro-Hungarian Empire until his liberal sympathies put him in a hopeless position after the revolution of 1838. He fled to the United States, arriving in New York in 1840 but going on from there to Wisconsin, where he built roads, bridges, and even a town called Haraszthy (Sauk Center today). Haraszthy was a promoter and also attempted to grow grapes in Wisconsin.

In 1849, the Haraszthy family headed for California. Haraszthy did not dig for gold; he planted it. Settling first in the Mission Valley north of San Diego, he began importing vines from Europe. In 1852, he purchased land near San Francisco's Mission Dolores and in San Mateo County. In 1858, he bought the sprawling Buena Vista farm in Sonoma, and for a decade he was the dominant force in the industry.

Haraszthy's land maneuverings gave him the opportunity upon which he capitalized with remarkable intuition. He brought in the *Vitis vinifera* from Europe in large numbers. Among the cuttings that apparently came from Europe was the Zinfandel. Some wine scholars, however, claim that the Zinfandel was native to California and Haraszthy discovered it. In either case, it was not until after 1870 (after Haraszthy had left California) that the Zinfandel was used by more than a few vintners.

Haraszthy was a sensation among California wine producers. According to the Cali-

Colonel Agoston Haraszthy.

fornia State Agricultural Society, by 1858 he had imported over sixty-five varieties. On the eve of the Civil War in 1861, he was at the peak of his prestige. He was appointed by California Governor John Downey to go to Europe to bring back "the choicest, the rarest, and the most profitable vines" he could find in Europe. Haraszthy swept through a number of European countries, visiting France, the Netherlands, Germany, Switzerland, Spain, and Italy. He purchased over 100,000 vines representing over 300 varieties, buying with the assurance that the California legislature would reimburse him for his expenses. The vines were said to be worth at least $30,000, and when Haraszthy returned he submitted a bill for $12,000. However, he had been accused of favoring the Confederate cause, and the California Senate Agricultural Committee, by a vote of 3–2, refused to accept the vines or pay the bills.

Haraszthy was understandably upset. For a year he held the vines, during which time they were not properly classified. When he began to sell them in small lots, the identification was generally unknown. Regardless, Haraszthy's original intent became reality. European grapes displaced the Mission grape in California.

The remarkable Hungarian was not through making contributions. He helped organize the Buena Vista Viticultural Society (later donating his 6,000-acre farm to it) and pointed out that certain fine wine grapes could be grown without the aid of irrigation in some areas. In 1862, he wrote and published an account of his journey to Europe, called *Grape Culture, Wine and Wine Making*. And he won an ally when his sons married General Vallejo's daughters. One of the sons, Arpad, learned to make champagne in France and later successfully introduced it in California.

Agoston Haraszthy never did regain political favor, and when some investments soured, he left California in 1868 to settle in Nicaragua, where he opened a sugar plantation and a distillery. On July 6, 1869, he disappeared and never was seen again. Reportedly, he attempted to cross an alligator-infested stream using the limb of a tree.

Haraszthy left behind a rich legacy in California. He had proved that the wine grower in that state could produce in quantity and quality. And the vines he had selected lived on and prospered.

At one point in the 1860s, there were 10½ million vines growing in California. The business was gigantic, and with the opening of the Union Pacific Railroad in 1869, the state began to export wines to the east coast and even to Europe.

Greed, however, got a temporary upper hand. Wine was mismade and adulterated. In the early 1870s, the wine boom collapsed. Even then California law did not permit any doctoring of wines—no flavoring, no coloring, no sweetening—but many of the winemakers were unwilling to make their wines under the sound principles of their predecessors. Some California wines were marketed as French or German wines. Fortunately, the emphasis shifted to more scientific winemaking and by 1879 the production of California wines totaled seven million gallons.

The greatest threat was yet to come: the vine louse called *Phylloxera vastatrix*, which manifested itself for brief periods in the mid-1860s and in 1874 in the Sonoma Valley.

The lush contours of the Napa Valley, home of many of California's earliest wineries (overleaf).

A very vicious pest, the phylloxera strikes swiftly, attacking at the vine's most vulnerable spot, the root system. The roots decompose and all nourishment to the vine is cut off.

It is likely that the phylloxera was brought to California on vines imported from Europe, most likely by Agoston Haraszthy. The irony, however, is that the phylloxera probably reached Europe in the first place on rootstock from *Vitis labrusca* grown in the eastern United States. It was double irony that the labrusca rootstock later became the lifesaver of most of the world's vineyards when the epidemic reached full force in the 1870s. In 1850, the powdery mildew oidium attacked French vineyards. The *Vitis vinifera* was susceptible but the *Vitis labrusca* was not, and French growers began importing the American vines late in the 1850s.

The phylloxera—an insect less than 1/10 inch in size—is undetectable for long periods, but once its damage is done it is lethal. It was first noticed near Bordeaux in 1868. Two years later Burgundy was overrun and in 1884 most of France had been literally decimated. France was not an isolated casualty. The bug struck Austria-Hungary in 1868, Germany in 1874, Spain and Portugal in 1876, Italy in 1879, and Africa in 1885.

By 1881 the phylloxera had reached crisis proportions in California—in Napa, Solano, Yolo, El Dorado, and Placer.

The cure for the afflicted areas came by transplanting the rootstock of the labrusca, which is tough and hardy and immune to the phylloxera, and grafting vinifera vines to it. The merger of species was successful, and even today most of the wine of the world is produced from vines that have labrusca rootstock.

The American wine industry—and particularly California's—also can be grateful to the University of California, which established the Department of Viticulture and Enology in 1880; at that time, the Board of State Viticultural Commissioners was set up. Eugene Waldemar Hilgard, the first professor of agriculture at the University, was the leader of the grape scholars. Hilgard was among the first to encourage the planting of certain grapes in specific regions. He also counseled in the methodology of wine production and led the battle against phylloxera.

In the 1880s, California winemaking was led by three giants: James Graham Fair, a millionaire United States senator; George Hearst, the publisher of the *San Francisco Examiner;* and Leland Stanford, the railroad baron.

Fair's elaborate operation on the Petaluma River concentrated largely on brandy. In 1894, the year Fair died, his operations produced 300,000 gallons of wine and brandy.

Hearst bought 400 acres in Sonoma County, but his vines were devastated by phylloxera. The misfortune only increased his determination to produce top quality wines; he grafted Médoc and Gironde vines to blight-resistant rootstocks and eventually reached production of 240,000 gallons. When Hearst died in 1891, ownership passed to his son, William Randolph Hearst.

Stanford bought 350 acres near San Jose in 1869 and built a 500,000-gallon capacity winery. Convinced of the virtues of California wine, Stanford expanded his empire in 1881 by acquiring 60,000 acres in the upper Sacramento Valley in Butte and Tehama counties. Even then, the property cost Stanford over $1 million. By 1888, the Stanford vines numbered nearly three million and his around-the-clock winemaking operations were turning out over a million gallons of wine. The climate of the upper Sacramento Valley was not ideal, however, and eventually production decreased and then was concentrated primarily on brandy. The crushing blow, however, came via a man-made circumstance, and it affected all of the American wine industry.

On October 28, 1919, the Eighteenth Amendment to the Constitution was ratified. It prohibited the manufacture, sale, and transportation of intoxicating liquors. For the next fourteen years—until Prohibition was repealed on December 5, 1933—wine production was virtually dormant. A few wineries continued to produce wine in limited quantity for sacramental purposes, and some sold grapes for the making of home wine, which was legal.

Grapes shipped to the East for home production had to have skin thick enough to withstand handling. The better red variety of grapes was thin-skinned and generally faltered under the rigors of shipment. According to Dr. Maynard Amerine, a professorial giant in wine, the most popular grape sold for home winemaking was the Alicante Bouschet. Consequently, most grape growers shifted to the Alicante Bouschet and thus drastically reduced the acreage of good red varietals.

Prohibition also had another damaging effect. Many skilled wine people—vintners and marketers—were forced to leave the business because of economics.

This incredible legislative misdirection caused a whole generation of Americans to forgo wine. It set back the industry for far more than the fourteen years of Prohibition. After repeal, wines that were not ready to drink were rushed to market, and it was not until the late 1930s—two decades after the start of Prohibition—that the vineyards began to right themselves.

In the modern era of winemaking, it is good to reflect on the past—on the toils and trouble that were a part of our ancestry. History often repeats itself, and the mistakes and misdirections of the past can serve as a guide to the future.

Our heritage is rooted in the past. In 1861, Charles Krug, an immigrant from Prussia, bought 800 acres in the Napa Valley. His work lives on today. Buena Vista was Agoston Haraszthy's monument over a century ago, and it still produces wine. The same is true of Schramsberg, founded in 1862 by Jacob Schramm...of Inglenook, founded in 1873...of Beringer, founded in 1877...Cresta Blanca, founded in 1882...Concannon, founded in 1883...Wente Brothers, founded in 1884...Paul Masson, founded in 1892. The list is endless.

The making of wine has come a long way since Father Serra planted those vines at the San Diego Mission in 1769. The industry has grown and prospered. In the mid-1930s, American wine consumption was 30 million gallons; in the late 1960s, the figure was over 200 million gallons.

A long way, yes. There is a still longer way to go.

Grape harvesters on the Hastings ranch near Pasadena, 1898.

A friend of mine whose interest in wine is superficial at best asked me a question not long ago. He wanted to know why Americans are so big on wine. I responded with another question: Why do people drink wine at all? That was my way of avoiding an answer to something I don't know.

I could guess but I really couldn't tell you why we're drinking twenty to thirty times as much wine as we drank three decades ago.

Are we more sophisticated? I doubt it. Peasant farmworkers in Italy and Spain drink wine by the gallon.

Is it a search for a newer, better taste? Perhaps. That sounds as if it has all the potential of being a fad kind of thing, but that hasn't happened in wine. The popularity has grown steadily, and only in the past few years has it shot up drastically.

Perhaps it's the ease with which people travel and, consequently, become exposed to new things. Maybe it's just American affluence. Maybe it's unhappiness with hard liquor. Or young people wanting to make a change from what their parents liked. Or the influence of women who prefer to sit down with their husbands or lovers and have a glass or two of wine and still be able to conduct an affair with them.

It may be all of those things, or a little of each. But I suspect that it's the taste—the special tastes now available in larger quantities to more people.

Until the refinements of the past few decades, it was not always possible to be eloquent about American wines. There were exceptions; in every wine there are exceptions. But a great deal of American wine was inferior, a victim of technological deficiencies and a general lack of knowledge at all levels of the growing process. I have tried some turn-of-the-century vintages, and they have been acceptable, even good and great wines. The quality was far from consistent, however. Prohibition was a stifling retardant to the wine industry, delaying progress of any sort for some twenty years. In fact, the aftereffects of Prohibition remain with us even today.

In an era of American specialization, the wine industry is unique. There are few specialists and many vintners who turn out a couple of dozen varieties of wine. This diversification is incongruous with modern life, but mostly it is a thorn in the flesh of the wine industry in America, particularly in California. Instead of turning out the wine best suited to a particular area, the winemaker has to be concerned with a multitude of varieties.

It all happened after Prohibition. Americans were eager to drink again and wine took time to produce, so hard liquor was dominant. Distributors weren't particularly interested in handling wine. If a distributor did condescend to sell wines, he didn't want to take just one variety. Wineries such as Beaulieu and Inglenook, which could have specialized in nothing but red wines, were selling rosé, champagne, port, and sherry—things they had no business making and still don't. So the wine producers had to have full lines of wines, and once they made that commitment, it was difficult

Most American table wines come in bottle shapes made famous by the great European regions.

2

for them to do anything else. And it still is.

To replant vineyards is a five- to ten-year program at a minimum of $1,000 per acre. If you're going to stay in business, you've got to use what's there. When Donn Chappellet came to Napa Valley and founded his vineyard up in the hills, he made Chenin Blanc. Nobody starts out to make Chenin Blanc if they have an alternative. Why did he also make a Gamay? Cabernet is the thing that sells for big money now. Chappellet made and sold Chenin Blanc and Gamay because they were already on the land and he wanted to get some wines on the market.

In the days after Prohibition, there was an interest in aromatic, sweeter type rosé wines, so there are now a lot of "rosé" grapes. Lots of people like Zinfandel and Sémillon and Sauvignon Blanc and Pinot Blanc. A lot of those plantings are still with us today.

I have the strong feeling that this boom — or whatever it is you want to call it — would have happened much earlier had it not been for Prohibition. It took us a long time to recover from that. Americans being the kind of impatient souls they are, they either couldn't wait for — or didn't have the time for — good wines when Prohibition ended. And even the people who did care for wines either settled for something less than the best or drank the wines of Europe. It wasn't exactly being a wine snob then to say that the only good wines were the imported ones. It is just that to say the same thing today.

In the 1970s, some American wines are things of beauty. It remains to be seen whether they will be joys forever — or for any length of time for that matter. To be a great wine drinker and taster you have to be willing to wait. And, sadly, most Americans are not waiters. A good bottle of Cabernet Sauvignon should not be opened for at least ten years. If you can buy a bottle of wine for four or six or eight dollars — whatever you pay for it — and if you can take that bottle, put it away in your cellar or your rack, leave it there until, say, 1980 and then one night sit down with good company and a fine meal and open it, you will have reached the consummate level of wine drinking. What should you drink in the meanwhile? There are plenty of alternatives that you will find in this book. They are not necessarily going to cost you a lot of money. Because I don't like to spend a lot of money on wine, I naturally assume that most people feel the same way. I hope it stays that way. I want wine drinking to be the right of everyone and not just the privilege of a few. A lot of the wine being drunk is junk — the pop wines, the fruit wines, the wines marketed for specific groups — but much is above average.

Even discerning Europeans are amazed not only at the quality of the very small wineries, but also at the kind of wine being turned out by the bulk wineries — wines like Gallo's Hearty Burgundy and Italian Swiss Colony's Zinfandel. It's not the kind of wine I drink often because I like a wine that offers excitement and intrigue, and these California burgundies are not going to give me that. You buy a bottle of Hearty Burgundy, you know exactly the taste you're going to get — which is fine; nothing wrong with that if that's what you're looking for in your wine. It's this very thing that amazes the Europeans. The table wines they've been used to — their *vins ordinaires* — are not only not that consistent but are quite often not up to that quality. When you consider that Gallo, for example, is a giant in the industry — it may produce almost half of all the wine made in California—that's an accomplishment.

At the same time, it's a source of concern to me. The large-volume producers have lab technicians and scientists, and their goal is a uniformity that will make the product standard and marketable. That standard of uniformity is very good but it's also very ordinary—like a tract house. If everybody lived in tract houses, there wouldn't be any reason for beautiful books on domestic architectural design. If everybody drank wines that tasted alike, there wouldn't be any reason for the existence of a book—or even a conversation—about wine. The soft drink industry in this country has sought good, uniform taste standards. Fine, but there's not a lot of intrigue in finding out whether Coke or Pepsi makes the better product.

I acknowledge that the bulk wineries in this country are turning out some pretty good wines. The bulk wines—the screw-top-bottle kind—are usually quite palatable. In Europe, they still have a lot of spoilage. Here it's pretty tough to buy a bottle of bad wine. You can make it bad yourself by holding it too long, but most of the wine you find on the racks and shelves of stores these days is going to turn out to be quite satisfactory.

In my wine appreciation course at UCLA Extension we explore kinds and types of wines and we come in direct tasting contact with what we are talking about. The experience—good or bad—is shared. You are on your own, of course, when you are reading this book. You will only be able to share some of the experiences if you are tasting and drinking the wine at the same time. Maybe it won't be the same brand from the same year—many of the choice California varietals not only are not available in their native state but are virtually unavailable elsewhere because of limited quantities and antiquated marketing laws. But different years of the same brand often will give you the idea.

Three of every four bottles of American wine produced today come from California. To understand American wine, then, it is mandatory to understand California wine—what it is, where it is being grown, who is growing it, how the wine comes alive, how it finally reaches you, and last—but definitely not least—how you, the wine taster and wine drinker, complete the final step of the process, bottle aging.

The vineyards of California have been placed in a regional classification system that is based on the amount of heat received during the growing season. The five regions as plotted by Drs. Winkler and Amerine of the University of California's Davis campus are primarily a guide for the grower, the enologist, and the viticulturalist, but they also provide you with a foundation knowledge of the California landscape. Full descriptions of the regions and their locations are displayed on pages 38-39.

To give you an idea what these regions mean in their general relations to the grape, it is wise to examine some of the prime California varietals.

The Chardonnay grape is recommended as excellent for Region I, and good for Regions II and III. It is not recommended for Regions IV and V.

The Cabernet Sauvignon grape is recommended as excellent for Regions I and II, good for Regions III and IV, and possible in Region V.

THE FIVE WINE GROWING REGIONS OF CALIFORNIA

Region I is the coolest area. Typical vineyards in this zone lie in parts of Mendocino, Napa, and Sonoma counties, the mountain areas north of Santa Clara County, part of Santa Cruz County, and Mission San Jose in Alameda County. San Juan Bautista in San Benito County and Gonzalez in Monterey County also are in this climatic zone.

Region II, the most important table wine region, comprises the major portions of the Napa and Santa Clara valleys and includes warmer areas in Napa, Santa Clara, San Benito, and Monterey counties.

Region III is moderately warm and covers the southern portion of Mendocino County, the warmest areas in Napa and Sonoma counties, the Livermore Valley, King City in Monterey County, Templeton in San Luis Obispo County, and Alpine in San Diego County.

Region IV takes in the central part of the Sacramento–San Joaquin Valley, from Livingston in Merced County to Davis in Yolo County, Cordelia in Solano County, the Cucamonga region in San Bernardino County, and Escondido in San Diego County.

Region V, the warmest district, includes the San Joaquin Valley, from Merced south and the region north of Sacramento.

Zinfandel, which is grown just about everywhere in the state, is recommended as good in Regions I and II, standard in Region III, and possible in Region IV. It is not recommended in Region V.

White Riesling is rated excellent in Region I and good in Region II; it is not recommended in the other three regions.

These are four examples and if they are rules, they are not hard and fast ones. Certainly you can occasionally find a good bottle of a particular varietal that has come from a nonrecommended area. And there are times when you might find a poor varietal from an area listed as excellent or good. Much depends on the winemaker, the grapes, the care, the skill—and luck.

One of the problems in judging solely by region is that many wineries today are given to blending. Consequently a wine may have a combination of grapes from Region I and II, or a winery in Region II may be the beneficiary of new plantings from a district in Region III, IV, or V.

In general, the table wines come from the cooler areas, and the dessert and aperitif wines come from the warmer areas.

Californians pride themselves on their weather, but the French and the Germans claim that is a weakness. They say it's important for a grape, for a vine, to suffer—to struggle through a snowstorm, for instance. I happen to think that's not necessarily true, although there's no question that weather is a prime factor in the vintage of the grape.

The California Wine Institute, an organization of immense assistance to California wine producers, likes to declare in its bounding enthusiasm, "Every year is a vintage year in California," but it is a simple fact that some years are better than others. Some years there is too much sun, some years not enough. Obviously our weather here is not as unpredictable as it is in parts of Germany and France, but it is variable enough. One of the big differences between the wines of France and the wines of California is that the French don't get enough sun and the Californians get too much. Too much sun will produce too little acid and too much sugar. It is a delicate matter of timing to know when grapes should be harvested. Extra days on the vines may taint a wine.

That very thing happened in much of the Napa and Sonoma valleys in 1972. There was so much sun that the grapes literally got burned. The growers in those areas suffered heavy losses, particularly in Zinfandel, Chardonnay, and Cabernet, the latter two being California's most expensive grapes.

The French worry about cold weather and the snow and sleet it brings. So do the growers in New York and other eastern vineyards. In California, the weather problem is quite the opposite.

There are five basic types of wines —red, white, rosé, sparkling, and dessert and aperitif wines (fruit wine is, to my mind, an oddball type that is only by the loosest of definitions a wine). In the appendices of this book you will find the Wine Institute's official descriptions of the qualities of the various wines. The descriptions are general, intended primarily as an aide to judges in competitions such as the Los Angeles County Fair.

The wine drinker's basic knowledge should begin with a basic understanding of the types of wines and the varietals classified under them. Consider the following, then, a beginner's course in varietals.

California Red Table Wines

Cabernet Sauvignon This is the premier wine of California, the Cadillac of the industry. It's a deep, rich red wine with an expansive bouquet and a flavor like no other wine's. In my opinion, the best Cabernet Sauvignons in California come from the Napa Valley. The Santa Clara Valley produces some nice Cabernets, too. The grapes those areas produce are quite distinctive. In taste they might be cousins, or even brothers, but there is a difference, believe me, and when you have tasted a number of Cabernets from different areas, you will know what I mean. In France, the Cabernet Sauvignon grape, which is also known as claret, is found in the Bordeaux region.

Zinfandel The origins of this grape are mysterious, but they seem to trace to Agoston Haraszthy, the Hungarian who apparently either brought it to California when he imported cuttings and rootstocks more than a century ago or discovered it growing as a native vine. In any case, the Zinfandel is a wine that is most often taken for granted when it should be given much more attention. The longer you hold a Zinfandel, for example, the closer in taste it will get to a good Cabernet Sauvignon. Eventually, there is a point at which it is hard to tell them apart. When young, the Zinfandel has a very fruity taste, almost like raspberries; and unlike the Cabernet Sauvignon, the Zinfandel can be drunk young. Zinfandels are generally underrated, and because they are, one can get excellent buys on superb wines.

Pinot Noir The red burgundies of France are made from this grape, which produces a wine light in color and usually soft and smooth to taste. Some excellent Pinot Noirs have been produced in California, but so have a great many middle-range Pinot Noirs. It is not an easy wine to produce in big quantities, and it usually requires a great deal of attention. If you want a good Pinot Noir, be prepared to pay a good price for it.

Gamay Beaujolais This is a red wine that is meant to be drunk young. A spin-off of the beaujolais wines of France, the California varieties are rich in fruity taste. The Napa County product usually is labeled only Gamay; wines produced elsewhere in California are generally labeled Gamay Beaujolais. In any case, it is a pleasant, uncomplicated, inexpensive table wine.

Ruby Cabernet A hybrid of the Cabernet Sauvignon and Carignane grapes, this is one of the newest wines produced in California. The idea was to find a grape that provides all of the potential of a Cabernet Sauvignon and the productivity of a grape such as the Carignane. Some wineries have been quite successful with this grape and claim to have produced better Ruby Cabernets than Cabernet Sauvignons. Frankly, I haven't found any great Ruby Cabernet to match a great Cabernet Sauvignon, but this is not to say that the Ruby Cabernet is an inferior wine. It is quite a good one, in fact.

Petite Sirah This is another overlooked wine and one you should start noticing. A grape that is grown in the Rhone Valley of France, it produces a big wine in California —one full of flavor and zest. I am partial to big wines, and as I have said, I don't take delight in spending money on wine. If you have a Cabernet Sauvignon taste but not the budget for it, drink Zinfandels and Petite Sirahs. You won't be disappointed.

Barbera This is a native of Italy that has done quite well in California. Again, it's a big wine with high acid and lots of flavor, and like the Petite Sirah, it thrives in Sonoma and Alameda counties. It is a wine that fits well with American-style Italian dishes.

Grignolino Light in color, it is almost a rosé. The Grignolino is another Italian native — very fruity, almost like strawberries — that is a good, pleasant, light wine. Like the Barbera, it's a nice complement to pasta.

California Generic Reds I'll have more to say about these later — for one thing, I'd like us to develop our own generic names — but most of these wines fall into three categories: burgundy, claret, and chianti. Varietal wines must contain a minimum of 51 percent of the name they claim to be; generic wines have no such restrictions. That doesn't mean that they're bad wines necessarily; it just means that you really don't know what you're getting in many cases. And chances are some blenders may be unable to tell you just what they did put together to make their burgundy.

California White Table Wines

Chardonnay The white burgundies of France are the equivalent of this, but they're not, really, because to me this is a very special California wine. I don't like to compare California to France or to anywhere, really. Each wine is unique and deserves to be judged on its own merits. It used to be that you could buy a very nice bottle of Chardonnay for two dollars; the French equivalent was twice as much or more. Now there isn't a significant price difference between the two. The reason for buying Chardonnay from California should be that it is a wonderful, distinguished wine — full bodied and strong in character. Napa Valley Chardonnay is especially good. For me, the standard of the best is the wines produced by Stony Hill and Joseph Heitz. Those are now being challenged by Mayacamas, Freemark Abbey, and Mondavi.

Sauvignon Blanc In France, the Sauvignon Blanc is used in making sauternes and some Loire wines such as Pouilly-Fumé. In California, it produces a nice, full-bodied wine, ranging from dry to sweet. Concannon's Sauvignon Blanc is a good example of the grape at its best.

Sémillon An exciting grape that also is used in the production of sauternes in France. Golden in color, it has many of the same characteristics as the Sauvignon Blanc and thrives in the same places — the Livermore Valley, as well as Napa and Santa Clara counties.

Pinot Blanc Like the Chardonnay, this is a white burgundy grape. Unlike the Chardonnay, which should be held, the Pinot Blanc should be drunk relatively young to take advantage of its freshness and flavor.

Chenin Blanc This wine is occasionally labeled White Pinot; one of the best-known French wines made from it is Vouvray. Chenin Blanc has done well in California — particularly in Napa County — resulting in a wine that is sometimes dry, as is Chappellet, while Charles Krug has a sweeter version.

Johannisberg (White) Riesling The rhine wines of Germany generally come from the White Riesling grape. This is a refreshing wine, fruity and satisfying but not terribly complex. The Napa Valley — and Souverain and Heitz in particular — has turned out some pleasing Johannisberg (White) Rieslings.

Emerald Riesling This is a cross between the Johannisberg Riesling and the Muscadelle. One of the newest varietals, it is a pleasant wine, fresh and pleasantly sweet in taste. Paul Masson's is a good example.

Fully ripened clusters of Cabernet Sauvignon await harvest.

The Chardonnay grape, split upon a redwood stake.

Traminer or Gewürztraminer Another kind of rhine wine, the Traminer is aromatic and spicy. In Europe the Traminer is grown in the areas where France and Germany come together; in California, it is grown well in Napa, Santa Clara, and Sonoma counties.

Flora This is one of the newest California varietals, a cross between the Traminer and Sémillon grapes. The wine has a great deal of potential, but since it has been around for barely ten years, it is early to make a decision about its overall quality. Schramsberg's Cremant is a most interesting example of what can be done with this grape.

Grey Riesling Another wine unrelated to the Riesling family, it is soft and quite mild. Livermore Valley Rieslings are among the best produced in the state. The true name is Chauce' Gris.

Sylvaner In many parts of Germany, it is known as the Franken Riesling and there are occasions in California when it is known as that or simply Riesling. Drunk fresh, the Sylvaner can be quite a pleasant wine.

California Generic Whites As with red generic wines, the California whites have retained the names of France—chablis and sauterne. There is some pretty good sweet sauterne produced and some quite good chablis, too. Because their names are mostly so general, they qualify as nothing but white wines. Instead of buying a bottle of "chablis," I'd prefer to be able to buy a bottle of "Napa Valley White." Such names would seem alien at first, but in the long run they would make the California generics more personal.

California Rosé Table Wines

Grenache Rosé The Grenache thrives best in the coolest of the growing areas, producing a wine that is both dry and semisweet.

Other Varietal and Generic Rosés Other rosé wines are produced from grapes ranging from Gamay Beaujolais to Cabernet Sauvignon to Zinfandel to Grignolino. Each has its own distinctive qualities. Generic rosé may be a combination of any of the other varietals. Some generic rosé is a combination of red and white wines.

California Sparkling Wines

Champagne California champagne is a generic wine, produced from varietal grapes such as the Pinot Noir, Chardonnay, Sémillon, Sylvaner, Chenin Blanc, and White Riesling. Champagnes, consequently, can have a variety of tastes, and it is up to you to find the kind and type (champagnes also range from very dry to very sweet). A lot of good champagne is made in California, and among the best is that made by Schramsberg. Just ask the Red Chinese, to whom President Nixon served it on his visit to China in 1972. Schramsberg's champagnes are made in limited quantity and not only are difficult to obtain but may be too expensive for some.

Other Sparkling Wines There are all sorts of novelty wines that fall into this category, the most prominent, I suppose, being the variety called Cold Duck. I'm told that Cold Duck is declining in popularity after a big boom on it, and as far as I'm concerned it's just as well. To me, Cold Duck is not much more than a flavored drink, a sparkling wine made out of anything the vintner happened to have around. Its name comes from the German *Kalte Ente*—"cold duck" literally, but slang for "hoax." It was a term the waiters made up for the concoction they would have at the end of the day, when they would take all the leftover wines, dump them together, and drink the mix with their snacks.

California Aperitif and Dessert Wines

Sherry All California sherries are generic blends. Most sherries come from the inland valleys—the San Joaquin is a big producer—and the southern region. Some good sherries are being produced, and I have the feeling they're going to get better and more consistent. One of the best recent varieties I've tried was from Eastside's Royal Host.

Port Like sherry, port is basically a generic wine in California. And like sherry, it comes from the same inland and southern regions, the finest coming from Ficklin. Many California ports are sweet and rich, the perfect dessert complement, but others are bland and neutral.

I t is important to know the wine label and understand the words and terms it contains. Often those are your only clues to selection—that and your prior knowledge of the vintner and the wine he has made. Varietal labeling has literally put California on the international wine drinkers' map. Varietal labeling means that when a bottle says "Pinot Noir" or "Chardonnay" on the label, the wine you are buying is composed of at least 51 percent of that grape. Of course no one is standing there looking over the winemaker's shoulder—although there may be inspectors who look in periodically. So it all comes down to the wine drinker. It's up to him—to you and me—to keep the winemaker in line, to make sure he's making wines that are true to type and true to character. And that simply means that a wine labeled "Pinot Noir" should have all the characteristics of a Pinot Noir—aroma, taste, everything. If you're saying you're not qualified to determine that, you may be right; it takes a little practice—more than a few tastings—to recognize what differences are there. But that is part of learning about wine.

Properly read, the label can contain important clues, but sometimes the very nature of the wine name on the label is the worst clue of all. In the same way that a varietal label means "what you see is what you get," a generic label means...well, nothing. I am against the continued use—and misuse—of the names of Europe as wine descriptions. Names such as burgundy, chablis, sauterne, and champagne have been used for more than a century principally because European immigrants who made wine in the style of their homeland probably couldn't think of any other names for their wines. The words have been used for so long now they are considered generic terms not only by California producers but also by Australians, Chileans, and others.

The persistence in the use of generic names merely tends to confuse the public. In the end, they become meaningless descriptions, since each one is made differently, in a different style, to a different taste. Give a Frenchman some wine labeled as California burgundy, and he doubtless will wonder just what it is. Taste three different California wines labeled burgundy, and it is more than likely that you will have trouble relating them to the same family of wine. I acknowledge that it will be difficult to eliminate generic names such as champagne, sherry, and port, since these names provide the consumer with instant knowledge about the type of wine. But an attempt should be made to change these, too. Champagne could be "Sparkling Napa Valley White" or "Sparkling Cucamonga Red" and sherries and ports could be given the proprietary names of particular vineyards and listed as dessert or aperitif wines.

A variety of wine glassware, some filled with pourings of California red and white generics, creates an attractive cluster (overleaf).

In actuality, you have to be your own best consumer protection. Since the only requirement of a burgundy and a chablis is that they be red and white wines respectively, there is nothing to stop the unscrupulous producer from calling wines coming from the same vat burgundy and claret. That kind of producer does not want you to become a discriminating wine drinker, of course, because with education and experience you will learn to pass him by when you are making wine selections.

I think that labels should tell stories, maybe even right down to the plot of ground the grape came from, when it was picked, how long the fermentation lasted, what were the sugar and acid counts. There are some labels in California today that give you that information. To me, knowing all of those things is a plus; they add to my enjoyment. I don't say you have to get involved to any' degree; I just say you should be involved because the making of wine is one of the few things left where we can demand integrity, where we can trace the steps. Frankly, if you don't care at all, then I'd suggest you forget wine and drink liquor and beer.

There are many ways besides varietal labeling, however, in which the labeling system does provide some protection for the consumer. When "Estate Bottled" appears on the label, it means that at least 95 percent of the wine must be made from grapes grown in the winery's own vineyards and made on the winery's own premises (adjacent to the vineyards). The law originally intended that in order to qualify for Estate Bottling the vineyards must be visible from the winery. (In these days of large holdings, however,

this "visibility" may be strained considerably, and wine can qualify even though the grapes are grown many miles away. Grapes that are purchased under long term contract also fall into this classification.) The label of Stony Hill, a small producer of excellent Chardonnay, reads, "Grown, produced and bottled by..." Many smaller wineries today are resorting to label language that refers to Estate Bottling in the classic sense, indicating that 100 percent of the grapes used to make the wine were grown on property immediately adjacent to the winery and then crushed, fermented, and bottled by the proprietor. Wine made from a variety of grapes raised by a winery in different areas would not qualify as Estate Bottled.

If a wine is labeled "Produced and bottled by," at least 75 percent of the wine has been crushed and fermented by the winery whose name appears on the label. (All wine—100 percent—made in California must come from California grapes; in New York the requirement is 75 percent.)

If the label says "Made and bottled by," the requirement is that at least 10 percent of the wine has been made by the winery. The balance may have been made from grapes or wines purchased elsewhere, then finished by the winery whose name appears on the label.

There are a number of other label descriptions: "Cellared and bottled by," "Bottled by," "Perfected and bottled by." These may identify wines from other producers that are finished and bottled by the winery named.

As you might expect, Estate Bottlings, classic or otherwise, seem to carry wines most true to type. This is not to say that good bottlings—even superior bottlings, on occasion—cannot be found that are not Estate Bottled. There are a lot of exceptions; I drink them often. More often I get what I expect—and get an exciting, interesting wine—when I buy one that is Estate Bottled.

The sad fact is, however, that as some producers get bigger and as they make more money and more people buy their wine, they are just not going to care about things like Estate Bottlings. We are still getting great Estate Bottlings from the small vintners, but most of the giants of the industry are ignoring it, or perhaps can't cope with it.

The same thing is true of vintage dating, which means that a date is put on a bottle, and all—or almost all—the wine in it must have been produced in that year. Vintage dated has generally meant that a wine comes from grapes grown and crushed that year. This may vary to some degree, but at least 95 percent of the wine must be made from grapes grown and crushed in the stipulated vintage year. Further, vintage dating has to do not only with the grapes of one year but also with the grapes of one area. (However, if the producer is responsible for all of the processes—the growing, the transporting, the making of the wine—even though he does these in different areas, he still can give the wine a vintage. But if the completed wine is taken somewhere else to age or finish and then bottled under a different name, it may not rate a vintage date.)

Thus another thing to look for on the California wine label is the geographical designation, such as Napa Valley or Santa Clara Valley. This is a guarantee that at least 75 percent of the grapes in the wine were grown and fermented in that area. The other 25 percent can come from elsewhere in California. All these rules and restrictions are designed to protect the term "vintage" for the consumer of California wines. Vintage-dated wine is like a history of the winery. If I know the wine in general and maybe the winemaker, too, then it is a part of my taste history.

A very exciting thing happened to me recently. I participated in a vertical tasting of Beaulieu Private Reserve Cabernet Sauvignon at Scandia Restaurant in Los Angeles. A vertical tasting means a tasting of wines of different years in the order of their production. The Beaulieu wines tasted began with the 1939 vintage and went until the early 1960s. It was a momentous event and we invited the Beaulieu winemaker, Andre Tchelistcheff, to tell us why each of them tasted the way it did—how the weather had been too hot, too cold, how the fermentation went. We just sat back and listened, and it was fascinating. It was like reading a biography of the winery, what they'd been doing for thirty years—'39 was good, '41 was great, '42 was greater, '47 was simply marvelous...and on and on.

The sad fact is that the experience—the vertical tasting of California wines—is almost impossible to duplicate. For the most part, you just can't find old vintage-dated California wines. And a lot of our wines aren't dated—we don't know when the grapes were grown or when the wine was made.

Do not mistake vintage dating for a sign of quality. It is not. Vintage dating is merely an identification; the wine inside the bottle holds the quality answer. Just because one year happens to be a particularly good year with one vintner is no guarantee that other vintners in the area should also have good wine. There can be climate variations within a small area, and since the individual producer controls the actual date of the harvest, he also controls the final condition of the grapes.

Thus it is essential to consider (1) the year, (2) the area, (3) the actual vineyard, if possible, and (4) the producer when you are selecting wine. The vintage date alone is helpful but it should be only one of the considerations. The general rule is that in every vintage there is some good wine and some poor wine. In every poor vintage year there may be some good wine. In every great vintage year there may also be some poor wine. Finding the best is not always easy because there simply are no guarantees.

One year at the Los Angeles County Fair we happened to have two bottles of Zinfandel — same brand name — from a famous volume winery. After judging them, I took both bottles, put a bag around each, and served the wine to the judges, asking them which one they preferred. I had marked them A and B. They loved A, thought it was wonderful, and they hated B. After they had made their judgment, I removed the bags and revealed the identical labels. It was no reflection on the judges. The fact is, the two bottles contained different wine, probably from grapes from different areas. When you produce in large quantities, it's inevitable that sooner or later your quality level is going to change.

My distress over the lack of consistency in that particular wine may sound like a contradiction of what I've said earlier about uniformity making for an ordinary product. It's not. There's no excitement in discovering that a wine you thought would be good is bad; there is excitement when you taste good wines from different places and different soils, each with its own characteristics. That is the mystique that makes wine so fascinating.

California laws also control additives to the wine during the wine-making process: "...grape wine produced in the State of California must be the produce of the normal alcoholic fermentation of the juice of sound, ripe grapes or grape products...without any other addition or subtraction whatsoever except as such as may occur in normal cellar treatment...provided further that no sugar or material containing sugar other than pure condensed grape musts and no water in excess of minimum amount necessary to facilitate normal fermentation may be used in the production or cellar treatment of any grape wine in the State of California."

The addition of sugar is permitted in France, and the addition of water is allowed in New York. The only major additive permitted in California is brandy, which gives the wine some extra body and alcohol. This doesn't have to be done often in California because usually the problem, if any, is too much sun (and enough body). The prohibition of additives other than brandy from California wines means the character of the product can't change.

It is a preoccupation of the beginning wine drinker in this country to want to know just what to stock in his new cellar. He wants to be an instant connoisseur, but, my friend, it just doesn't work that way. You can go through this book and make yourself an extraordinary list of wines from those I have mentioned. You can then search out those wines and put together a pretty fab-

Three fine vintages of Beaulieu are sampled at a private tasting at the winery.

ulous collection. But if you haven't a solid foundation in wine appreciation, you will have nothing. Could a primitive man—a man not familiar with great artists—be brought out of the wilderness and instantly appreciate a Picasso?

My advice to a beginner is to drink a lot of standard stuff. Start with Gamay Beaujolais and Petite Sirahs, not necessarily Cabernet Sauvignons and Pinot Noirs. Drink a lot of Gallo and Italian Swiss Colony, a lot of Red Mountain. Try some CK wines from Charles Krug and some lesser, lower-priced Louis Martinis. Lay a foundation, begin to train your palate to look for distinctions of taste and quality, and look for varietal character. Does it taste like Gamay Beaujolais or like something else? Like what? Is it a true Cabernet Sauvignon? Taste. Believe me, you will find out.

It is vital not to become "label conscious." Rather, be "wine conscious." The whole marketing theory is geared to make the middle range of American consumers label conscious. The people at some large California wineries want you to walk into a store, walk up to their shelf area, and take a bottle of their wine—because it must be good, it's ours, isn't it? Well, it may be good indeed, but that's not the point. I'd like a buyer to walk into a store in search of a bottle of good Chardonnay, not a brand. That's true discrimination in wine buying.

Some day I'd like to see a winery picketed —not by Cesar Chavez but by a consumer saying, "You've taken all the character out of your cabernet." I'd like to see a relationship between the grower, the winemaker, and the consumer—one in which the consumer actually writes a letter to the winemaker or to the grower that says, "I

thought your wine was great," or "I thought your wine was terrible." Maybe when we get more of that we'll have more of an understanding of what it takes to look for, what it takes to buy.

I don't have any trouble, frankly, sitting down with the French growers and winemakers and telling them their wine was awful. The French seem to be big enough to survive those things. But in America some producers take criticism personally, maybe because they're newer and consequently less confident in what they're doing. They shouldn't be less confident, though. We should always be big enough to admit our mistakes and, at the same time, cope with our successes.

The important thing to remember is that we as consumers actually dictate the style of the wine. Many winemakers will take advantage of what is in style at the moment. At the moment the style is fast wine—get it out, buy it, drink it.

A good French example of this is the wines of Burgundy. The makers of burgundy, when necessary, add sugar to their wine to give it more body and more alcohol; in the United States, chaptalization may appear necessary at times but is not a frequent practice. Chaptalization may be a useful tool—I'll grant that—but it's tampering with my wine in a way I don't like.

There are a number of different ways to make Chardonnay—with a lot of the fruit showing or a lot of oak in the taste and aroma or a little of both. In red wines, a large share of American wine drinkers prefer a wine that's soft, mellow, and even slightly sweet. Some winemakers are catering to that but it's not my style at all. I prefer a big, gutsy wine, a wine that has gusto. I don't like little, flimsy wines; some people call them elegant; I call them thin.

Mostly, I am discouraged by this growing impatience—of the wine drinker who cannot be satisfied, who wants it now, and of the winemaker who answers the need and gives it to him now. In 1972, at least one California winemaker harvested his Beaujolais grapes in late October and had them in a bottle in November and in the marketplace shortly after that. It was an interesting American wine experiment. It's like drinking good apple cider—drinking to quench your thirst—and it can be quite pleasant. Don't misunderstand me. I don't think all fast wines are bad. And I'm not ever about to condemn a man because of his taste. It's just that I don't want this enthusiasm for "now" wines to overrun an appreciation for great wines. Maybe the same fellow who will drink a bottle of wine that was put together in just a few weeks is also capable of buying a great bottle of Cabernet Sauvignon and holding it until 1980. I hope so.

Ask me what the rules are on holding wine, and I'll have to tell you that there are none—or rather that there are guidelines but nothing more than that.

As a rule, most white wines will not last more than five years. The exceptions are Chardonnays (and white burgundies), which generally can be held up to ten years.

Among red wines, Gamays don't age very well. Pinot Noirs can be held for a long time but not as long as fine Cabernet Sauvignon, which almost always should be put on a shelf for at least ten years. Zinfandel is a versatile wine. You can drink it early if you like fruit in your wine. If you like a more complex wine, hold it. If it is a good Zinfandel, it may become difficult in years to distinguish it from the Cabernet Sauvignon produced in the same year. I suspect this same thing may also be true with Ruby Cabernet, although no one knows for sure at this stage because we haven't got any old vintages, and I don't know if we ever will because it's not the style of wine people usually save.

You'll have to discover for yourself the precise moment a wine is ready to drink. There is no shortcut, no way of finding out other than opening the bottle at the preferred time and tasting the product. If it is bad, good, or somewhere in between, well, you will have learned something about the next bottle. You will have educated your palate.

Tasting a wine really comes to four things: (1) you can hold the glass up and examine the color; (2) you can smell the wine, important because smell tends to be the most informative sense; (3) you can taste the flavor in your mouth and spit it out; or (4) you can swallow it and judge the aftertaste. A wine that is really a great wine speaks to you for a long period of time after it has gone down. It literally lingers in your mouth.

To check color of wine, you should hold it to the light. The color should be pleasant, true to its character, and free of foreign particles. Color is very important to the overall pleasure of the wine. The rich full red of an exceptional Cabernet Sauvignon, for example, will be apparent when compared to weak, thin Cabernet Sauvignon.

For smell, the taster should literally push his nose all the way into the glass after swirling it a bit to release the bouquet. It is a good idea to smell the wine immediately after it is poured, then again in a few minutes. The smell of some wines changes in a few minutes. Some dissipate quickly, others need air to develop.

The correct method of tasting is to swirl the wine in the glass and then to draw it into the mouth. It should be sucked into the mouth with a little air. Is the taste agreeable, satisfactory, too sour, too acidic, too sweet for its type?

Then swallow the wine and evaluate the aftertaste. Is it smooth or bitter, is it pleasant and satisfactory for the type? Bitterness could be the result of poor cellar work; the wine could have been too full of stems when it was made; it could have been left too long in the skins or picked too soon.

The acid content of a wine is quite important. Achieving a fine acid balance is often the difference between good or poor wine. Acidity is akin to the skeleton of the human body. A guy walking around with a broken bone limps. Wines limp, too, if the skeleton (the acidity) is not right. When the balance is right, then everything's in place and the acid holds it all together. Wines high in acid are very sharp in the mouth; wines low in acid droop, are limp or flat.

But a most important factor—and I can't stress this enough—is the aroma and the bouquet. When wines are very young, they exhibit a lot of their native fruit—the fruit of the grape itself. The aroma is a fruity smell —that of Chardonnay is fresh and lush. After the wine has been in the bottle for a long period of time, it develops an additional smell called the bouquet. The bouquet is different from the fruity smell, designated as the aroma. Both are very pleasant yet distinctive in good wines. In his later years, Maurice Chevalier was unable to taste wine because of doctor's orders. Supposedly

then he would go into the great restaurants of Paris and order an exceptional bottle of wine—not to drink but to smell.

After you have looked, smelled, tasted, and swallowed a wine, don't be timid about giving your opinion. Listen to other opinions, weigh those against yours, and determine just where your taste level is. It is easy to be influenced by labels. If you should have a formal tasting party, it's a good idea to put the wine bottles in paper bags to hide the labels, or pour it into the glasses in another room just before drinking—particularly if you are serving a wine from a screw-top bottle. You may discover some surprising things about your taste level.

There are a lot of things to consider in the tasting and the drinking. You start with whether the wine is sound. Is it going to improve? Is it ready to drink? Is it at its peak? Is it worth tasting, much less drinking?

Soundness merely has to do with whether it's any good at all—not whether it's great. Then you examine the varietal character and whether the wine is true to it. What good is a wine that says Pinot Noir but tastes like a Cabernet? Is it true to the soil from which it purports to come? Was the winemaker trying to make something great, or was he just trying to make something?

Another thing about wine tasting is that it's easy to get out of practice. It's not like riding a bicycle—once you learn how, you never forget. With wine, you must be tasting constantly—daily—to keep reminding yourself what varietal character is. The palate is like a muscle and it gets out of shape. In the same way, it gets tired. If you try to taste too many wines at a sitting, the palate will play tricks on you. In actuality, the best time to taste is in the morning, before you have breakfast. If you taste, say, two wines then and you're an experienced taster, it's possible to retain those tastes all day.

Another kind of tasting—and it's one that most consumers don't often come in contact with—is tasting wines before they are ever put in the bottle. That's when the big buyer has to make a decision to buy or not to buy. Those are tough decisions because a lot of wines taste very much the same at the beginning. They don't start to change for at least six months after fermentation. I buy wines for Scandia Restaurant in Los Angeles, and I've bought young wines in great quantity with much risk. Believe me, I've trembled doing it. Obviously you've got to be very careful in tasting young wines—and not just in the cask but out of the bottle as well. I could give you young wines that sell for two dollars a bottle along with young wines that sell for twenty-five dollars a bottle, and in most cases the two-dollar bottle would be preferred. The reason is the lesser wine can develop fast at a lower level, while wines that are young but of high quality come along slowly—that's one of the reasons that they are so high in quality. So it may take years for that wine to really come around and show what it has. Only a very experienced taster can see that at the beginning. An inexperienced taster would prefer a lesser wine if it appeared more ready to drink than the greater bottle.

The whole spectrum of wine tasting is exciting to me. I enjoy tasting average wine and then good wine, all kinds of wine. If I've had mediocre wine for, say, three or four nights in a row, then having the good wine on the day after that makes me appreciate it all the more. The taste is greater and so is the experience. Rich French food is fabulous but no one could stand to eat it every day.

And then there are those truly special tasting times. You may have had a bottle of wine in storage for an extremely long time that you've been anticipating tasting and drinking. Knowing the man who made the wine and knowing the problems he may have had with it are important to me. Maybe there was a hard rain that year, maybe it was a tough financial time for him, or maybe he had problems in his winery. If you've lived through all these problems with the winemaker and then you come across a bottle of wine that really does it for you, you will have a very strong feeling about it.

But it absolutely astounds me when I see so many Americans condoning bad taste disguised as progress. Beautiful, charming residential areas are sacrificed for the sake of steel and glass skyscrapers; rustic areas are destroyed and landscaped to build tract houses. All in the name of progress. Who can fight it, people ask.

Well, I'd like to fight it in wine. I'd feel better, though, if the army around me were bigger. The more a human being gets used to mediocrity, the more he forgets about the exceptional. That's the way modern life is structured.

I don't say that the intrusion of big business into the wine industry has to be bad. I warn that it could be bad.

In the last decade or so, Inglenook Vineyards has been bought and sold two times. They have gone from being a moderate-volume producer—around 20,000 cases of wine at most—to being a giant—hundreds of thousands of cases. It is owned by Heublein now (Heublein also owns Beaulieu) and markets a whole line of wines: Estate Bottled, non-Estate Bottled, all kinds of wine. There are other corporate giants. The Nestlé Company owns Beringer, the Rainier Brewing Co. controls Robert Mondavi Winery, and National Distillers owns Almadén.

With all the potential problems, there remains an incredible amount of potential greatness. We have all the makings of greatness in California, and in some cases it has been realized. It's time we stopped talking about the great French vintners and started talking about some of the thoroughbreds we have right here.

Take Joseph Heitz. Year in and year out his winery makes superb Chardonnay. He knows what to do with the grapes when he gets them, and he has the sources—grapes from a plot of ground on the floor of the Napa Valley owned by Zinfandel Associates and from another plot of ground at the University of California's experimental station at Oakville.

Heitz gets his grapes on the Napa Valley floor and makes premier Chardonnay. Stony Hill gets its grapes in the hills above the Napa Valley, and its Chardonnay is equally superb. Ridge is turning out marvelous Zinfandels and Cabernet Sauvignons. Schramsberg makes a brilliant champagne, one of the best you can buy anywhere (if you can buy it). Hanzell in the Sonoma Valley also makes an excellent Chardonnay. Sebastiani makes fine Barbera, while the Concannons make fine Sauvignon Blanc in Livermore and Mirassou great Gewürztraminer in San Jose.

These are all quality people—and there are more than a few more, as you will note when you read the Wineries section, which follows this one. This is not to say that the big wineries—the volume producers—cannot turn out great wine if they set their minds to it.

To me, one of the greatest California wines of my lifetime was produced by a volume vintner, Cresta Blanca. They made a sweet Sémillon, a "Premier Sémillon," in the late '50s that was so good it tasted like a Chateau d'Yquem. In France, where the famous Chateau d'Yquem is made, the grapes hang on the vines for a long time and become almost raisinlike, owing to the action of a mold, *Botrytis cinerea*. When they're harvested they look like tiny pieces of coal. Cresta Blanca decided to attempt to match that wine under hothouse conditions, injecting spores of *Botrytis cinerea* into the grapes after harvesting. The wine that resulted was fabulous and it sold for something like six dollars a bottle, at the time an outrageous price for California wine. The wine sold out, of course, but it was not a sensation, probably because it came at the wrong time and only a few people were interested in sauternes, which still are not big sellers. It might have been a different story if they had done something comparable with a Cabernet Sauvignon.

In 1971, Guild, another large producer, marketed a new wine called Winemasters Pinot Noir, and they entered it in the Pinot Noir category at the Los Angeles County Fair. The wine was a sensation—a magnificent, big, gutsy wine made in a new style from grapes grown in a relatively new area (Mendocino County). I'm chairman of the judging committee, and in all the years I've served, we had never given a very special award—a Sweepstakes Award—to the best of all the wines in the four judging categories—white, red, dessert, and champagne. There are sixteen judges and you need at least twelve votes to give the Sweepstakes. That wine made it easily; it was almost unanimous.

Cresta Blanca and Guild did prove a point. This is what all big wineries should be doing. They should be saying to themselves: Okay, we make a lot of wine for the sake of commercial sales; why not make one wine for the sake of art? But many of them won't do that and the reason they won't is that they claim all their wines are already art. Some big producers are very defensive, very protective.

When I started teaching my course in wine in the late '50s, a lot of people thought I was crazy. There has been tremendous interest in it with capacity attendance for each semester. Two salesmen from a major commercial winery had attended one of my classes. I don't know who they were and it wouldn't have mattered if I had. At one particular tasting I said something to the effect that this company made a good wine for the money, but it could not be classified as a great wine. Soon after that a furor developed over that statement. The heat it generated was, to my mind, extraordinary. The winery felt all their wine was great. They had lost the ability to see their own wines in true perspective. Today I still feel the same way about their wine. You get what you pay for —a good middle-range wine that's always dependable, never bad. And never great.

The giant California producers are Gallo and Italian Swiss Colony. After that—and far back in total volume—come Guild, Almadén, Paul Masson, The Christian Brothers, and Inglenook.

Paul Masson is a major producer that is making an effort to upgrade its wine. For many years Paul Masson didn't have many vineyards of its own—an incredible fact in view of the volume of wine it was turning out. But the vineyards that furnished them with their grapes were being snuffed out by urbanization, and so in 1952 they— and the Mirrasou brothers—approached the University of California and asked for some recommendations on where to plant new vineyards removed from urban sprawl.

The university didn't just suggest some land at random; it suggested a prime piece in the Pinnacles area south of San Francisco, bordering on Monterey County. The vines on that land are young and it's really too early to tell, but the signs are encouraging that they will keep improving over the next few years. Paul Masson may have done a lot of blending in the past, but with their new land they're able to do less of it.

There's nothing wrong with blending if it's done to make something more palatable. But there are vintners who are not so much blenders as manufacturers. Some of the best blending wineries are The Christian Brothers and Llords and Elwood. Even Joseph Heitz blends some of his lower-priced wines.

Almost all wines are blended slightly, adding a little bit here and there to make it better. If you are a vintner and you have two or three consecutive vintages that are not very good—or one that was good and one fair—you may blend the two and try to make one palatable wine. The French do a tremendous amount of blending. You won't find many Champagnes and Ports that aren't blended, and all Sherries are blended.

California winemaking has rebounded from the dark ages of Prohibition with remarkable vigor. One important reason for the emergence was the arrival of Andre Tchelistcheff at Beaulieu in 1938. Prior to the appearance of Tchelistcheff, California winemaking techniques usually had been in the hands of Italian cellar men, who made wines in the Italian fashion—that is, wines matured in very large wood, with grapes that were slightly overripe, and left in the cask for a long time before bottling.

Tchelistcheff introduced and perfected the first use of cool fermentation of white wines, rational malolactic fermentation and aging in small casks (fifty gallons).

With the advent of the Hanzell Winery in Sonoma, winemakers began to consider the possibility of producing wine commercially in stainless steel, using inert gases as antioxidants for racking and bottling. The University of California at Davis had been suggesting these things for a long time, but they were ignored by wine producers simply because the techniques could not be utilized in antiquated buildings.

In 1966, Chalone Vineyards and Beaulieu Vineyards began the technique of fermenting Chardonnay in new French oak. This had previously been done by Martin Ray, but with less than resounding success. The formula discovered by Chalone and Beaulieu, however, served to upgrade the Chardonnay.

Most important is the discovery of new grape-growing areas. For a long time—in the early days at least—it was thought that the southern part of California was the best for growing table wines. That proved to be untrue. A search began for new areas, eventually found in the north, around San Francisco.

Then older areas were abandoned—willingly or unwillingly—and vintners sought other ideal areas.

Today we are exploring in places abandoned long ago—Rancho California, San Diego County, the San Luis Obispo area, and Monterey and Mendocino counties. Some of those areas are producing some very good wines already—I've tasted a very good Emerald Riesling from Temecula in Rancho California and a nice new Zinfandel from Templeton in San Luis Obispo—but it's hard to tell because some vines don't peak for ten to fifteen years.

In many ways, vines are really like human beings. They usually start slowly; maybe you'll get a ton or two per acre. As the years pass the vines mature and the yield may multiply by four, five, or six times. It tapers off as the vines get older. A good vine can last fifty years. In Genesis it says, "Be fruitful and multiply." That's the life story of a good vine.

We have done a lot to improve the health and vitality of our grapes and vines. The viticulturalists at Davis have helped in the development of sturdier plants, and it is doubtful today that a pestilence such as phylloxera could ever again decimate vineyards the way it did late in the nineteenth century. Those techniques developed here have helped to protect and improve the quality of European wine, too.

Mechanical harvesting is another American innovation, although it remains to be seen whether it is a good thing. Cesar Chavez doesn't think so, of course, and I'm not so sure I don't agree with him, for a different reason—how will it affect the taste?

For the most part, I refuse to make a comparison between the wines of America and the wines of Europe. The differences of climate and soil are too wide. The conditions in California are not at all the same as France's and certainly not the same as Germany's. There are portions of northern Italy that have some of the same characteristics as California, but that doesn't mean a great deal since you could take areas of the world where no grapes are being grown and say they are similar to California. What would that prove?

Even experienced winemakers and wine drinkers argue about "ideal conditions." Some say they can be too ideal, that there is too much sun in California, too much good weather and good soil. They say that the grape must suffer to be truly great. Other people say it doesn't matter. There are the people who argue for mountain slopes and those who argue for valley floors. The valley vines grow in richer soil, the mountain grapes in rocky, more desolate soil. The mountain grapes are far less productive, of course, and there are problems with deer and birds. Strangely, it's the vineyards on the valley floors that have the problems with frost—good or bad, depending on whom you talk to.

I suspect the best conditions are those of sun—but not too hot a sun—during the daytime and cool breezes at night. The conditions in the Napa Valley are like that and the grapes there do very well.

Of course, temperature is one thing and soil is quite another. The soil around Livermore is very gravelly, very rocky, quite similar to the soil around the white wine areas of Burgundy and Bordeaux in France. For years we thought that was the only place to grow wine in California. We were wrong. In recent years our Chardonnay has come from grapes grown in soil that is completely different—much smoother and richer—and our Chardonnay today is superb, the best we have ever produced. Maybe the improvement in winemaking techniques has something to do with that, but time is showing us that some of our old judgments and assumptions were not necessarily correct.

The Germans and French are major contributors to the California heritage. The French brought their marvelous flair for wine, for making the soil come alive, and the Germans brought their usual efficiency and perfection. But no influence has been stronger than that of the Italians—the Sebastianis, the Mondavis, the Martinis, the Pedroncellis, the Bonesios, the Guastis, the Gemellos...to name a few. You could add the Gallos to that list, too, although theirs is a different style of winemaking. The Italians have a great love affair with the soil and a marvelous enjoyment of life. And do they love the produce of the soil, wine!

Wine is just as important to an Italian as it is to a Frenchman, although the Italian treats his wine with less fanfare. The French will sit around and look at wine and talk about, almost bow down to it—Americans are much the same, or they try to be—and it's almost as if the wine is the whole reason for getting together. Italians sit down to a meal and the wine is there and it's only an incidental—though necessary—part of the meal. They'll eat or sing or dance and have a good time and wine will be part of all of it.

This is a generality, of course, but many of Italy's winemakers are not making wines as complex as those of France or California. Many make wines that are the same, year in and year out. I like them because I can drink them and not worry. Once I was talking to a fellow in Italy, and I said to him, "There's so much wine in Italy—more than there is in France—so why don't you talk about it more?" and he said, "When you're as rich with wine as we are, you don't have to talk about it. We think talking about it would be bragging."

The Italians bring a buoyant joy to wine-making that I think the wine industry needs. But that's changing, too—and tomorrow will decide whether it's in the right direction. The jug producers aren't going to change and neither are the Mondavis or the Martinis. They've always made some quality wines and always will. But now all of a sudden Gemello is getting more intense about his wines, Parducci is selling wines for six dollars or more a bottle, Pedroncelli is making very interesting wines. They're changing, and by the most literal of definitions, they're no longer Italian in my opinion. It's even changing in Italy. Enough people have told the Italians they make great wines, and now they're starting to say it themselves and to ask bigger prices for them.

Frankly, much of this comparing conditions and soils and techniques doesn't excite me. It's a part of a wine education to know why and how, but in terms of priorities of learning, it should be far down on the list. Really, there is no way of knowing whether a soil or a technique will work or not until it has been tried. If it makes a great wine, I don't know why, I don't care. The wine is good. And that's all I care about in California.

Old, thick-boled vines, pruned for the winter, stand at the Bertero vineyard in Gilroy, California.

Statistics show us that the consumption of wine in the United States has increased substantially during the last several years. As interest in wines has escalated, wineries have expanded their ability to meet the market demands. The "boom" has also fostered the growth of many new wineries.

California currently produces about 84 percent of the nation's wine, or some 252 million gallons annually. Not surprisingly, Californians also lead in the consumption of wine and, in 1971, they accounted for slightly more than 20 percent of the total national volume.

In 1957, U. S. wine consumption was 1.44 gallons per capita; in 1971 it has increased to 2.43 gallons, a gain of nearly 70 percent. This figure pales by comparison to the figures of France and Italy, where adult per capita consumption of wine is approximately forty gallons annually. The Wells Fargo Bank of California, in a recent report, projects U. S. adult per capita consumption of 3.4 gallons by 1980, still a modest sip compared to a European's enjoyment of wine.

Louis G. Gomberg, industry consultant and analyst, predicted in *Wines & Vines* that the American market in 1973 would consume approximately 345 million gallons of wine, or about eight bottles for every person in the nation. This is an interesting prediction, because in 1969, also in *Wines & Vines*, 30 major industry experts estimated that within ten years U. S. produced wine sales would exceed 337 million gallons. The fact that their figure was probably surpassed in only

four years dramatically underlines the American consumer's new-found interest in domestic wines.

Undoubtedly, much of the wine consumed has been of the so-called "pop" variety, such as Cold Duck, Boone's Farm and Annie Greenspring's fruit wines. The "pop" wines, in my opinion, are antithetical to the understanding and appreciation of table wines. They are, simply, an alcoholic form of soft drink and are understandably popular among young people.

Marketing experts have attributed the current wine boom to the kind of society we live in, where incomes are increasing, as are education and leisure time—all factors that go into promoting the consumption of wine. These findings clearly suggest the importance American winemakers are beginning to place on the value of advertising and its influence on the market, which is you and me.

Wineries are spending more and more dollars on advertising each year. California wineries are, by far, the heaviest spenders in the nation. Advertising, no matter how well it is handled, is probably the last criteria by which wine should be judged. Media exposure does not make a great wine, it only makes a familiar label. The discriminatory wine drinker will still find the answer to a winery's capability in the bottle, not on television or a magazine page.

A substantial number of wineries today, large and small, are reluctant to enter wine judgings such as the Los Angeles County Fair or any other county or state fair judging. These judgings are generally for the im-

3

provement of the breed. There is fear among some of the wineries that their image or sales will suffer if they are not awarded the gold medal. Nothing could be further from the truth. Emphasis should be on the making of good wine within the limits of the competition and the medals will take care of themselves. Those that bypass American judgings often enter foreign competitions with, perhaps, the thought that there is nothing to lose and everything to gain in a foreign competition.

The most interesting judging of all, however, and the most important, is that competition which is enjoyed between America's own wines and the consuming public.

Which, in a somewhat inconclusive manner, leads to the following section, a series of personal evaluations of some of California's more important wineries, many of which are unknown beyond the state's borders, and for many, probably unknown within, too. Many of the wineries mentioned cannot ship outside the state. Others are so small, that the only hope a buyer has of obtaining a bottle is to travel directly to the winery.

When it was first suggested I write this book, my main reservation was that such a book would be a great disservice to the small winemaker, especially the small winemaker producing superb but severely limited quantities of wine. The very exposure of these men and their excellent work provokes problems for them and their potential customers. Quality winemaking is a painstaking process. When a winery is as small as some discussed, production is limited to only a few hundred cases annually. There is almost no way for the winery to meet the demands of the market place.

And, of course, the usual result of limited quantities and increased demand is higher prices. Even eight, ten and twelve dollars per bottle of wine is no deterrent to the connoiseur who is impatient for a particular bottle of Chardonnay or Cabernet Sauvignon.

But the domestic wine industry, especially in California, is of great interest and, some thirty years after Prohibition, we are seeing wine being produced that challenges the very best being offered by France, Germany and Italy. This is exciting evidence that this nation, while temporarily deterred by an unfortunate law, has found the soil and the technological skills to compete on an equal basis with wineries that have hundreds of years of experience and heritage.

On the following pages I have attempted to explore those wineries I believe to be important. Obviously, many wineries have been omitted. The reason for the omissions has nothing to do with the wineries, but reflects on the shortcomings of my own tasting experience. The wineries discussed are those I am familiar with and whose product I have tasted many times. To pass judgment on those I have not tasted would be a disservice to the wineries, as well as to you, the reader.

Any book on wine that tends to be specific also tends to become obsolete on the day it is published. Particular bottles of wine may no longer be available and, as in other industries, personnel changes will occur. Up to the final days of publication, revisions in both areas were accomplished to the best of my ability and understanding.

Every attempt was made to assemble complete data on the wineries covered here and in the New York section. Where data is missing, it is because the information was not available from any source.

N.C.

Best Bottles Code

| X = Good, interesting wine |
| XX = Better |
| XXX = Possibly great |
| XXXX = Great wine if aged properly (great wine in complete balance) |
| *Comer* = Improving bottles |

THE VISIONARIES

Not long after the storied California Gold-rush, a handful of men of unique vision devoted their intellect and energies to other, more certain, treasures that awaited in the bountiful earth.

It is difficult today to appreciate the imperatives of those early pioneers who cultivated the rich soil of California's hills and valleys, planted vines of European lineage, and watched them mature with luscious fruit. Their dream, like that of all pioneers, eludes those of us spoiled by its realization today, more than a century later.

Today, in places named Sonoma, Rutherford, St. Helena and Russian River, architectural landmarks stand as proud monuments to their foresight, and serve as fascinating reminders of California's long romance with wine.

On the following pages are shown some of the most handsome and familiar of the many wineries built by those men of vision, each structure an individual substantiation of their faith in a new world of wine.

Page 65
California's most bountiful wine country, the beautiful Napa Valley, is slightly more than an hour's drive from San Francisco.
Page 66
From the air, Château Chevalier, with its gentle, rolling vineyards sheltered by clusters of trees, gives a visual impression that is as French as its name.
Page 67, top
On a hill overlooking the Valley of the Moon in Sonoma County, the Hanzell Vineyard winery proudly crowns its terraced vineyards, its architecture patterned after the famous Burgundy château, Clos de Vougeot.
Page 67, bottom left
The copper roof of Inglenook's magnificent winery thrusts above the vineyards that surround it.
Page 67, bottom right
At the Charles Krug winery, in St. Helena, the old carriage house has been converted to an aging room.
Pages 68/69
Silhouetted by a high August sun, the Rhine House, at Beringer, is a picturesque Victorian mansion that serves as a tourist attraction and tasting room.
Pages 70/71
Reposing in the glowing warmth of Beaulieu Vineyards' executive tasting room, Andre Tcheli stcheff reminisces about his thirty-five years as one of California's most influential and dynamic winemakers.
Page 72
This ivy encrusted Norman tower has been standing at Korbel's Russian River vineyards since the 1880's, a symbol of the pride and heritage of one of California's finest producers of sparkling wines.
Page 73
Hanging above the entrance to the Buena Vista Vineyards cellar is this hand-carved plaque, proudly acknowledging the winery's colorful founder, Colonel Agoston Haraszthy.

ALMADÉN VINEYARDS

Alcoa Building
One Maritime Plaza
San Francisco, California
94111

Owner:
National Distillers

Winemaker:
A. C. Huntsinger

Vineyards:
7,100 acres

Capacity:
Small oak cooperage
2,192,232 gallons
Large oak cooperage
637,365 galloons
Redwood cooperage
7,957,937 gallons

Blanc de Blanc Champagne XXX
Grenache Rosé XX
Gewürztraminer X
Solera Cocktail Dry Sherry X
Cabernet Sauvignon (Paicines):
Comer

The important Paicines vineyards, located in San Benito County.

Almadén Vineyards, the largest of the so-called premium wineries in California, bottles approximately 20,000 cases a day. Its history did not begin with wine—its founder, Etienne Thée, an émigré from France's finest wine district in Bordeaux, came to California more for gold than for the grape. As it turned out, gold was fickle but the grape was not, and in 1847 Almadén's founder began, in the area of Los Gatos near San Jose, a wine dynasty that has now grown into California's most productive giant premium winery.

Aided by Charles Lefranc from Paris and assisted by European cuttings and the merging of the Thée and Lefranc families through marriage, the vineyards did extremely well in drawing national and international renown with wines that without doubt deserved it.

A later marriage of one of Lefranc's daughters to Paul Masson continued the French amalgamation. The winery prospered and precipitated young Paul to move into his own property at Saratoga, laying the foundation for another giant California premium enterprise, Paul Masson Vineyards.

Following a dormant period during Prohibition, Louis A. Benoist of San Francisco, with the help of Frank Schoonmaker —everyone's favorite wine connoisseur—greatly expanded the winery and vineyards, leading to the present ownership by National Distillers.

Perhaps more than any other large wine enterprise, Almadén foresaw the present boom in wine consumption. Beginning in 1958, in excess of 4,000 acres of new vineyards were planted at Paicines and Hollister in San Benito County to offset the inroads of urbanization in the Los Gatos area. This was an unprecedented move of extraordinary expense and risk, although the risk may have been

The state plaque at Los Gatos.

tempered considerably by the advice and counsel of the department of viticulture at Davis, which assisted in locating this area as a fine property for premium grapes. The area echoes with the legend of the adventurous Joaquin Murietta, the noble bandit who sought refuge here.

The risk seems to have been worthwhile—the wines here have turned out to be more than satisfactory and in time may even be great. They are still in the process of proving themselves—both the "great" varietals Cabernet Sauvignon and Pinot Chardonnay—and only time and taste will tell. The

Cabernets thus far seem to be holding their own in terms of overall taste and flavor, while the Chardonnay still has a way to go. Other wines, such as Johannisberg Riesling, Gewürztraminer, Sylvaner, and Sauvignon Blanc, have done reasonably well.

Almadén is a most intriguing giant enterprise in that it seems to have made wines on variously good levels. The top of the line is the Almadén Blanc de Blanc Champagne, which is remarkably good for such a large undertaking. Their popular priced champagne, Le Domaine, is also a remarkable value for it is good—not great—and a welcome companion for those who wish an inexpensive, reasonably good sparkling wine.

The generic wines of Almadén are also good for the money; often bottled in gallon and half-gallon sizes, they are not a burden to one's pocketbook. Almadén provides a very good line of dessert wines with such items as flor-type sherries, Solera Golden, Solera Creme, and tawny port.

The Almadén people, although not always making wines of great complexity, are providing an extraordinary amount of fairly decent wine at a more than reasonable price, and with the aid of the new vineyards, no American should have to worry that he can't have a satisfactory glass of wine at a not-too-high price.

One is not certain whether this is the way that Etienne Thée and Charles Lefranc would have wanted Almadén to go. Possibly quality is sometimes forsaken for quantity. But Almadén seems to have found a satisfactory middle-of-the-road direction with occasional movement toward wines of character and interest.

Dino Barengo's weathered brick winery, now 38 years old, once served as a grain barn.

BARENGO CELLARS

3125 East Orange Street
Acampo, California 95220

Owner and Winemaker:
Dino Barengo

Vineyards:
24 acres

Capacity:
Storage 1,750,000 gallons
Fermenting 300,000

Dino Barengo is no stranger to California wines. He was with Acampo Winery when Cesare Mondavi (later of Charles Krug Winery) was its president. In 1943 Barengo managed the winery after it was acquired by the Gibson Wine Company, another fine name in the California wine panorama.

The winery is situated north of Lodi at the end of a row of tall palm trees—a large complex of silver-painted buildings housing aging cellars, fermenting rooms, and a vinegar plant.

The Barengo winery is quite typical of San Joaquin Valley facilities capable of large production. There is no pretense of the romantic winemaking image; the wine here is produced on a mass volume basis and the buildings reflect that goal. Barengo himself runs the winery in a no-nonsense manner and is responsible for all of the winemaking.

The vineyards are planted to Ruby Cabernet, Zinfandel, Carignane, Sémillon, Mission, and Tokay. The wines that are produced are generally standard bulk wines, often sold to other wineries for blending and marketed in half-gallons and gallons. The varietals are interesting because they are inexpensive, sound, good early drinking wines. They include Ruby Cabernet, Zinfandel, Pinot Noir, some Chardonnay aged in American oak, and a unique table wine, Muscadelle du Bordelais.

There is also an assortment of fruit wines such as Ambermint, a mint chocolate wine, Cremocha, a coffee-flavored wine, and Cremapri, an apricot-flavored wine. There are some specialty items such as May wine under the Dudenhoefer label. Barengo is the only producer of this wine in the United States. Harvest wine is a fortified port, a wine specifically marketed for the Eastern and Midwestern markets. Some good sherries are made

by Barengo: a dry sherry that is a blend of submerged culture, flor, and baked wines, and Pedro Ximinez, a dark-colored wine from grapes of the same name, which is unique to California. Some champagne is made for Barengo by other producers using Barengo wine as a base. The wines are bulk process and are fairly good but not complex.

There is a good quantity of fine wine vinegar produced by a solera process quite similar to the Orleans barrel process.

Some of Barengo's wine is sold in five-gallon glass demijohns, not legal in California but allowed in Nevada and Idaho.

BEAULIEU VINEYARD

57 Post Street
San Francisco, California 94104

Owner:
Heublein, Inc.
Winemakers:
Andre Tchelistcheff and
R. G. Peterson
Vineyards:
745 acres
Capacity:
Storage 1,200,000 gallons

Private Reserve Cabernet
Sauvignon XXXX
Beaumont Pinot Noir XXXX
Chablis XX
Chardonnay Beaufort XX
Burgundy XX
Beaurosé Rosé X
Champagne Brut: *Comer*

Andre Tchelistcheff at work in Beaulieu's laboratory.

The name Andre Tchelistcheff has been synonomous for over three decades with the best that Beaulieu Vineyard has been able to produce. Among wine drinkers there are many who believe that he owns the place, but such is not his lot. In reality he is the winemaker—prestige enough, for he may have been the leading winemaker in the entire state throughout those thirty years.

Tchelistcheff has often been referred to as a winemaker's winemaker. I prefer the title "a wine drinker's winemaker," for he has always made his beloved Private Reserve Cabernet Sauvignon with the interested, knowledgeable, and certainly appreciative wine drinker in mind. In other words, he has made wine not only for sale but, more important, for art's sake. It is at Beaulieu that some of California's finest Cabernet has been made, the kind of wine that provides the complex experience with all the nuances that make wine tasting exciting, enduring, and terribly rewarding.

Elsewhere I have described the dinner in the wine cellar dining room of Scandia Restaurant that Mr. Tchelistcheff came to, at which we tasted all of his Private Reserve Cabernets from 1939 up to and including 1960. He commented upon each of the wines as if he were talking about his own children, detailing in depth the birth of the wine and leading to the graduation to the bottle. To lay bare, before knowledgeable wine drinkers, all of those wines, representing thirty years of labor, was an awesome risk. He won hands down. Would be that other wineries would assume the same risk. It is a great thing to go back thirty years in California wines and judge the wines and listen to the winemaker expound about them as they are revealed in their glory and in their weaknesses. This was perhaps one of wine drinking's finest moments.

Andre Tchelistcheff came to Beaulieu in 1938 and almost at once became a legend in winemaking. He was able to bring the best of European winemaking modes to the high degree of skill developed in California. He is a diminutive Russian gentleman with French influence whose greatest gifts to California have been his fine Cabernets and his publicly stated desire to have a law similar to that of the Appellation Contrôlée, whereby all of California's vineyards would be laid out according to where the particular grape varieties grow best.

It was not enough for him to specialize in Cabernet Sauvignon. His Beaumont Pinot Noir has been in the forefront of that variety—an especially difficult accomplishment because of the problems that the treacherous Pinot Noir grape provides.

The Beaulieu story begins with the Georges de Latour family who founded the winery in 1900. Arriving with Bordeaux and Burgundy experience, de

superb wines called "The Founders Wines," all named for him. The name Georges de Latour may indeed be as important in the Napa Valley as the names of Charles Krug, Beringer, and Schramm, and as important as Sebastiani in the Sonoma Valley.

Samuel Sebastiani and Georges de Latour, during those early days of winemaking in California, bartered a great deal for grapes and wines and argued at length over varieties and price—the valley still fairly resounds with their voices. So hard was their bargaining and so heated their discussions that some of their sessions seemed to conclude at the point of their never speaking to one another again. Yet somehow, through the grace of the grape, peace was

Peterson, a young, dynamic enologist whose interest is as a consumer as well as a professional. If Mr. Peterson is allowed to follow the dictates of his own conscience upon the retirement of Mr. Tchelistcheff, the fortunes of the winery and the tastes it produces may well be secure.

There is concern on the part of most wine drinkers that since the winery is now owned by Heublein, Inc., a corporate giant, the wine may lose much of its character and style. Suffice it to say that Heublein has, in its wisdom, allowed the winery to continue with both Mr. Tchelistcheff and Mr. Peterson and has indeed provided the necessary capital and drive to maintain the momentum of good taste begun in 1900. I hope that they will continue this policy and

plete the line there is dry sauterne, sweet sauterne, Sylvaner Riesling, and the recently included Gamay Beaujolais.

Some of the best generics, such as chablis and burgundy, are made at Beaulieu; these are good enough to restore a wine drinker's faith in generics and generally are a decidedly

A sign on the Silverado Trail.

good buy. A 1968 Beaulieu burgundy, for which a virtually hand-inscribed label has recently been made, is selling in excess of four dollars and is probably worth it, although one would not like to get into the habit of spending that kind of money for generics. Rounding out the line are the champagnes, which have improved considerably in recent years, and a line of aperitif and dessert wines including sherry, port, and Muscat de Frontignan.

The back labels of Beaulieu wines have always been the most advanced of any of California's wineries, for they state from which grapes the wine has been made. For example, the burgundy label will describe which grapes are in the wine, such as Gamay, Pinot Noir, Petite Sirah, and Mondeuse—a practice that hopefully other wineries will follow.

It is not difficult to fall in love with Beaulieu wines and Mr. Tchelistcheff, whose retirement is imminent. Thankfully, the people at Heublein, to date, have allowed the romance to flourish.

The tasting room at Rutherford.

Latour had no trouble finding his way to Beaulieu in the Napa Valley. When he died in 1940 he had brought to the valley the great Beaulieu estate and vineyards as well as a whole line of

restored and their undeniable friendship continued.

Georges de Latour's wife took over for her husband until she died in 1951—the year that produced one of the great Private Reserve Cabernets, one of my favorite California Cabernets alongside my most revered favorite of all, 1947 Private Reserve Cabernet Sauvignon.

Andre Tchelistcheff today is ably succeeded by Richard

not tamper with a good thing, for without question some of California's finest wines have been made at Beaulieu, which is not limited to the Pinot Noir and the Cabernet but also makes such fine wines as Beaufort Pinot Chardonnay and Beauclair Johannisberg Riesling. To com-

BERINGER-LOS HERMANOS VINEYARDS

St. Helena, California

Owner:
The Nestlé Company, Inc.

Winemaker:
Myron Nightingale, Sr.

Vineyards:
800 acres

Capacity:
Storage 2,000,000 gallons
Fermenting 240,000 gallons

Malvasia Bianca XX
Barenblut X
Zinfandel : *Comer*

The Rhine House is a stately landmark identifying Napa's oldest winery.

The Beringer Brothers is yet another California winery and winemaking tradition with a heritage of European winemaking, begun in 1876 at the winery's founding at Los Hermanos by Frederick and Jacob L. Beringer. Influenced by his experience with the best wines of France and Germany, Jacob is probably one of the few original winemaking pioneers who came to

America with a single ambition —to plant a vineyard and build a winery. It wasn't long before he persuaded his brother to leave an established New York business to join with him in the wine enterprise.

The greatness of Beringer wines, from the founding to modern days, is a legend.

The winery itself is a must stop for travelers, for it is a fascinating attraction with its beautiful old home, now called the Rhine House, and its maze of tunnels, cut a thousand feet into the limestone hills a century ago by Chinese labor. The tunnels are a great attraction as well as a useful wine tool in

providing perfect wine storage, with temperature variations of no more than a degree or two the year around. Much of the cooperage of Beringer is as old or older than the winery itself and is decorated in the European tradition.

The Beringer Brothers winery —until 1971, when it was sold to the Nestlé Company—was and has been the winery longest family-owned in the Napa Valley and perhaps in California. The family produced superb if not memorable wines from the winery's founding in 1876 into 1971. In recent years the winery was led by Otto Beringer, the grandson, and the daughters of the brothers. In fact, the daughters or family who ran the winery were referred to as the dowager winemaking group; it is to their credit that they kept the winery going in the face of the great winemaking changes that have been taking place. Their land is excellent for the wine. However, recently the wines have not been at as high a level in quality as the Beringer family-owned wineries in recent years have had to make the choice of either selling out or plunking their money back into the winery to buy new equipment and cooperage and acquire new plantings, not an easy thing to do. It is to the credit of the Beringer family that they per-

A blend of the old and new.

Many of the old bottles of Beringer of the '40s and the '50s in my own cellar are living testimonials to the greatness of the Beringer tradition.

Nestlé, with its new winemaker, Myron Nightingale, has literally reequipped the winery and spent a fortune to bring in the best and finest equipment for winemaking. At this stage the quality of the wines does not yet match the effort and the expense. This winery will be most interesting to watch; as its wines become available one can see if money and corporate management can revive the winery and restore the Beringer name to its rightful place among the makers of great wines.

Casks and barrels of wine age in one of the numerous limestone tunnels.

A newly gunited "limestone" cavern.

wines of the earlier period were.

The family, under the direction of Otto Beringer and Roy Raymond, its winemaker during the later stages of family ownership, battled mightily to put Beringer back on its original level of high quality, and it was probably this battle that precipitated the sale to Nestlé. Many of the severed as long as they did.

The Beringers have made some of the state's finest Cabernet, Zinfandel, and Pinot Noir, The whites, represented by Grey Riesling, Chenin Blanc, Sauvignon Blanc, and Chardonnay, although good, did not seem to have the same complexities that the reds often developed. A featured wine was an old specialty of the Beringer house, Barenblut (blood of the bear), which was a hearty blend of Pinot Noir and Grignolino; it was always a wine that could be counted on to be assertive, big, and flavorful.

BROOKSIDE VINEYARD COMPANY

9900 "A" Street
Guasti, California 91743

Owner:
Beatrice Foods, Chicago, Illinois
Winemaker:
Earl McCauley
Vineyards:
In excess of 1,210 acres
in San Bernardino County
and at
Rancho California Temecula
Capacity:
Storage 8,500,000 gallons

Assumption Abbey
Angelica XXX
Emerald Riesling (Temecula) XX
Johannisberg Riesling XX
Cream Muscat XX
Petite Sirah : *Comer*

The Brookside Vineyard Company, like so many of its contemporary vintners, pushed by the popularity of wines, launched a search for new lands on which to find grapes.

Seven years ago Brookside started to investigate the Mesa Grande area of Rancho California at Temecula, which was part of the old Vail cattle ranch. The area, according to the University of California agricultural scientists, could be classified as Regions *II* and *III*, the same as many other good grape-growing areas in the state.

Thus began an exciting project that has meant a return of grape growing to southern California, where for the past fifty years the vine has steadily given way to urban development. These were not Mission grapes or the Criola; they were the Johannisberg Riesling, Petite Sirah, Emerald Riesling, Zinfandel, and Chardonnay.

Predictions by agricultural scientists or vintners about the quality of the wines from a gamble with new grape soil was just that—a prediction. The

A memorial to the town's founder.

proof could come only in the wine.

Brookside took the gamble, invested in the land, and planted a total of fifty-six different varieties of grapes in a thirty-five-acre experimental vineyard. Initial indications from the quality of the plant were high, as the vines literally burst forth on the soil where only cattle had roamed for at least a hundred years.

The grapes were beautiful and three years later the first wines

Ontario airport's landing path is directly over Brookside's vineyards.

were made. It appeared from these first wines that Brookside had won the gamble. Although none of the wines were, in themselves, considered great, they were exciting because they were interesting, good to taste, and with enough flavor in them to promise that the vines and the wines would improve. The most exciting of these wines was the Johannisberg Riesling, which had considerable flavor in depth, fruity nose, and a good finish, perhaps the best white wine Brookside had yet made. The reds didn't seem to be quite as interesting, but time again will tell.

Brookside believes that this is only a beginning. Plans are already being made to build a winery at Rancho California and other vintners are watching the Brookside experiment.

The Brookside Vineyard Company is not new to the California wine industry, for the Biane family has been grape growers and producers of wine for five generations. The company is now run by Philo Biane; his ancestral roots go back to Théophile Vaché, who came from France to locate in the wine business at Monterey in 1832. Some of his early plantings near Hollister in San Benito County may have been the forerunners for the vineyards now used by Almadén.

The great success of the Biane family in the wine business really began in the most unlikely of places, downtown Los Angeles, where a business of wines and spirits was established, offering to Angelenos wines and vinegar made at the old San Bernardino winery.

Wine families have a way of blending themselves into greater wine families and so it was that Marius Biane in 1892 came from France to go to work for the Vaché family at Brookside—and, of course, he married the boss's daughter, Marcelline.

The next region for the Bianes was the Cucamonga district. In 1916 Marius's sons Philo and François were employed by Garrett & Company (remember Virginia Dare?), and in 1952 the Bianes made their move by establishing again the Brookside Vineyard Company in their own style at Ontario and Guasti.

The Bianes today make wines under such labels as Brookside, Vaché, and Assumption Abbey. With a tradition for altar wines, the Brookside winery negotiated with the Benedictine monks of the Assumption Abbey of Richardton, North Dakota, for the use of their abbey's name. The Benedictines are a Roman Catholic order that lives by the rule of the founder, and a beautiful creed, *ora et labora*, "to pray and work." The best of the Brookside wines, particularly the varietals, are made under the Assumption Abbey label.

The Brookside winery produces some eighty different wine products ranging from varietals such as Johannisberg Riesling to brandies, wine vinegars, so-called cooking wines, mixes, wine jellies, sparkling wines, fruit wines, and dessert wines.

The various dessert wines are indeed quite good, particularly the Sherry Crema, Cream Mar-sala, and Sherry Palido. The varietal wines—Zinfandel, St. Emilion, and Cabernet—still must be proved. They are very reasonably priced, make good buys and, as the new plantings at Temecula become older and more seasoned, the varietal wines should develop—or be

The main winery is an imposing 100 feet wide and 600 feet long.

able to develop—complexity.

The southern California area in which Brookside is located has never been particularly popular with the so-called wine cognoscenti of California or the East Coast, so Brookside decided to take its case to the people and embarked on an ambitious plan to set up its own retail outlets, called Brook-side Wineries and Tasting Cellars, all over the state. A grandfather clause in the law allowed this branch winery concept and so there are now in excess of thirty Brookside Wineries and Tasting Cellars dotting the state as well as two in Arizona. This gives people an opportunity to taste Brookside wines and saves the winery from having to entrust the sale of its wines to retailers, who are probably more moved by famous-name labels than by an interesting, reasonably priced line of wines.

Make no mistake, Brookside wines are not great, complex varietals, but in the overall stream of wine drinking, they have a decided and deserved place.

San Secondo de'Asti, the church at Guasti, was named for Secondo Guasti.

DAVID BRUCE

21439 Bear Creek Road
Los Gatos, California 95030

Owner and Winemaker:
David Bruce, M.D.

Vineyards:
37 acres

Capacity:
Storage 45,000 gallons
Fermenting 6,000 gallons

Chardonnay XXXX
Zinfandel XXX
Cabernet Sauvignon XX

The growing, making, and tasting of wine has for decades attracted the medical practitioner. A good number of physicians have fallen in love with the grape, interesting themselves not only in establishing extensive wine cellars for their own use but also in actually making wine for public con-

David has established a fine wine facility; as proof, the 1968 David Bruce Chardonnay is without question one of the finest Chardonnays made. The wine is full, rich, complex, and abundant with Chardonnay character. The 1967 Chardonnay was much lighter by comparison and by no means a great wine, but

The 1969 Chardonnay is, in the view of some wine drinkers, even better; it should be—it sells for twenty-two dollars a bottle. One thing is certain— David is making wines of considerable interest and character, and for a relatively new and small winery this is not easy to accomplish.

Looking jaunty, Dr. Bruce strikes a pose in a spacious room of his home.

sumption. It may be that many physicians and other professional men want to give expression to certain artistic impulses that lead joyfully and unerringly to winemaking.

A dermatologist from San Jose, David Bruce had been most severely bitten by the grape and there appeared to be no antidote other than the purchase of vineyards in Los Gatos. He did so in 1961 and, with family participation, the vineyard was planted to Chardonnay, Cabernet Sauvignon, Pinot Noir, and Johannisberg Riesling.

The winery came later, in 1964, with a new one following in 1968 that has already been outgrown because of the demand for David Bruce wines.

David is learning well. The 1968 Chardonnay may be one of the biggest Chardonnays ever made. There appears to be a difference of opinion among wine lovers about this wine. Some believe it has slightly oxidized (which gives it complexity, they say), while others believe that it is no longer good to drink. It will not last long, but the majority view is that it is a wine undeniably great.

Dr. David Bruce.

The winery produces small quantities of Pinot Noir, Cabernet Sauvignon, Zinfandel, Johannisberg Riesling that it calls "White Riesling," Grenache, and Petite Sirah.

These wines are good but yet not exciting in the various years tasted. Experimental wines such as Pinot Noir Blanc and Zinfandel Blanc, red grapes made into white wines, stimulate the curiosity but do very little for the palate. The Chardonnay is here to stay as is David Bruce.

BUENA VISTA VINEYARDS

Old Winery Road
Sonoma, California 95476

Owners:
Vernon Underwood,
Phillip A. Gaspar,
Peter and John Young

Winemaker:
Albert L. Brett

Vineyards:
320 acres

Capacity:
Storage 75,000 gallons
Fermenting 20,000 gallons

Zinfandel XX
Gewürztraminer X
Green Hungarian X
Cabernet Sauvignon : *Comer*

An imposing cellar door identifies the historic Haraszthy Cellars in Sonoma.

Winemaker Al Brett.

The Buena Vista story is really the story of Agoston Haraszthy, which is told in the *Yesterday* chapter of this book. It was at Buena Vista that Haraszthy's interest in California wines fully blossomed, and it was here that he brought some of Europe's greatest varieties for planting and study. He may have brought the Zinfandel here or found it — no one is quite certain.

For many years some of the state's finest Zinfandel has been grown and made at the winery under the aegis of Frank Bartholomew, who was chairman of the board of United Press, under the direction of one of the state's unheralded winemakers, Albert Brett.

Buena Vista was dying on the vine, as it were, in 1943 when Frank Bartholomew, with the dream of the rehabilitation of the winery — almost as ambitious a dream as Haraszthy's — brought the winery back slowly. Through his connections, which were worldwide, he got the Buena Vista label on some of the country's leading hotel and restaurant wine lists. They were well rewarded with some very interesting wines, not limited to Zinfandel but also including Green Hungarian, a specialty of the house, and some of the state's finest Gewürztraminer, a fresh and spritely wine indeed. Buena Vista has also made good Cabernet Sauvignon, Chardonnay, and Johannisberg Riesling. On occasion they have even tried a so-called vintage Port 1954, which has been one of the better ports made in the state.

Presently the winery is in the hands of men whose names are new to California winemaking — men who were wise enough to retain Al Brett as their winemaker. Further wisdom was reflected in the purchase of vineyards in Napa Valley, which may be somewhat sacrilegious according to the Haraszthy Sonoma philosophy but is likely to provide a great deal of substance to Buena Vista's red wines of the future.

There is no question that Buena Vista is a winery on the move, and already there has been considerable improvement, as reflected in the taste of the newer cask bottlings of its Zinfandel.

It would appear that everything necessary to make the winery produce excellent wines is being done. The reds from Napa Valley should provide quite a stimulus to both the winery and the consumer.

BYNUM WINERY

614 San Pablo Avenue
Albany, California 94706

Owner and Winemaker:
L. Davis Bynum

Vineyards:
26 acres

Capacity:
Storage 10,000 gallons
Fermenting 1,200 gallons

Amber Dry Sherry XXX
Private Reserve Cabernet
Sauvignon XXX
Ruby Cabernet XX
Port XX

The Bynum tasting room is just another storefront on an Albany street.

The label "Barefoot Bynum" may sound like just a catchy and interesting name to some people, but for many the label means a line of wines that is reasonably good, sold in bulk, and inexpensive. For those unable and unwilling to spend three to six dollars on one twenty-four ounce jug of wine, Barefoot Bynum wines are both a moral and practical victory.

Barefoot Bynum is really Davis Bynum who, appropriately, was figuratively barefoot when, with little capital, he opened his own winery in Albany, California, in 1965, not far from the University of California at Berkeley.

Bynum states that he situated his winery in the heart of town so that its customers could see all of the winemaking processes. I suspect however that he started there so that he could more easily sell the wines that he purchased and perhaps finished at his little plant. He could run the whole operation by himself. The project prospered and the little winery moved to new premises in St. Helena, California, without giving up Barefoot's first plant.

Davis Bynum is a most interesting man. His wine background was bolstered by his father, Lindley Bynum, a California historian of note and the author of perhaps one of the first California wine consumer books, *California Wines and How to Enjoy Them*. It is now out of print and a rarity.

Davis is one of those "bootstrap" winemakers who learned to make wine simply because he wanted to, more from benefit of the bottle than by the book. He is as much an enthusiastic wine drinker as he is a competent winemaker.

There are three labels at Bynum Winery—Barefoot Bynum (which for me makes wine drinking less pretentious), Davis Bynum for so-called premium wines, and Davis Bynum Private

Reserve for special bottlings. One of the more interesting Cabernets in recent years was the Davis Bynum Private Reserve 1966, which, although not a great bottle, had enough complexity and interest to make it a notable achievement for such a small and young wine establishment. The other reds—Pinot Noir, Ruby Cabernet, and Zinfandel—are pleasant. Of the whites, three are pleasant, but not necessarily distinguished—Johannisberg Riesling, Chenin Blanc, and Franken Riesling. There is a good line of rosés, the Cabernet rosé particularly—made of Cabernet Sauvignon grapes—and Zinfandel rosé and Grenache rosé.

Some of the best of California's dessert wines come from this winery—an amber dry sherry, some ports, and other sherries. These desserts are surprisingly good and show what a small winery can do if it uses its head.

CHALONE VINEYARD

P.O. Box 855
Soledad, California 93960

Owner:
Gavilan Vineyards
Winemaker:
Richard H. Graff
Vineyards:
40 acres
Capacity:
Storage 3,000 gallons
Fermenting 3,000 gallons

Chenin Blanc XXXX
Pinot Blanc XXXX
Chardonnay XXX
Pinot Noir: *Comer*

The growing of grapes for winemaking is a difficult task even under optimum conditions. Under adverse climatological conditions, it is virtually impossible. At Chalone Vineyards the impossible is almost overcome.

The Chalone Vineyard lies the Chalone bench in the Gavilan mountain range, in Soledad, California. There Chalone has had over sixty years of grape-growing experience. As a winery, Chalone's career has been short and checkered. Wine was first made at Chalone in 1960 and then, after a dormant period of five years, the winery resumed operation in 1966.

A view of the upper and lower sections of the vineyard inspires one with awe at the prospect that any wines can be made under such marginal growing conditions. The average annual rainfall is eleven inches. The vines, then, must struggle, giving expression to the wine myth that vines must suffer in order to produce great wines. At Chalone this is certainly true.

Originally, the vineyard was part of the section of land discovered by a Frenchman named Tamm, whose objective was to find soil conditions similar to those in the northern section of France. In the area of Chalone Vineyard, Tamm found similar soil—chalky, with very little organic matter—and planted the first vineyard.

The Chalone property as it stands today was planted in 1916. William Silvear planted Chardonnay, Pinot Blanc, Chenin Blanc, Pinot Noir, French Colombard, and Aligote—a noble selection of grapes at an inappropriate time: the year before Prohibition.

During that period grapes were grown at Chalone, but no wine was made. However, some of the grapes were made into champagne by Oliver Goulet at Almadén Vineyards for Silvear. The champagne was labeled Soledad Champagne, and, according to old-time wine drinkers, it was remarkably good.

Silvear died when he fell out of a tree that he was pruning at his home near Watsonville. His wife sold the vineyard to a winemaking group in 1960. As its winemaker, they hired a young Australian, Philip Togni, now the winemaker for Chappellet Vineyard. He made Chardonnay, Pinot Blanc, and Chenin Blanc and achieved some noteworthy, albeit brief, success. In 1962, the grapes were sold rather than used for winemaking.

Winemaker Richard Graff.

In 1965 a new era, the present one, began under the aegis of Richard Graff, the present winemaker. Recently out of the navy, Graff worked for other vineyards before coming to Chalone, where he dreamed of the possibility of producing distinctive high-quality wines. He enrolled in special courses on wine and winemaking at the University of California at Davis. He produced the 1966 Chalone wines: Chardonnay, Pinot Blanc, Chenin Blanc, Pinot Noir, and champagne. Those wines were not sold under the Chalone label, but by other wineries. The champagne, which will be released sometime in 1973, will carry the handsome Chalone label.

The struggle to revive Chalone is almost as great as the struggle of the vine with the soil, and Graff has done yeoman's work in restoring equipment, reconstructing the winery, and preparing the soil. Largely as a labor of love, Graff has almost single-handedly made Chalone what it is today, a fine producer of top varietals. The limitation of the winery as to quantity—it cannot produce more than 1,000 cases in the most bountiful of years—is a serious handicap.

The 1969 and 1970 wines reflect considerable promise, for the style of the wines is full, rich, and deep, finding much favor with a growing market of wine drinkers. The winery has benefited from a unique watering system, devised by Graff, of plastic tubing carrying a measured amount of water to each vine. At many small wineries, this must be done by hand, giving the vines a "drink" in this very dry area of California. The water must be trucked five days a week from Soledad in the Salinas Valley to a storage tank high in the slope above the vineyard; from there gravity

The austere Chalone Vineyard property is located in spectacular countryside.

feeds water down through the plastic tubing. If Rube Goldberg were growing the grapes at Chalone, this is the way he would do it.

The cooperage for fermentation and aging is now French Limousin oak which, according to Graff, gives considerable

The indispensible water truck stands in front of the winery.

character to his wines. The white grapes are picked and crushed into a wooden basket press; pressed, the juice runs, with the help of gravity, into the winery, where it ferments in sixty-gallon casks. This can be a very time-consuming and laborious method of fermenting,

but it always makes for good—possibly the best—interesting and exciting wines.

The character of the wine is different from that fermented in stainless steel tanks. Chalone is not the only winery where aging in oak is practiced, but it may have been among the earliest to stick to it. A refinement at Chalone, however, is that the wine is always fermented in *new* casks.

The emphasis at Chalone in recent years has been not only on quality but also on increasing the quantity. New plantings

should help. It is questionable whether Chalone will ever be a truly large producer of wines.

Chalone is the embodiment of the concept that a good wine must be handmade. There is always a continuing discussion among Chalone wine fans as to whether the old-fashioned techniques of the winery or the vines grown on limestone soil are responsible for its character. The Chalone wines always have something to say in a most interesting style, evolved by Graff, who, more than any other person, has brought back the wine pioneer spirit to Chalone—and to California.

CHAPPELLET VINEYARD

1581 Sage Canyon Road
St. Helena, California 94574

Owner:
Donn Chappellet

Winemaker:
Philip Togni

Vineyards:
100 acres

Chenin Blanc XXXX
Johannisberg Riesling XXX
Cabernet Sauvignon : Comer

The rust-colored roof of the winery projects above the sanguine California landscape.

For some, moving from the comfort of Beverly Hills to the hills of Pritchard in the Napa Valley would be a nightmare—leaving a plush, sophisticated area for a rugged, wooded one. For Donn Chappellet it was a dream come true after vast contributions of money, sweat, and family dedication.

Donn's winery was founded in 1969 on the premise that he would make the very finest wine and that compromise would be something that he would leave behind in Beverly Hills.

He is one of the new breed of California vintners that came to winemaking not by way of an economic pursuit nor a Davis Department of Enology education, but simply by way of wine drinking. Donn has been drinking wine conservatively, deliberately, and intelligently for many years, and his constant tasting and joy may have been responsible for the establishment of one of California's great new wineries.

To use the word "great" of new wineries is often an exaggeration; however, here it seems to be close to the truth. In the few short years of Chappellet, the winery has produced some first-quality, quite possibly great,

Donn Chappellet.

wines. Among the first was Chappellet Gamay, a blend of 1969 and 1970, which many believed to be quite fruity, light, and with just the right measure of tartness. I found the style of this wine to be too light for my taste and am grateful that Donn has pulled the vines in favor of Chardonnay and Cabernet Sauvignon.

Another first was Chappellet's 1968 Chenin Blanc, which was delightfully dry and crisp to the taste and with its considerable body may have set a new style for California Chenin Blancs. Up to that time many California wineries producing Chenin Blancs made them principally as secondary wines, sweet to semidry, considering them not especially important but something nice to round out the line. Chappellet took Chenin Blanc seriously and consumers who tasted it did the same. Subsequent Chenin Blancs, including the 1970, have improved, particularly in overall balance, so that Chappellet Chenin Blanc is used at our house as a principal wine with a fish course, replacing some current Chardonnays that are not as complex or as interesting.

The winery makes a limited supply of Johannisberg Riesling. In 1969 and 1970 the wine was excellent for its type, with a personality that probably reflected Donn's interest in growing grapes in the hills. It is his belief that the best wine comes from the hills—Pritchard of course, not Beverly.

The winery, with its well-educated, wise winemaker, Philip Ivor Togni, will un-

measure up to the 1969. The flavor has been zealously guarded by not fining the wine —that is, not clarifying it—and so perhaps this may set a style for other winemakers to follow.

Donn Chappellet was a very successful executive with one of the largest food-vending and industrial-catering companies in the world. He and his lovely wife, Molly, and their five children moved to the Napa Valley in 1967. It may be that Chappellet will make his mark as so many earlier California pioneers did in making good wine as a family enterprise. The family has style, interest and, perhaps most important, they love wine.

glimpses the vineyard with the house high above and then the road plunges back into the trees. The car stops and the visitor climbs a flight of rustic stairs to double glass doors going into the office. If he looks up sharply before going in he sees a startling roof soaring into the heavens. The office is bright with plants, paintings, antiques, and other art objects. Molly Chappellet has made a far more charming room than the seasoned winery visitor expects.

The visitor continues through doors at the back of the office into the winery. He has probably been talking until then. Now he gasps, falls silent for a few moments, and begins babbling something about cathedrals. The impact of the building is as unique as the building itself. The 60° temperature adds to the solemnity.

The floor plan is a huge triangle 200 feet on each side. The roof consists of three enormous triangular slabs rising steeply from the outer walls to a point almost 50 feet above the floor at the exact center of the building. The slabs are separated to allow an observation platform looking in three directions high above the center point of the floor. The immensity of the room is broken only by a few slender steel columns painted yellow. Lights from the working level are reflected from the warm texture of the ceilings. A shaft of sunlight may strike

down through the cavern. Precise rows of casks march across the floor. On the far side, tall stainless steel tanks stand on their concrete pads and less familiar adjuncts of the modern winemaker's trade hang in profusion on the wall.

The exterior of the winery is equally striking, if less easy to

The winery building.

appreciate because the great bulk of the building is set low in a clump of trees. The roof slabs are dramatic, both for their size and the wide bands of Corten steel that cover them. Corten is a roofing material that weathers into warm reddish earthen tones in accord with the setting. Ridges between the bands give texture to the roof.

The winery lacks for nothing that contributes to good wine. One of the things that impresses most about Donn Chappellet and his love for wine is that he is tremendously independent. His feelings about making great wine are so intense that he rarely has time to spend with visitors, famous or no; the daily effort is to maintain the vineyard and make the wine, with plenty of time to enjoy both with a glass of wine. After all, it was a glass of wine that moved Donn to the notion that he could make California's finest wines. Who knows? He may do it.

The main office fronts the winery interior. At left hangs a John Altoon painting.

doubtedly attempt to make the finest in Cabernet Sauvignon and Chardonnay. If the limited edition of 1970 Chardonnay is any indication of the future, then the wine should do well.

I was bowled over by the 1969 Cabernet Sauvignon, which is a "big one" with all the goodness and richness of which Cabernet is capable, and is a wine that will probably outlive me. The 1968 Cabernet Sauvignon, also quite good, does not

If Donn did nothing else in the Napa Valley, he would still be known, and indeed remembered, for the modernity, beauty, and efficiency of his new winery structure, which may be the forerunner of many others.

I like wine writer Roy Brady's description of the winery as "the Chappellet domain." He goes on to describe it in the December-January, 1972, edition of *Wine World Magazine.*

A first-time visitor has no way of being prepared for the winery. The road climbs steeply up from Lake Hennessy as it twists and turns through the trees. One

THE CHRISTIAN BROTHERS– MONT LASALLE VINEYARDS

P.O. Box 420
Napa, California 94558

Owners:
The Christian Brothers

Winemaker:
Brother Timothy

Vineyards:
2,000 acres

Capacity:
Storage 20,000,000 gallons
Fermenting 3,700,000 gallons

Pineau de la Loire XXX
Cabernet Sauvignon XXX
Johannisberg Riesling XX
Pinot St. Georges X

The winery and the novitiate at Mont LaSalle stand in the center of 200 acres of vineyards.

The Christian Brothers have a long tradition of winemaking in California, particularly in the Napa Valley.

The order, a part of the Catholic Church, is dedicated to the education of youth. It was founded in 1680 in Reims, France, by St. Jean Baptiste de la Salle and is made up of men who are not priests, but who have taken the vows of poverty, chastity, and obedience.

The principal winery, at Mont LaSalle in Napa, California, was constructed in 1903, although the Brothers began making wine as early as 1882 in Martinez, California. Since then the Brothers have constructed an efficient yet most picturesque aging and champagne cellar in an old stone landmark at St. Helena, California, and in addition have built a new winery in the same general area that is a model of modernity, simplicity, beauty, and efficiency.

Brother Timothy, a tall, dynamic, kindly man, is so identi-

fied with the operation that when one drinks The Christian Brothers wine one's imagination conjures up a picture of the gentle Brother Tim drinking a glass of wine amidst a lovely Napa Valley setting. No other personality in the modern era of California winemaking so personifies the beauty and love, as well as pride, that goes into the production of California wine. Brother Tim has been a forceful figure both in the industry and at the winery in the advancement of the cause of civilized wine drinking, and no other personality stood for quality winemaking as well, long before the present wave of wine popularity in America.

Brother Tim has been ably assisted by Brother Gregory and Brother Frederick, and Brother Eric, in the vineyard growing and winemaking facilities.

The Brothers have always been in the forefront of the industry, running full-page ads in magazines and newspapers all over the country even before wine became popular. Soon another Christian Brothers advancement, their wine museum in San Francisco, will be open to visitors.

Although it makes quality wines, The Christian Brothers is also a volume winery, producing wines in great quantity, always with the idea that the wines should be generally ready to drink on purchase. It does not always offer wines of great complexity, but rather, through skillful blending of its wines, something good to drink at any given moment, and at a reasonable price, without the necessity of aging the wines for long periods of time.

Some so-called connoisseurs complain that the wines are light and without enough varietal character. In perspective, however, the wines are most satisfactory and pleasant to drink. They are wines for the everyday table. The Rieslings and Cabernets are particularly good buys and really quite excellent, and from time to time there have been

Brother Timothy, cellarmaster of the largest church-owned producer of wine in the world.

An aerial view of the ultramodern facility in the Napa Valley.

some memorable wines with The Christian Brothers label.

The Christian Brothers make Chardonnay in a style different from that currently in vogue. Their belief is that the Chardonnay should not be overflowing with the taste of oak, and many wine lovers seem to agree. The Chardonnays generally show more fruit and little, if any, oak. There is at the moment a school of taste that prefers Chardonnay with much fruit, so it is not uncommon for wine lovers to enjoy The Christian Brothers Chardonnay as a welcome relief from the so-called oaked Chardonnays.

Currently the Chenin Blanc, marketed under the name of Pineau de la Loire and also made to show considerable fruit, is a favorite.

The reds—Pinot Noir, Gamay Noir, Pinot St. Georges, and Zinfandel—are in the lighter style, not necessarily heavy bodied or complex. These wines, at the price, are among California's best values.

The private office at the Greystone Cellar in St. Helena.

The altar wines, under the Mont LaSalle label, were the first Christian Brothers wines, made way back in 1882 and still among the best in altar wines. An interesting new product of the winery is an excellent brandy— one of the best yet made in California. Labeled XO Rare Reserve, it is aged ten years in wood and 50 percent pot-still brandy. It is limited in its distribution and expensive when you do find it— but it is worth every effort.

With rising prices, it is most comforting to know that Brother Timothy is still around, making good wines at popular prices. For that alone The Christian Brothers and Brother Timothy will continue to be as memorable as a good glass of wine. It is such men as Brother Timothy who give the lovers of California wines assurance that even though a winery is of volume character, it can still produce honest and good wines at prices that encourage pleasant drinking.

CONCANNON VINEYARD

P. O. Box 432, Tesla Road
Livermore, California 94551

Owner:
Concannon Family Corporation,
Joseph S. Concannon, Jr.,
President

Winemaker:
James Concannon

Vineyards:
350 acres

Capacity:
Storage 400,000 gallons
Fermenting 60,000 gallons

Sauvignon Blanc XXXX
Cabernet Sauvignon Limited
Bottlings XXX
Muscat de Frontignan XXX
Johannisberg Riesling XXX
Petite Sirah XX
Prelude Sherry X

Winemaker Jim Concannon tests a new vintage in the winery lab.

If you stand and listen in the Livermore Valley, traditionally known as a California premium white wine district, you are likely to hear Joe, Jr., proclaim, "We can make as good a Cabernet Sauvignon on this soil as anywhere in the state." Strong words, from a man whose Concannon Vineyard has been producing some of California's best white wines in the Livermore Valley for almost a hundred years. After tasting some of his Cabernet Sauvignons, limited bottlings, I say he may be right. For the Cabernet, completely different from that which is made in the Napa Valley, has enough varietal character to identify it as a Cabernet while developing its own personality derived from the so-called white-wine soil of the Livermore Valley.

Making good red wines has been an interesting, successful experiment, which the Concannons enjoyed doing as much for the challenge as for the wines themselves. They also commercially pioneered the red varietal Petite Sirah and were probably the first to do so in California, showing the way for a number of others. The Petite Sirah is usually a straight-forward wine, with not a lot of complexity but with a good deal of body and flavor so as to make it a most flavorful companion to an everyday meal.

The whites are extremely good, particularly the Sauvignon Blanc, which seems to be a house specialty; when it is made in limited-edition bottlings it is quite possibly the finest Sauvignon Blanc in California. Sauvignon Blanc as a varietal does not seem to be popular these days.

Joe Concannon inspects the estate's vineyards.

However, when the Concannons do it well it is a wine with considerable flavor, with a style they have developed as their own, and with a crisp, pleasant dryness that makes the wine welcome with superior fish. The Johannisberg Riesling is another fine Concannon white wine, followed in descending order of my appreciation by the chablis, dry sauterne, and moselle. The Château Concannon, a sweet Sémillon, although very different from a French sauterne, has a pleasant style of its own and is appropriate as an after-dinner sweet wine; with some bottle age it can develop most interesting characteristics.

A favorite of mine for dessert is the winery's Muscat Frontignan, a wine of 18 percent alcohol providing the unique odor and flavor of Muscat. Muscat is not always welcome in "experienced" wine homes but I find it to be one of the most nearly unique of wines—pleasant in taste and smell. The only problem with California muscatel is that it has had poor public relations.

Another experiment at Concannon is a line of champagnes, which are sold only at the winery. The brut is probably the best, with very little sugar content.

The new sherry produced by Concannon, Prelude Dry Sherry, should improve as more of it is made, but I found it somewhat disappointing. Knowing the family and the dedication of its wine-maker, James Concannon, I can predict later editions of the wine will be much better. The Prelude may be just that—a prelude.

The Concannons take pride in the fact that since the 1880s, a bottle of Concannon wine has graced the table of every pope. The history of the Concannons is already legend in the Livermore Valley. It began in 1847 in Ireland with James Concannon, who founded the vineyards in 1883.

A religious man, James Concannon, assisted by his faith and by the archbishop of San Francisco, Joseph S. Alemany, first produced wines for religious purposes. This tradition certainly was helpful during the Prohibition period. The winery had its greatest expansion and success during the period of Captain Joe Concannon, one of five sons of James Concannon, who died in 1911. Captain Joe worked until his death in 1965, and today the tremendous duo of Joe, Jr., and Jim faces the popular wine boom well armed with fine wine and a rich tradition.

CRESTA BLANCA
WINE COMPANY

One Jackson Place
San Francisco, California

Owner:
Guild Wine Company

Winemaster:
Lawrence Oroccia

Old, thick-boled vines stand in the Livermore vineyards.

It has been difficult to figure out what is happening to the Cresta Blanca Wine Company these days. Undoubtedly it is going through a transition, apparently one for the better. In recent years it is one of the few wineries that have not profited by the boom in wine drinking, nor does it seem to have improved its wines. Operations have been moved to Mendocino County where Guild Wine is resuscitating the label.

The company most certainly has a noble and interesting past. It was begun by wine pioneer Charles A. Wetmore in 1882, when he purchased a portion of Rancho El Valle de San Jose in Livermore.

For almost fifty years he was recognized as a great authority on California wines. He was well known not only in California but also in France, where he studied. He was also in the first class of the University of California. As well as anyone else Wetmore helped to put over California wines, as the Cresta Blanca name won awards at the Paris Exposition of 1889.

The finest Cresta Blanca wine was one made in the late '50s by Myron Nightingale, now the winemaker at Beringer. (Mr. Nightingale seems to move from one challenge to another.) It was an experimental wine, called Premier Sémillon, which came

closer to approximating the taste of Château d'Yquem than any other wine in the state. The taste of French sauterne in general and of Yquem in particular is perhaps the most nearly unique of all wines and is almost impossible to duplicate. The flavor is caused by the *Botrytis cinerea,* a fungus which gives the sauterne of France its character but apparently is difficult, if not impossible, to duplicate in California, because the humidity is too low.

The Premier Sémillon, one of California's first wines to sell for more than five dollars, was, in almost hothouse conditions, in-

The storied Premier Sémillon.

fected with the fungus. The result was magnificent—the best thing ever done at Cresta Blanca—and may have indeed shown that a large corporate-owned winery could make not only a good wine but a hallmark wine when it wanted to.

Since the days of Myron Nightingale the winery has slipped for some reason. In 1971 it came under new management, the Guild Wine Company, and if it is put back together Cresta Blanca may rise again. There is activity under the leadership of its new president, Herbert Drake, that bodes well for the future. A recent offering of Zinfandel was not from the winery's original vineyard in Livermore, but rather from Mendocino County, where Guild has large plantings. The wine was typical of Mendocino County—full, big, and with different Zinfandel character from that found in the home vineyard. The change of vineyards may be for the better for the reds; the whites may be a different question.

With new capital, able leadership, and first call on some choice Mendocino County plantings, the Cresta Blanca label may again grace some premier bottlings of American wine.

CUVAISON, INC.

4560 Silverado Trail
Calistoga, California 94515

Owner:
Cuvaison, Inc.,
a California corporation*

Winemaker:
Thomas Cottrell

Vineyards:
15 acres

Capacity:
Storage 20,000 gallons
Fermenting 17,000 gallons

Chardonnay grapes, ready for the crush.

Founded in 1970 on a good Napa Gamay vineyard in Calistoga, California, Cuvaison is a prime example of the many fledgling, small, but quality-minded wineries that are finding their way into almost every grape-growing section of California. Up from the laser industry, in the San Francisco Bay area, Thomas Cottrell, Ph.D., a research scientist, and Tom Parkhill, an electrical engineer, came to the Napa Valley with considerable daring, little money, and less experience. Together, they have been making principally two wines, Chenin Blanc and Gamay.

The first wines were of the 1970 vintage, which was hampered by the "big freeze" of 1970 when 80 percent of the crop was destroyed, and so the wines are not full of varietal character, nor do they have the freshness for which both varieties are well known. However, there is such demand for wines from small wineries that the wines sold out anyway.

Cuvaison, emphasizing slow, cold fermentation, improved its wines with the 1971 Chenin Blanc, Grey Riesling, and Napa Gamay, which is labeled Gamay

Vivace to distinguish it from the 1970 production. Chardonnay has been made in two styles, one with less oak than the other. Both bottlings of the Chardonnay showed varietal character but not enough to make them great. With more time and experience, Cuvaison's Chardonnay and its other wines are likely to challenge some of the older, more established small and medium-sized wineries.

The winery is unique in that, as of 1972, there was no winery building. Equipment was limited but good, with four jacketed stainless steel fermenters, a Willmes press, and a crushing platform on a cement slab enclosed by a cyclone fence. That is a winery, because it works.

Innovative, Cuvaison was the first American winery to use carbonic maceration, a technique used to produce a beaujolais-style wine. The technique is to crush imperfectly a small amount of fruit and then add grapes that are placed uncrushed in closed vats. In this condition, the grapes continue living without oxygen and, through the phenomenon known as carbonic maceration, part of the grapes' sugar changes into alcohol without the usual intervention of yeast cells. The time the juice is left in contact with the solid matter of the grapes varies from wine to wine and is determined by whether the wine is meant to be kept many years or to be drunk young. The berries are black and the winery is able to get much color. The fermentation is finished as if it were a white wine. The process —new here, old in France— is called *cuvaison* (fermentation in vats), and accounts for the winery's name.

There is some customer resistance in this country to this style of wine, due to residual CO_2 (carbon dioxide) in the bottle. This European technique, not much used in California, may become more popular as Cuvaison learns more about it and the wines it is producing.

*In a state of merger at time of publication.

EAST-SIDE WINERY

6100 East Highway 12
Lodi, California 95240

Owner:
East-Side Winery
Cooperative,
with 130 members throughout
the area
E. C. Haas, General Manager

Winemaker:
Lee Eichle

Vineyards:
Owned by members of the
Cooperative

Capacity:
Storage 4,500,000 gallons
Fermenting 1,000,000 gallons

Royal Host Cocktail Sherry XXXX
Royal Host Gold XX

The East-Side Winery at Lodi.

East-Side is one of the oldest and largest cooperatives remaining in California, founded in 1934 with the objective of making good wines from the most desirable soils of Lodi on the "east side," where the winery was established.

The production is divided into several bottlings, the first of which is wine in bulk, sold in the East under the Pastene label. The varietals, such as Ruby Cabernet, Grey Riesling, Sémillon, and Chenin Blanc, are sold under the brand name of Royal Host. Rounding out this line is a hybrid variety of Muscat and Sémillon grapes identified as Gold.

East-Side's fame, however, has come from its dessert wines and brandy. The brandy is sold as Royal Host, both straight and as a blend, while Conti Royale is sold as a ten-year-old straight brandy. The dessert wines include cocktail sherry, dry sherry, cream sherry, tawny port, and ruby port, and are consistent winners at the Los Angeles County Fair, the only official wine judging in America. During the 1972 Fair, Royal Host Dry Sherry shared a Sweepstakes Award with Heitz Cellar's 1969 Chardonnay, Lot 2-92Z; the two were judged the outstanding wines in a competition that had over four hundred entries. The sherry is made even more notable by the fact that table wines in America are outselling dessert wines; it must have been extremely good to have pleased the palates of the judges.

The sherries are baked in 20,000-gallon concrete bakers, from which small quantities are taken and stored in reused brandy casks that stand above the sherry bakers for a period of two to three years. The resulting wine is often used in a blend with bulk wines and may account for some of the richness and depth of flavor of the Royal Host sherries.

The table wines are of interest mainly because of the reasonableness of their price. They are good but not complex or outstanding. The Ruby Cabernet and the Chenin Blanc, however, are improving constantly. The dessert wines and the brandy at East-Side provide the great excitement.

FETZER VINEYARDS
Route 1, Box 361-X
Redwood Valley, California 95470

Owners:
Bernard A. Fetzer and Kathleen
M. Fetzer

Winemakers:
Bernard A. Fetzer and
James Fetzer

Vineyards:
90 acres

Capacity:
Storage 50,000 gallons
Fermenting 25,000 gallons

Zinfandel XX
Cabernet Sauvignon X

A relatively new winery, the Fetzer Vineyards was founded in 1968 and in the same year made one of its finest wines, a Zinfandel.

Whether its future wines can be as good is a question that only time and taste will tell. The Cabernet Sauvignon, Pinot Noir, and Carmine Carignane have not developed the same interesting taste characteristics as that first Zinfandel. Later Zinfandels have been relatively good but the 1968 still reigns as the best.

The white wines—Mountain Sémillon, Green Hungarian, Chardonnay, Sauvignon Blanc—are not quite as good as the reds and of course this may be due to the fact that the region is as far north in the state as winemakers care to go. Bernard A. Fetzer, the founder of the winery, seems to believe that his vines benefit from the difficulties with which they are faced in order to survive. The whites don't bear this out, the reds may, and of course the Zinfandel does. The reds are aided immeasurably by aging in French oak casks.

Mr. Fetzer, member of a famous lumber family in the area, is quite independent, so there is no public tasting room. Tastings are by invitation only.

Mendocino County is just being rediscovered by wine drinkers. The first taste for them ought to be the 1968 Fetzer Zinfandel.

Pat Fetzer shows off the winery.

The handsome buildings at Fetzer are less than ten years old.

Winter ice fronts the terraced Mendocino vineyards.

FICKLIN VINEYARDS

32046 Ave. 7½
Madera, California 93637

Owners:
Walter C. Ficklin, and
David B. Ficklin, Jr.

Winemaker:
David B. Ficklin

Vineyards:
Substantial amount of acreage at
Madera in San Joaquin Valley

Capacity:
Storage 40,000 gallons
Fermenting 4,500 gallons

Tinta (Madeira) Port XXXX
Vintage Port (Special
Bottling) XXXX
Emerald Riesling X

Unquestionably, Ficklin produces the finest port wines in the state of California. The most famous of its wines is the Tinta Port, which is a blend of choice Portuguese grape varieties. The vineyard is planted to Tinta Cão, Tinta Madeira, Alvarelhão, Souzão, and Touriga.

A small amount of vintage port is produced—bottled usually three years after the vintage and bottle-aged approximately ten years before being sold. These wines, referred to as special bottlings, are in very small quantity; those that have been tasted have been properly sweet, rich with port character, round with great depth of flavor. The 1951 was made exclusively from Touriga grapes, while the 1957 was made wholly from Tinta Madeira and pot-still brandy distilled from their own grapes.

On occasion David Ficklin is known to take some of the regular Ficklin port, the Tinta Madeira, assign it to a special space at the winery, and just leave it to sit in the bottle for years. This was done with the 1955, although no vintage or bottling date appears on the label. It turned out to be a wise experiment, as the wine seems to have benefited a good deal from the added bottle age, acquiring more richness in its flavor.

Specialization in Portuguese grape varieties has made Ficklin the most unique port-type winery in California. It was founded with the unheard-of notion that the winery become a port specialist, and is family-operated by David Ficklin and Walter C. Ficklin, Jr. Their father, Walter C. Ficklin, Sr., planted the vineyards in 1912 but it was not until 1948 that the present character of the winery asserted itself with the first port wines.

Most vineyards in the central valley feature strong-limbed vines, such as these.

The principal port wine, the Tinta Madeira, is labeled Tinta Port and can be compared to Portuguese wines—the Tinta Port is similar in style to a Portuguese ruby port. Making great port wines as the Ficklins do may be a very fine comment on the qualities of the Fresno district. There are some who believe that this district can make the finest dessert wines in the world and would do so if there were more interest on the part of the growers in making it, as well as the wine drinkers in drinking it. Some wine writers believe that Ficklin ports are good not only because of the soil but also the judicious use of beverage brandy for use in arresting the fermentation and ultimately giving the wine more depth and interest.

In recent years an infinitesimally small amount of Emerald Riesling and Ruby Cabernet grape varieties have been planted and made into respectable table wines. The Emerald Riesling shows considerable fruitiness, while the Ruby Cabernet shows some finesse. The wines are sold at the winery to customers who happen to come in and ask for them. In addition, a small amount of heavy-bodied red wine of a very curious variety, the Raboso Piave from the northeastern part of Italy, is also produced in some years. But the major production and interest at Ficklin is still the best port in California, the Tinta Port.

FREEMARK ABBEY WINERY

3022 St. Helena Highway
St. Helena, California 94574

Owners:
A partnership including
Charles A. Carpy,
Frank L. Wood,
William P. Jaeger, Jr.,
Richard G. Heggie,
James C. Warren,
R. Bradford Webb,
John M. Bryan

Winemakers:
J. Luper and R. Bradford Webb

Vineyards:
A variety of vineyards in the
Napa Valley

Chardonnay XXX
Petite Sirah XXX
Cabernet Sauvignon XX
Johannisberg Riesling XX

The increase in wine consumption in America has served to bring many new glasses of wine to the American table. One of the best and most distinctive is from Freemark Abbey, a winery that has had its roots in St. Helena since 1895, when it was founded by Antonio Forni.

The winery literally closed its doors prior to the present wine boom, but was revived by an amazing collection of gentlemen who have formed a partnership that grows grapes and makes wine.

If I were going to select a number of men with which to start a good winery operation, there could be no better choice than the Freemark Abbey group, among whom are R. Bradford Webb, the chemist turned winemaker who was responsible for Hanzell Vineyard's first great wines; Charles Carpy, whose family has been in the Napa Valley since the 1890s; Frank "Laurie" Wood, who has been carefully tending the vines of some of the best vineyards in the Napa Valley; and James C. Warren, the eldest son of former Chief Justice Warren, who has sold some of the best vineyards and vineyard sites in the Napa Valley as a real estate broker.

Gathering this elite group

Winemaker Jerry Luper.

The main building at Freemark Abbey dates from 1895.

brings together all of the good things that a winery must have— good vineyards (resource material), winemaking know-how, and vineyard site selections—so when the winery reopened, this group assured the project's success. If for no other reason, the winery would have done well simply because from the day it reopened its doors it had a great selection of grapes, resulting in such

fine varietal wines as Chardonnay, Johannisberg Riesling, Pinot Noir, and Cabernet Sauvignon.

The winery has also had access to a most interesting Cabernet Sauvignon from the Bouche vineyard, called Cabernet Bouche. Brad Webb has made Johannisberg Riesling in a heavier, bigger, drier style—with some consumers complaining that the wines lack freshness and fruitiness. It is a most interesting dispute, but I find this style of Riesling most enjoyable for its assertiveness, taste, and flavor, a welcome diversion from the lighter,

Contemporary winemaking facilities contrast with the interior of the seventy-eight year old building.

fresher Johannisberg Riesling styles.

The 1967 Cabernet Sauvignon has turned out to be a remarkably good wine for a first effort and lends credence to the hope that great Cabernets will come from Freemark Abbey. As is true with many wineries, Freemark Abbey has found Pinot Noir difficult to make with strong varietal character, but at least the winery has the grapes that give them a chance to do it.

One of the best things the winery has done is to make a full-bodied, rich, strong-flavored Petite Sirah 1969, which has been a far better wine than the 1968 Pinot Noir. Petite Sirah has still not found great and universal acceptance by the American palate, but this is a wine to watch for.

All of the Freemark Abbey wines have been well made—not always, however, with great complexity. As each year passes the wines are gaining in style and character. The 1970 Chardonnay was just such a wine. As a result it is challenging the finer Chardonnays of the state. The Rieslings, Cabernet Sauvignon, and Pinot Noir no doubt will also make such challenges. The winery is one of the best examples of a new operation and is a shot in the arm for those of us who are concerned about the future of California winemaking. Freemark Abbey is here to stay and, some of us think, just in time.

GEMELLO WINERY CORP.

2003 El Camino Real
Mountain View, California 94040

Owners:
Mario and Kay Gemello
and Louis C. Sarto

Winemaker:
Mario Gemello

Vineyards:
None

Capacity:
Storage 62,000 gallons
Fermenting 20,000 gallons

Cabernet Sauvignon XXX
Zinfandel XX

Mario Gemello has been making wine at the present winery site in Mountain View for over thirty-five years. He has done extremely well with Cabernet Sauvignon, especially the 1960 bottling, one of the finest I've tasted. Curiously, Mario has made fine Cabernet Sauvignon without the winery's owning any vineyards. He has acquired grapes from vineyards by contract only. His Cabernet is from the Gaspar and the Smith vineyards, located on Pierce Road in Saratoga, California. It is said that this area is the one from which wine pioneers Paul Masson and later Martin Ray made their Cabernets. The Gemello Zinfandel, Petite Sirah, Barbera, and Carignane are made from grapes grown in the Morgan Hill area, from a vineyard generally known as the Prusso Vineyards.

The winery formerly emphasized nonvintage wines, but under the relatively new partnership of Louis C. Sarto and Mario and Kay Gemello, the winery is now stressing vintage reds and whites. It was often the practice of Mario to hold vast quantities of red wines in cask for six to ten years before bottling, as was done with the 1960 Cabernet—a very fine wine—which was bottled in 1966. There are those winemakers and wine drinkers who believe that this is too long; they probably represent the majority view, which is always disproved by a bottle of wine such as the 1960 Gemello Cabernet Sauvignon.

A typical start of production for red wines is to ferment them for a long period of time on their skins, then age them in oak or redwood puncheons or tanks, and bottle the wine only as sales warrant. In keeping with the Italian fashion, little if any attention was given to bottle

The storage and aging cellar creates a handsome display.

aging for many years. This is changing as the new vintage-dated varietals are coming into bottle.

The wines of Gemello are highly distinctive and show well the good qualities of the Santa Clara wine district, an area threatened, regretably, by "civilization." Mario's father, John Gemello, born in Italy's wine district of Piedmont, began Gemello's winemaking career in 1934, selling a considerable

Winemaker Mario Gemello.

quantity of wine out the front door, on the highway, directly to the consumer. Today lesser-priced sound wines of Gemello are featured under the secondary label Mountain View.

The winery has embarked on a special program, including lengthy fermentation, a minimum of fining, and longer wood aging when necessary, with the use of French Nevers and Limousin oak. This is beginning to show throughout the line of wines, particularly Cabernet Sauvignon, Zinfandel, and Gamay. Much more in the way of complex wines can be expected of Gemello in the future—only, however, if the vineyard contracts can be maintained.

GUILD WINE COMPANY

500 Sansome Street
San Francisco, California

Owner:
Guild Wine Company

Vice President, Production:
W. E. Kite

Winemaster:
Lawrence Oroccia

Vineyards:
Variety of vineyards located in
Mendocino, San Joaquin, and
Fresno counties

Capacity:
Storage 50,788,000 gallons
Eight wineries are operated with
an annual processing capacity
of 200,000 tons of grapes

Winemasters Guild Pinot Noir
Mendocino County XX

Ceremony Old San Francisco
Brand Port XX

Winemasters Guild Lodi
Creme Sherry XX

February rain clouds build over the main winery at Lodi.

The Guild Wine Company can be best described as large, for it is made up of over a thousand growers formed into a co-op of wineries. It is the third largest producer in the United States. It is always difficult to assess the quality of such a large enterprise as it relates to the great wines of America. There are many labels here, such as Winemasters Guild, Virginia Dare, Cresta Blanca, Garrett, Cribari, Cook's, Roma, etc., all different in quality and price.

Suffice it to say that a wide variety of wines is made, all stemming from an interlocking of companies including the Garrett Wine Co., the Italian Vineyard Co. (founded, incidentally, by Secundo Guasti), Guild, Alta, Roma, and Cribari. No doubt there are others, but for our purposes these will be sufficient to characterize the operation.

Much of the wine is made for bulk bottling but there have been some interesting new things coming out of the conglomerate, so much so that the enterprise may indeed earn a place of distinction among wine producers.

At the 1971 Los Angeles County Fair wine judging, for the first time in almost three decades, the sixteen judges agreed to give a Sweepstakes Award (best out of 400 entries) to one of Guild's new wine varietals, Winemasters Guild, an exciting, rich, full-bodied Pinot Noir. The wine was distinctive

The entrance to the tasting room.

and truly remarkable, inasmuch as it came from grapes grown in Mendocino County, where Guild has large holdings. The judges were surprised by the quality of the wine as well as the origin of the grapes. Indeed, some of the judges complained that it was really not Pinot Noir. Others said that this was perhaps the way Pinot Noir tasted when grown from grapes in Mendocino County. All agreed that the wine was good, perhaps even great.

Guild itself may have been surprised by the award and it is to be hoped that this kind of wine will be the forerunner of many more. The wine obviously was not made by luck, so there is no reason to believe that more will not be forthcoming. Bulk wine is fine, but complex wine is better.

There have been some other examples, particularly the dessert wines, which are marketed under the Ceremony or Old San Francisco labels. These wines, made from grapes grown either in the Lodi district or central California, are among the state's better dessert wines, particularly Ceremony Old San Francisco Brand Port, which has been aged in small cooperage and is a consistently good and satisfactory wine of this type. Inexpensive price is another of its virtues and so is the quantity available.

But it is from that award-winning Pinot Noir that one can take hope. It proves that a corporate entity can make a fine wine — so fine that it can greatly surprise sixteen consumers whose wine experience together totals 100 years. It will not take 100 years before Guild turns out another fine varietal under the Winemasters Guild label.

HANZELL VINEYARDS

18596 Lomita Avenue
Sonoma, California 95476

Owner:
Mary Schaw Day

Winemaker:
R. Bradford Webb,
Consultant Enologist

Vineyards:
Approximately 25 acres

Capacity:
Storage 6,000 gallons
Fermenting 3,600 gallons

Chardonnay XXX
Pinot Noir : *Comer*

The winery at Hanzell was patterned after the Burgundy château, Clos de Vougeot.

Some of California's greatest Chardonnay has been made at Hanzell Vineyards, especially the ones made under the leadership of James K. Zellerbach of the Zellerbach Paper Company, the former ambassador to Italy who also served as chief of the Marshall Plan.

Mr. Zellerbach fell in love with the wines of Romanée-Conti and Montrachet of Burgundian fame and dreamed the great dream of producing wines in California as interesting as those he remembered from France. He set out to make great Chardonnay and Pinot Noir, and lived long enough to fulfill his dream with Chardonnay but not long enough for the Pinot Noir.

The vineyard was planted in 1952 as it is today to approximately ten acres of Pinot Noir and eight acres of Chardonnay; the latter has been increased to sixteen acres in recent years. To fulfill his dream, Mr. Zellerbach equipped his winery with experts and with the finest of winery equipment. With its stainless steel tanks, small Limousin oak barrels, and a modern laboratory, the entire winery complex was designed by the best brains money could buy, assisted by some which money could not buy—great enology and viniculture experts from the University of California at Davis. The winery today still stands as a model for other small wineries insistent on the highest quality operation.

The Hanzell name is a contraction of Mrs. Zellerbach's first name, Hannah, and the first syllable of Zellerbach.

The Hanzell Chardonnays of the middle and late '50s are probably the best produced in Sonoma County and indeed may be among the best ever made in California. It was often a pleasant experience to taste the Hanzell Chardonnays blind along with great French wines and to observe the challenges the Hanzell wine made to the so-called superior Montrachets of Burgundy. The Pinot Noirs have been reasonably good but not in the same class as the Chardonnays, although recently in a twenty-three-entry California Pinot Noir tasting, the Hanzell 1967 performed extremely well. These Chardonnays have been made with the beautiful and happy marriage of fruit and

Built by the late James D. Zellerbach in the '50s, Hanzell was designed to equal the great wines of Burgundy.

wood, with less emphasis on the wood than other fine Chardonnays of California. Perhaps this is a good thing for those who enjoy the fruit of the Chardonnay grape more than the qualities that wood can give.

Hanzell was among the first producing wineries to employ such now-accepted techniques as cold fermentation, nitrogen sparging, and the use of Burgundy oak barrels in the production of Pinot Noir and Chardonnay—Burgundy wines. The Pinot Noirs are normally sold with three years of bottle age and the Chardonnays with one. Mr. Zellerbach did not need

to make any money on his "winery plaything," but he had such pride in California wines that he believed a small, premium winery could indeed make superb California Chardonnay and charge enough to make a profit. Hanzell was among the first to charge what was then a high price for its wines, in excess of four dollars a bottle. The wine is now selling at ninety dollars a case.

When Mr. Zellerbach died in 1963, the Hanzell lovers were terribly worried about the "Burgundy dream" at Hanzell, and they were right, for the executors of the estate planned no further making of wine. Some of the grapes and wines of that time are found in bottlings of other wineries, notably Joe Heitz's early Chardonnay, which again

proved to be some of California's finest.

Fortunately, in 1965 Douglas N. Day, a good and kind gentleman who retired from his position as a chain-store executive, bought the Hanzell property and continued to make Pinot Noir and Chardonnay, with his first vintage of 1965 released in 1967. There was great concern among Hanzell lovers over whether Douglas and his charming and efficient wife, Mary,

would continue the winery in the tradition of quality set by Mr. Zellerbach. Some believed that Douglas would bring a chain-store approach to the making of Hanzell wines, expand the vineyards, and turn the winery into a volume operation. Nothing could have been farther from the truth, as succeeding vintages of Pinot Noir and Chardonnay have proved.

Unfortunately, Mr. Day died in 1970. However, Mrs. Day took over and, to her credit, is doing it well. Chardonnay at Hanzell continues to be a complex wine with considerable flavor, expensive but so far worthy of the price. The dream continues.

HEITZ WINE CELLARS
500 Taplin Road
St. Helena, California 94574

Owner and Winemaker:
Joseph E. and Alice Heitz

Vineyards:
30 acres in the Napa Valley
immediately east of the
Silverado Trail

Capacity:
Storage 90,000 gallons
Fermenting 19,000 gallons

Chardonnay XXXX
Cabernet Sauvignon XXXX
Angelica XXXX
Johannisberg Riesling XXX
Pinot Noir XXX
Pinot Blanc XX
Grignolino XX

More than any other person in the state, Joe Heitz typifies the new breed of winemaker involved in winemaking in California. He has combined the best of both wine worlds—he is a graduate of the University of California at Davis, Department of Enology, and a serious, dedicated wine lover. In many commercial operations, these two worlds do not necessarily blend. But Joe Heitz appears to make wine as much for his own consumption as he does for commercial profit. He is a wine-drinking idealist.

Fiercely independent and self-sufficient, Mr. Heitz makes his wines in a style that dares you to be critical of them. He says that they are the best and, surprisingly enough, more often than not they are. By no means, however, should the Heitz name be blindly accepted as a guarantee of greatness. But you can be sure the wine will be quite good and, reflecting Mr. Heitz's personality, have a good deal of character.

Since wine growing and winemaking have become such expensive pursuits, Mr. Heitz represents a breed that is just beginning to make its mark on the California wine scene. He may be the first graduate of Davis to establish his own winery from scratch. Many of the sons of winemaking families, past and present, have had the good fortune to come, after graduation from Davis, to land that had been seasoned with generations of growth and experience and assisted by considerable capital and the finest of equipment. Mr. Heitz started in the early 1960s with nothing but the

ability to make good wine.

In the beginning, Heitz Cellars took a page out of the Burgundy shippers' book by moving up and down California, finding grapes and buying wines to make into cash under the Heitz banner. Starting a vineyard and winery overnight is impossible. It takes almost five years to grow the first grapes, at considerable expense, so young graduates of Davis generally seek employment from large wineries, and more often than not remain there. To begin a wine estate is no small task, and Joe began with wines rather than grapes. Unable to finance vineyards from the beginning, Joe pur-

Iconoclastic winemaker Joe Heitz.

chased wines from such places as the then inactive Hanzell Vineyards in Sonoma. After careful finishing, they were offered as his own. One was a Chardonnay, one of the finest I've ever tasted. There are those who credit him (I am one) with showing the way for the making of truly fine Chardonnay.

Following this Burgundian approach, many wines were found, selected, tasted, finished, and matured by the young winemaker, and it was not long before Mr. Heitz's reputation was made as a quality selector and producer. He set the tone for his establishment by offering wines aged longer in oak than others, and wines held back from sale so they could benefit from longer bottle aging. As a natural consequence of this, the wines were more expensive than those of the competition, and so Joe Heitz was among the first to sell Chardonnay at six dollars a bottle and Cabernet Sauvignon 1968 Martha's Vineyard at more than ten dollars a bottle.

Joe has succeeded in putting out some of the state's finest wines, particularly Chardonnay, Cabernet Sauvignon, Johannisberg Riesling, and Pinot Blanc.

Shortly after Joe established his reputation he acquired an old winery built in 1898, and approximately thirty acres of Grignolino, a leftover from the former owner, who made wine of Grignolino grapes a specialty. These grapes continue to be a favorite of Joe's and he makes a sparkling and a still Grignolino, both of which he prefers to talk about more than the Chardonnays and Cabernets, which seem to cause the most excitement. He loves to provide wine, such as the Grignolino, for everyday use, and he makes a considerable quantity of wine that ranges in price from two to four dollars. He makes a lot of generics, such as chablis, burgundy, sherry, port, and champagne, and offers a lower-price Cabernet Sauvignon from time to time. Many of these wines are inexpensive, and not the best, nor are they claimed to be. They do provide something that Joe deems extremely important, wine for his table and yours at a modest price. He insists strongly that his expensive and "great" wines should only be drunk on "great" occasions.

Since Mr. Heitz began his winery with his wife Alice, sons Rollie and David (who is a student of enology at Fresno State) and daughter Kathy, he has attempted to acquire more in the way of wine acreage and has built a beautiful new winery that will help to produce more wine and provide him with something he never had before—an office. He has established an excellent relationship with some of the finest grape growers in the Napa Valley, who continue to sell him some of the finest grapes in the area. Because of his ability to buy wine grapes from several sections of the Napa Valley, the Heitz wines will often reflect the differences of the areas from which his grapes come. In buying Joe's wines, one must keep this in mind and expect that Joe will always make a good wine but that it will vary from vintage to vintage.

One of his favorites is a very sweet wine that has been associated with the Mission grape, perhaps the first *Vitis vinifera* grape to be planted in California; it is said to have taken its name, Angelica, from the city of Los Angeles. Heitz Cellars has always managed to provide some of the finest Angelica. It is not inexpensive, but it is without question a truly unique, fine dessert wine. It has always been a mystery where Joe finds this wine and some of his others—but what is more important, he does find

them. On some of his labels, Joe will indicate—as he has on his Pinot Blanc 1968—that the wine was produced from grapes from Fred McCrea's vineyards, which is the Stony Hill Vineyard. Otherwise, there is no way of

The Heitz tasting room.

knowing where the grapes came from and this is part of the interest.

Joe does like to make his wines big and complex. So if one wants wine with a great deal of character and depth of flavor, a Joe Heitz wine is a good gamble. Pinot Noir, one of the more difficult grapes to grow and a wine that has not made as great a splash as Cabernet Sauvignon, is one with which Joe has done extremely well. Starting with his 1963 Pinot Noir and with several vintages thereafter, he has furnished promising bottlings. His Chardonnays—some of them labeled U.C.C. No. 81 (1968), for example, the grapes of which came from the University of California Experimental Station in the Napa Valley—are his greatest successes.

His family is as wine oriented and as dedicated as he. Heitz Cellars is a family operation; it may be one of the last in the Napa Valley making wines in the styles that represent the winemakers as wine drinkers first and above all else.

New equipment stands outside the old winery at St. Helena.

INGLENOOK VINEYARDS
Rutherford, California 94573

Owner:
Heublein, Inc.

Cellar Master:
A. Del Bondio

Senior Winemaker:
Tom Ferrell

Assistant Winemaker:
J. Richburg

Cabernet Sauvignon
(Cask Bottling) XXX

Pinot Noir
(Cask Bottling) XXX

Charbono XX

Pinot Chardonnay
(Cask Bottling) X

Gewürztraminer X

Inglenook Vineyards, another jewel in Napa Valley's tiara of vineyards, is owned by Heublein, Inc., and while the corporate entity has helped Beaulieu (another Heublein acquisition), Inglenook may have suffered initially from too much help. The early corporate-made wines just did not live up to the glorious reputation of the old tiny mighty Inglenook.

I can recall as if it were yesterday the great bottles of Inglenook's Cabernets and Pinot Noirs, among the finest wines yet tasted by this writer, showing what the soil of the Napa Valley can do in the hands of the generations of skill and experience of Inglenook's original owners.

I recall with great emotion the soulful, extraordinary great taste of a 1941 Inglenook Cabernet Sauvignon I drank in 1960 in the beauty of Inglenook's tasting room with John Daniels, the grandnephew of the founder, Gustav Niebaum.

Mr. Daniels was a most complex man, as indeed were some of his wines, for he was not only dedicated to fine winemaking but was also interested in the advancement of his industry. Perhaps more than any other individual, he led the fight for varietal labeling in California and for greater honesty in labeling. While concerned for the consumer, Mr. Daniels was generally not at home to the visiting wine lover for he believed that wine-making was a full-time occupation not to be intruded upon. He put his work in the bottle and in the law, not in the visitor's tasting room. In 1963 he sold Inglenook to United Vintners, ending the winemaking reign of the Niebaum family, which had begun in 1879 when Captain Gustav Niebaum founded Inglenook, a Scots word for "cozy corner." The name was given the winery not by Captain Niebaum, but rather by the former vineyard owner, W. C. Watson.

Captain Niebaum has been variously described as a Finnish sea pirate, a fur trader, and a businessman par excellence. Whatever attributes he had, he parlayed with great dedication into one of California's finest wine estates. From the very beginning of Inglenook until the days of the early 1960s, his wines were considered to be among the finest.

There was always friendly, if not spirited, rivalry between the two great estates, Beaulieu and

The Inglenook Board Room and private tasting area.

Inglenook, as to whose Cabernet or Pinot Noir was the better.

The Inglenook acquisition poses a troublesome question for California's wines in general, and Heublien in particular; can a little old winery in the West find happiness in the superstructure of corporate winemaking? The answer immediately appeared to be no, as the winery went from a small 29,000-cases-a-year producer to a 2,000,000-cases-a-year giant. With that kind of quantity, not all the wines could be in the great or exciting "traditional Inglenook style."

Those of us who have revered the wines and the name were at first turned off by Inglenook's producing several lines of wines in huge quantities, including the Navalle line together with Vintage bottlings of standard wines from a variety of north coast districts that formed the bulk of the production. Where were the great wines of yesteryear, and would they ever come again?

It was thus with suspicion yet open palate that I tasted Inglenook's renaissance

of "new" wines from its Reserve Cask and Estate bottled wine selections.

Gratefully and thankfully, the wines bring back the memory of the old days, as they are decidedly improved, with style, varietal character, and the quality that has apparently been missing since the Daniel days.

The best of the bunch from a newly improved bottling is a 1970 Estate Cabernet Sauvignon Cask-30, a rich flavorful Cabernet, nicely balanced and softened with Merlot that has been produced from Rutherford Vineyards in the heart of the Napa Valley. The wine will obviously improve into one of distinction and be worthy of the name. Too bad there were only 4,500 cases, but how else are you going to produce a great wine without restricting the quantity and isolating the vineyards? Apparently

Built by a Finnish sea captain, the main winery at Rutherford is one of California's most distinguished landmarks.

Heublein, the corporate giant, has retrenched, learned its painful lesson well. The 1970 Pinot Noir Cask K-150 is obviously the best Pinot Noir made since the old days, and it too is from a single vineyard. It is nicely balanced and bodied but it weakened a bit at the finish. Perhaps with the additional bottle age required, elegance will develop. Only 1,500 cases of this one. Interesting was a 1970 Red Pinot Cask G-23, which is 86 percent Pinot St. George. The wine has considerable richness, is relatively high in alcohol, and reflects well its varietal character. Both clean and excellent for its type, it too suffers from small quantity, 1,500 cases.

One of my old favorites at Inglenook has been the Charbono. The vintage of 1970 does well by the wine, which has been blended 10 percent with Barbera. It is an intense, fairly big wine which will need much more

bottle age. The quantity is now up to 4,500 cases. More would be planned except that grapes are unavailable.

The Chardonnay has been much improved, beginning with the 1972 vintage, which provided a clean, fruity wine with little oak showing. The wine is full-bodied, dry, and will undoubtedly improve with at least another year or more of bottle age. Tasting the 1975 version from the barrel, great improvement is reflected, for here is a more concentrated Chardonnay style, better balanced with oak, and a wine that will be a "longer liver" with a bright, complex future. The Gewürztraminer, beginning with the 1973, has also improved as much as the others, perhaps more so, for it sells out its meager supply immediately.

A taste of the 1974 Johannisberg Riesling, done in the current California fashionably slightly sweet style, is no longer dull and flabby, and is now a full, rich, concentrated with flavor wine that makes it beautifully sippable.

The 1973 Cabernet Sauvignon

is for my money the most improved of all, for it is really a throwback to the old days, with intense Cabernet flavor produced in a fine year from choice Cabernet grapes from the floor of the Napa Valley. With the aid of new American oak, Inglenook here has produced an extraordinary estate bottling, which in four to five or perhaps six years should develop complexities and drink generously well.

It is obvious that these estate-bottled wines can stand on their own and attract great attention. The others, less expensive and lesser lived, are sound value for the money. The Navalle brand is in the $2.00 range, while the Inglenook Vintage line hovers around $2.50. In both lines there is a full range of generics with the Navalle line featuring varietals, French Colombard, Chenin Blanc, Ruby Cabernet, and Zinfandel. It is also obvious

that these lesser lines will help pay for the more interesting, far greater Estate and Reserve Cask bottlings.

The quality of all the wines has been upgraded, especially, of course, the Estate and Reserve Cask bottled wines; so much so that I had to ask the questions why and how. The how is largely due to the able direction of a young man, Thomas Ferrell, thirty, perhaps the youngest senior winemaker of a major winery in California. An enology graduate from U.C. Davis, he is as much a wine drinker as he is a winemaker. That combination, of course, has been responsible for many great wines at other wineries and in other eras.

The why stems from an "attitudinal change" at Inglenook. The direction will be to make, in addition to the so-called volume district wines, greater Estate bottlings and even greater Reserve Cask bottlings. Ferrell is desperately in love with the idea of making great Estate and Reserve Cask bottlings, and as a consequence will be responsible for them while others will be assisting to produce the district bottlings.

The Inglenook name is great and rich and it is not simply a name—it is a monument in California wine history. Whether Heublein will enrich the tradition remains to be tasted, although the new Cask and Reserve Cask bottlings should do it. Obviously they can if they wish to and at the moment they do.

It may be that Inglenook with its new lines is showing the way for all future corporations in winemaking, for this may be the only way the balance sheet can survive in these days of corporate finance—a sort of General Motors approach, where something is made for everybody's taste and everybody's pocketbook. Whatever the winery does I am sure it will be done as well as a corporate giant can—but for me they need only duplicate those great estate bottlings of old, for those were wines of feeling and depth, the kind that Gustav Niebaum and John Daniels would have enjoyed and appreciated.

KORBEL & BROTHERS, INC.

Guerneville, California 95446

Owners:
Adolf L. Heck and Paul R. Heck

Winemakers:
Paul R. Heck and Alan Hemphill

Vineyards:
700 acres

Capacity:
Storage 750,000 gallons

Champagne Nature XXX
Champagne Brut XXX

Years ago when putting on a Wine and Food Society dinner I petitioned the Korbel winery—just as I had, earlier, the Wente winery—for the very best of the Korbel champagne. My feeling was that their best was the Korbel Natural, a dry champagne—even drier than brut, for it had literally little or no dosage. Their response, by correspondence, was No, I could not have it. I asked why and was told that the wine was too dry for the American palate and that Americans would

feel that this wine was too dry or perhaps bitter. How times have changed! Now this wine has become not only one of Korbel's hallmark wines but also has been copied by almost every other producer of premium champagne in the state. The style is one that Americans have learned to appreciate, as it, more than any other, seems to have captured the fancy of those who like their champagnes dry and French. More often than not this style is compared to those of the French champagnes.

It goes without saying that after long persuasion the winery elected to let me have the wine and the Wine and Food Society people to whom it was served immediately took to it as a favorite. And so it has been throughout the country.

The Korbel people have been making fine champagne along the banks of the Russian River at Guerneville since 1886, when the winery was founded by the Korbel brothers. Later, in 1954, the Heck brothers took over and

made it into what it is today.

The Heck brothers, aided by a thirst for good California champagne and a *Consumer's Guide* article many years ago that pronounced a Korbel label a "best buy," probably have done more to put over California's sparkling wine than any other label. Certainly their wine has to take its place among the fine

A winter fog lifts above a newly pruned vineyard at Russian River.

The old Board Room.

California sparkling wines, along with Shramsberg, Kornell, Paul Masson, and Weibel. The line includes Korbel Brut, Extra Dry, and Rouge, a sparkling burgundy—certainly one of the best of the sparkling wine lines. It is to the Hecks' credit that the wines are as good as they are, considering the large quantity of production that has been urged on them by a great demand.

Not content with only sparkling

Cooperage is over 100 years old.

wines, the Korbel winery has gone into the table-wine business and has done quite well with Cabernet, Pinot Noir, chablis, sauterne, Grey Riesling, rosé, burgundy, sherry, and port. Not all are as good as the sparkling wines, but there is constant improvement and occasionally a "sleeper" is found—often enough so that there springs great hope for this line of wine as well.

The Heck brothers are without question among the most consistent of quality sparkling wine makers. For almost a full generation their sparkling wines have represented the standard to which other wine producers have aspired. Much credit should be given this winery for showing the way and it is hoped they will do nothing to tamper with that standard. It is unlikely that they will.

HANNS KORNELL CHAMPAGNE CELLARS

Larkmead Lane
P.O. Box 249
St. Helena, California 94574

Owner and Winemaker:
Hanns J. Kornell

Vineyards:
None

Capacity:
Bottling 30,000 cases
bottle-fermented champagne
per year

Sehr Trocken XXX
Champagne Brut XXX

Hanns J. Kornell is one of the most interesting winemaking gentlemen in the Napa Valley. Someday someone is going to write a best-selling novel about him and it should be almost as interesting as his champagnes.

Hanns makes only champagne under his label Kornell Cellars and probably makes as much champagne for other wineries as he does for himself.

His list of former wine employers reads like a wine Who's Who, beginning with Fountaingrove, the Gibson Wine Company, and the American Wine Company, makers of Cook's champagne.

Hanns Kornell.

There is a tradition of winemaking, especially champagne, in the Kornell family going all the way back to 1848 in Germany. Hanns had to leave Germany in 1940 as a penniless refugee.

A refugee and penniless no longer, he is making some of California's finest champagne—brut, extra dry, pink, and a Muscadelle du Bordelais, all bottle-fermented. Some still wine is produced, but as yet nothing in the class of the sparkling wines.

Recently, Hanns made a wine for the Nature lovers of champagne which he appropriately calls Sehr Trocken—a great example of what can be done with Johannisberg Riesling grapes. On its first time out it

A million and a half bottles of champagne age in the Kornell cellars.

won a gold medal at the 1971 Los Angeles County Fair wine judging. More is planned for this wine. It will soon challenge the Nature or Naturel sparkling wines of the most famous California sparkling wine makers, such as Korbel, Paul Masson, Almadén, and Weibel.

Life has been very fruitful

The winery at St. Helena.

and rewarding for Hanns, who started with nothing in this country and wound up in 1958 with the old Larkmead Winery in St. Helena, where he is now located. He purchased it from the Italian Swiss Colony Company. Hanns married a lovely native of the Napa Valley, Marilouise Rossini, whose roots in the valley go back to her grandfather's generation.

Not long ago Hanns gave a party for a wedding anniversary celebration which the valley wine family is still savoring—both the anniversary and the Hanns Kornell Third Generation Brut Champagne. Hanns must have been very proud on both counts.

In the 1960's a new generation of winemakers staked their claim in California's fertile valleys and hills. Armed with superior education, technology, and unresolved differences with traditional methods, they sought escape from the confinements of conventional businesses, and pursued self-realization in an ancient and respected industry.

They came, these men of imagination, with attitudes and energies that clearly challenged the *status quo* with resources too persuasive to ignore. New visionaries invaded the vineyards, resourceful successors of those pioneers of a hundred years ago who first planted and gave root to *Vitis vinifera* in a virgin land.

Today, along the highways and back roads that bisect California, they have erected their own distinguished landmarks to join with those of the men who preceded them. Rich vineyards, yielding some of the world's choicest fruit, surround virtual castles erected to the glory of wine.

Their names bode well for the future of American wine, and, like the land they cultivate, send forth sturdy affirmation of their success: Davies, Heitz, Graff, Chappellet, Travers, Mondavi, Bennion, Mirassou, Webb, Strong, Bruce, Green. They, and their contemporaries, are the prodigies, the men of new vision who have earned worldwide recognition for American wines.

Page 113
During a rainy February afternoon, a storm is dissipated by the pure colors of a rainbow as it arches over a winter-bare vineyard, pointing, perhaps, to a modern version of the pot of gold.
Pages 114-115
On the flat Napa Valley floor, the handsome winery of Robert Mondavi disguises its efficient technology behind the walls of buildings evoking the mood of early California missions.
Pages 116-117
As dynamic and as bold as a hard-edged painting, the crisp, clean lines of Windsor Vineyard's new winery, built in 1970, converge in the sky-blue water of a reflecting pool.
Pages 118-119
The magnificent winery of Donn Chappellet, built in 1969, dwarfs its machinery under soaring wooden beams, and creates a cathedral-like reverence in the awe-struck visitor.
Page 102
Situated on a knoll near Calistoga in the Napa Valley, the nearly completed Sterling Vineyards promises to be one of the most spectacular and popular of California's wineries.
Page 121
The Paul Masson Champagne Cellars, built in Saratoga, California, in 1959, remains one of the most handsome wine buildings in the world, and annually attracts some 200,000 visitors.

CHARLES KRUG WINERY

P.O. Box 191
St. Helena, California 94574

Owners:
C. Mondavi & Sons,
Mrs. Rosa Mondavi, President

Winemaker:
Peter Mondavi

Vineyards:
800 acres

Capacity:
Storage 3,500,000 gallons
Fermenting 230,000 gallons

Cabernet Sauvignon XXXX
Chardonnay XXX
Chenin Blanc XX
Johannisberg Riesling XX
Mountain Zinfandel XX

A memorable structure at Krug is the old carriage house, now converted to an aging cellar.

The Charles Krug Winery, one of the first in the Napa Valley, is really the product of two families, the Charles Krugs, wine pioneers, and the Cesare Mondavis, latter-day innovators.

Charles Krug, one of the first to recognize the value of producing wine from European grape varieties, became involved with the grape in 1858. With the use of a cider press he made some 1,200 gallons of wine that year for John Patchett of Napa, the first wine made in Napa County by a process other than the old Spanish method of fermenting in skins. Born in Prussia in 1825, Krug immigrated to Philadelphia as a teacher at the age of twenty-two and taught in the Free Thinkers School of August Glasser until 1848. Deeply disturbed by the political situation in his native land, he

returned to Prussia to participate in an attempt to overthrow the reactionary parliament. The revolt failed and Krug, together with the other ringleaders, was imprisoned. Fortunately for California wine, he was freed in 1849 when the prison doors were opened by the adherents of a new uprising at Baden and Rheinpfalz. Pursued by the police of Hesse, Krug fled to Philadelphia.

He came to San Francisco in 1852, and was engaged as the editor of the *Staats Zeitung,* the first German paper ever published on the Pacific Coast. He stayed with the paper until 1854 and then went to Crystal Spring, San Mateo County, where he

located on a government claim near the farm of Agoston Haraszthy. In 1856 he was appointed clerk in the refining department of the United States Mint, where he remained until Haraszthy, along with associates, opened a gold and silver refinery. In 1858 Krug bought a Sonoma farm from Haraszthy and planted twenty acres of vines. In the same year he made the famous wine for Mr. Patchett of Napa.

In 1860 Krug left Sonoma and moved to St. Helena, where he married the daughter of Dr. Edward Turner Bale. Settling on a tract of land that formed part of the Carne Humana grant, he built his first wine cellar and planted vines in 1861.

The winery and the vineyards became models and the Krug

winery and ranch became one of the most attractive and productive in the Napa Valley.

Krug was named a state viticultural commissioner and became the first president of the St. Helena Viticultural Association. Most important, his wines gained international reputation and were marketed not only in California but also in the eastern United States, Mexico, Germany, and England.

Eventually the ranch was run by his daughters, Lolita and Linda, with subsequent ownership in the hands of James K. Moffitt. In 1894, while the winery was still under Moffitt ownership, Bismarck Bruck, a cousin of the Krug daughters, took over operations and made wine up to the time of Prohibition and grape juice for a few years thereafter. Upon Repeal, the vineyards and cellars were leased to the Napa Wine Company.

The second part of the Charles Krug wine story begins with Cesare Mondavi, founder of C. Mondavi & Sons, who was born in Ancona, Italy, in 1883, and came to America in 1906, working first in the iron ore mines in Minnesota. He returned to Italy long enough to marry his childhood sweetheart, Rosa, who today is the president of Charles Krug Winery. They had four children, Mary, Helen, Robert, and Peter. The two sons have made considerable contribution to the California wine industry, Peter operating Charles Krug Winery and Robert Mondavi establishing his own.

In 1922, Cesare moved his entire family to Lodi, California, where he launched a wholesale business in grapes and other fruit. Upon the repeal of Prohibition, the venture was expanded to include winemaking. At one time Mondavi owned the Sunny St. Helena Winery but it was not until 1943 that the biggest decision was made. Mondavi acquired the Charles Krug Winery in which the Mondavi family has continued to invest time, money, patience, and hard work.

By the time Cesare died in 1959, the Mondavi-Krug winery was one of the best equipped and most efficient in the country, ably directed by the two sons, university graduates with post-graduate emphasis in viticulture and viniculture. The winery has produced some of the finest Cabernets, notably the 1951 and 1958 vintages. The Cabernets of the 1960s are also quite good, perhaps as good as any made in California. The red wines, which include the Gamay, Pinot Noir,

New vineyards frame the winery at St. Helena.

and Mountain Zinfandel, in general have considerable character.

The white wines have good varietal character, particularly the Chardonnay, on occasion the Gewürztraminer, and the slightly sweeter Chenin Blanc, which was one of the first Chenin Blancs to be made as a varietal in the state.

When the Tinta Madeira port is made it can be quite pleasant, as is a Moscato Canelli, a sweet muscat.

The winery also makes some subordinate wines, Mondavi Vintage and the CK line, a very inexpensive wine sold in half-gallon and gallon containers. They provided a great deal of taste and comfort to me during my salad days when I enjoyed particularly the Barberone and the chablis. The wines, sound and quite flavorful, are not complex or great but they are satisfactory to drink. I use them by decanting the gallon containers into tenths, thus insuring against exposure to air. This way the wine will last for a longer period of time and be available when-ever the mood dictates. (A half-gallon or gallon jug will, after opening, begin to oxidize.) Decanted, this wine doesn't cost more than fifty cents a tenth— good yet inexpensive drinking.

Anyone interested in a chatty, newsy letter from Charles Krug should write to Francis Gould, care of the winery, and ask to be put on the list for Bottles and Bins.

Peter Mondavi poses in the winery's tasting room.

LLORDS & ELWOOD WINERY

315 South Beverly Drive
Beverly Hills, California 90212

Owners:
J. H. Mike Elwood,
Irene J. Elwood,
Richard H. Elwood, and
Mary G. Elwood

Winemaker:
J. H. Mike Elwood

Vineyards:
125 acres

Capacity:
103,000 gallons

Dry Wit Sherry XXXX
Rose of Cabernet XXX
Champagne Superb Extra Dry XX
Castle Magic Johannisberg
Riesling XX

J. H. Mike Elwood was one of Los Angeles' most successful retail wine and spirits operators from 1933 to 1961. Long before wine became popular, Mike Elwood waited on customers with such evangelical zeal in the sale and promotion of wine that he became a myth among his competitors. Any customer, including some of Hollywood's greatest stars, going into his store without any wine knowledge came out not only with wine but with an education about the tasting, drinking, and buying of wine.

During his twenty-eight years as a retailer, Mike learned much about the great wines of the world, a body of knowledge that not all winemakers are fortunate enough to acquire. Exposure to those wines convinced him that finer wines could be made in California. In 1955 he took the plunge and built his own winery in the Santa Clara Valley, approximately forty miles southeast of San Francisco.

Allied with Mike is his entire family, notably his son Richard, who worked with him at the store and now is doubling as a vineyardist and executive in the administration of the winery.

At a time when wineries were not yet making much money, Mike and Richard began by buying grapes and making wine to satisfy their own palate and style. Most of their wines have been good, sound ones; their greatest success has been with dessert wines.

They do not vintage-date their wines for they feel that they can find grapes and blend wines that cannot carry a vintage date and yet are superior to vintaged varietals. Their table wines generally carry a cuvée number or bin symbol that enables you to distinguish one batch of wine from another.

The table wines, although not possessed of great complexity, have been solid, good, interesting, and more than satisfactory. The Cabernet Sauvignon has been aged in cask and has enough Cabernet Sauvignon flavor so that it can be identified as a Cabernet. The Pinot Noir, labeled Velvet Hill Pinot Noir, is favored by some wine drinkers as one of California's better Pinot Noirs, while others state that it is not characteristic of the grape. The rosé, labeled Rose of Cabernet, is made exclusively from Cabernet Sauvignon grapes, a rare wine these days, and is a fuller, bigger rosé than most California rosé wines. The Chardonnay, labeled Rare Chardonnay, is not as big and full as some, but it is a sound bottle and provides a style not unlike some of the medium-priced white burgundies of France. The Johannisberg Riesling, described as a Spät-Iese, labeled Castle Magic Johannisberg Riesling, is a wine patterned after a German rhine wine, which is generally sweeter than most Johannisberg Rieslings in California.

The dessert wines, which were the first to be made, are without question some of California's finest. The Great Day D-r-r-y Sherry, the Dry Wit Sherry, the Judge's Secret Sherry, and the Ancient Proverb Port round out the line. You can see that Mike not only likes to make wine but he likes to find curiously interesting names for it. The Dry Wit Sherry is perhaps one of the more interesting California sherries, lingering on the palate and pleasantly dry. It is one of the few that can be enjoyed strictly as an aperitif wine in the same manner as a good dry sherry from Spain.

The winery intends each year's sherries and ports to be very near the same through their use of the solera method of aging,

A simple building houses the winery.

extensive tasting, and careful finishing prior to bottling. Tasting has proved their methods to be correct.

The winery is past the experimental stage and good wines are beginning flow, particularly from vineyards that were not yet planted when the Elwoods began their facility. As time and wines pass, the table wines should become as interesting and exciting as the dessert wines. The Elwoods mean to do this with better vineyard resources that they will control or own, assuring them of fine grape supply and the opportunity to make wines in the truly great class.

LOUIS M. MARTINI VINEYARDS

P.O. Box 112
St. Helena, California 94574

Owner:
Louis M. Martini Corporation

Winemaker:
Louis P. Martini

Vineyards:
850 acres

Capacity:
Storage 1,900,000 gallons
Fermenting 100,000 gallons

Cabernet Sauvignon XXXX
Moscato Amabile XXXX
Gewürztraminer XXX
Pinot Noir XXX
Zinfandel XXX
Barbera XX

Louis Martini is not just a winemaking name in the Napa Valley—he is today the elder statesman, not only in Napa Valley but perhaps for the whole industry. He has struck it big in the Napa Valley, but not without first making great contributions of his own, particularly in making wines that are not only among the best in the state but that can compete with those of the world.

Few will challenge the quality of Louis Martini's Private Reserve and special selection wines, particularly Cabernet Sauvignon and Pinot Noir. In tasting the older Cabernets of the '40s and the '50s a consumer can only sit back and enjoy to the fullest what California Cabernet Sauvignon and Pinot Noir are all about.

I remember sitting one day at the home of Jack Davies of Schramsberg Vineyards complaining about the lack of good Pinot Noir in the state and suggesting that perhaps Pinot Noir ought to be eliminated from the California wine scene and Cabernet Sauvignon be planted in its place. Promptly I was served a bottle with no label on it. After tasting the wine I observed that Jack had really put me in my place, as well he should, by serving me Louis Martini's 1957 Pinot Noir, about as fine a Pinot Noir as I have tasted. One must be careful about pontifically pronouncing what should or should not be grown in the state, for

Louis Martini, Jr., stands in the entry to the new tasting room at the St. Helena winery.

California is full of Jack Davieses who will pull out wines like Martini's Pinot Noir to set the record straight.

Louis's wines have been setting records straight since Prohibition, when he was making wine at Kingsburg in Fresno County. When he moved his family to St. Helena (in 1939) Martini began to make wines seriously with three great vineyard areas.

Louis had come to the United States by way of Italy and had made wine in a small way in San Francisco. He had then further practiced his skill with Secondo Guasti, the great southern California wine pioneer, and had completed a stint in Italy to study enology. By 1933 Louis was well equipped to begin making the wide variety of wines that has taken the winery from its humble beginnings to the giant enterprise it is today.

Louis has somehow managed to make his wines good, often complex, despite the size of the business. Part of this, at least, is no doubt due to the assistance of his son Louis P. Martini, who is a recognized industry leader, and to the grandsons, who are also earmarked for the same work.

Louis Martini's wines, particularly the private reserve or special selection reds, have been exciting and interesting, not only the Cabernet Sauvignon and the Pinot Noir but also the Zinfandel and the Barbera. The whites have also been quite good, particularly the Gewürztraminer, which on occasion rates among the state's finest wines.

Martini also makes a line of wines for jug drinking that is probably among the best jug wines of the state, some of which are labeled "Mountain Pinot Noir", "Mountain Barbera", etc. The regular line of varietals— that is, not the special selection—

is also worthy of drinking, as is the line of mountain generics, such as Mountain Chianti, Burgundy, etc. In latter years the winery has added to its vineyards from areas in Sonoma County as well as in Napa County, and so a fairly decent supply of Martini wines is assured.

To me, one of the most interesting wines of all, and certainly the best in the state of its type, is a sparkling wine made from

although I think better—and is a most refreshing, light, delicate, fruity wine showing to full advantage complexities of the muscat grape. Lately the wine can be obtained only from the winery, although some California restaurants enjoy serving it. It is a difficult wine to obtain, principally because it should be transported in refrigerated trucks and drunk soon after home delivery to capture all of the wine's nuances and to avoid spoilage.

A smudge pot stands ready as fog begins to cloak the nearby hills.

the Muscat of Alexandria grape called "Moscato Amabile," which is a takeoff from Asti Spumanti—

Incidentally, this wine is an excellent introduction to the Muscat type and demonstrates the full beauty of this delightful taste.

Louis Martini and his son have brought much to the Napa Valley, not only the strength of his personality and a dedication to art but new advances and

admirable concern for great winemaking.

He was among the first to express in print (in *Time* magazine) his concern about so-called pop wines; he said he believed that this trend could lead to the ruin of California's great table-wine industry, if winemakers could manufacture wines more by laboratory blending than by making straight table wines from great grapes and letting nature take its rightful course. When Louis's opinion was made public the "pop" wine people retorted "sour grapes." Time has proved that there is room for both, but at Louis Martini's there is room only for good grapes, good winemaking, and a great concern for the consumer.

No other winery has made a greater effort to hold prices down. It would be easy for Martini to raise his prices, considering the demand, and yet his prices remain stable and, considering the quality, his wines as a rule are an excellent buy.

I wrote the Martinis recently, asking them if they were going to sell, as so many others have done, to large corporations. The answer was an emphatic "no." I suspect this is because the Martini family wants not only to make fine wine but to enjoy the good life of winemaking in the Napa Valley. I hope that they never sell and I wonder whether they realize how important they are to us, the wine consumers, who think of them as one of the last bastions of California's great winemaking families.

PAUL MASSON VINEYARDS
Saratoga, California 95070
Owner:
Joseph E. Seagrams & Sons
Winemaker:
Joseph Stillman
Champagne Master:
Norman Damico
Vineyards:
4,000 acres, principally in the area of the Pinnacles, near Soledad, California, and in the Santa Clara Valley, the home of Paul Masson's mother vineyard
Capacity:
Aging 5,000,000 bottles of champagne
Bottling 11,000 cases per day

Champagne Brut XXX
Emerald Dry Riesling XXX
Rare Souazo Port XXX
Gamay Beaujolais XX
Cabernet Sauvignon (Pinnacles):
Comer
Johannisberg Riesling
(Pinnacles) : *Comer*

The champagne cellar at Saratoga is one of California's most spectacular showplaces and a popular tourist attraction.

Paul Masson as a winemaker and a winery once represented all that was good in California wine. Today the name has a broader meaning. Now it stands on a label that sells in excess of 4,000,000 cases a year. Although born in Burgundy in 1859, Paul Masson's roots in California go back to the 1850's, to the days of Etienne Thée and of Charles Lefranc, whose daughter he married. The establishment of his own vineyard took place in 1892. Today the giant Masson enterprise makes wine in enormous quantities with a quality that will satisfy the beginning wine drinker but often loses him as he begins to become more experienced. The wines of the enormous enterprise are generally quite satisfactory considering the cost and quantity, but are not wines with great excitement, complexity, depth of flavor, or

The Paul Masson monogram.

tremendous character. They are good for what they purport to be: relatively inexpensive, everyday wines that are charming and pleasant to drink.

Things are changing at Paul Masson and there is a strong movement to improve to wines of complexity, particularly with the vineyards at the Pinnacles in Monterey County, a region that was only an experiment ten years ago but one that now appears to be moving fast, as evidenced by the Pinot Noir and Cabernet Sauvignon from this region. The Pinot Noir is Vintage Cuvée Blanc de Blanc, while the Cabernet Sauvignon is Vintage Cuvée 843. Both are limited bottlings.

Paul Masson was a man who lived by this quotation: "Who

loves not women, wine, and song, remains a fool his whole life long." He was a great man, with a strong fascination for all of the arts and a tremendous zest for life. He made his name famous by producing champagnes and then he moved on to table wines. He was perhaps California's most exciting wine figure after Haraszthy. In 1936, Masson sold

the California wine industry a giant step or two forward.

The people at Paul Masson, under the foresighted leadership of Otto Meyer, have done more than just make good wine for large segments of the wine-drinking public. They have also made a contribution to the arts by staging beautiful symphonic music experiences high atop

clearly on the move, anxious to upgrade their image and reputation. They feel that the new area in Monterey County is the key to that goal.

Paul Masson always has produced better champagne than table wine. Some of the state's finest sparkling wines, both the brut and the newly introduced Blanc de Blanc type, are

before the judging, in 1892.

Paul Masson's winery was partially destroyed by the San Francisco earthquake of 1906 and was not wholly rebuilt for several years. Its reconstruction was finally completed with building materials from St. Joseph's Church in San Jose, which had been destroyed by the same earthquake.

The Pinnacles vineyards at Soledad.

his mountain winery at Saratoga to Martin Ray, the stockbroker turned winemaker. Joseph E. Seagrams & Sons, the big liquor distillers, acquired the Masson name and premises from Ray in 1942. Seagrams then formed a partnership with Alfred Fromm, Franz Sichel, and Otto Meyer, all from famous wine families in Germany. These men have not only spearheaded the great growth of Masson, but also moved

their vineyards at the mother winery and vineyards near Saratoga overlooking the Santa Clara Valley, one of the most scenic spots in all the world.

The winery also has been busy making such pleasant wines as Rhine Castle and Emerald Dry Riesling, both slightly sweet white wines. Of the reds, the Gamay is of rather light body but generally has enough flavor to make it a satisfactory wine for an everyday dinner.

As the vines at the Pinnacle vineyards mature and reach full production, the Paul Masson wines should improve immeasurably. The Masson people are

Masson's. It is surprising that Paul Masson made fine champagnes for over fifty years because he came from Burgundy with a solid wine background in red and white burgundies but without any champagne experience. He was still making champagne until shortly before his death at eighty-one. His champagnes won gold medals at the Paris Exhibition in 1900, no small feat considering that the wine was introduced in California only eight years

Today, the modern Masson empire, equipped with stainless steel tanks and all of the latest winery equipment, stands on the threshold of a new era. If successful, the Pinnacles will turn Paul Masson into the world's largest producer of so-called premium wines; not great wines, but wines satisfactory enough to be ranked by experienced wine drinkers as good.

The dedicated men at Paul Masson may yet turn out wines of intriguing character and, as is true of any other winery, large or small, time and taste will tell.

MAYACAMAS VINEYARDS

1155 Lokoya Road
Napa, California 94558

Owner:
A limited partnership, with
Robert Travers as managing
partner

Winemaker:
Bruce E. Meyers

Vineyards:
40 acres

Capacity:
Storage 30,000 gallons
Fermenting 10,000 gallons

Chardonnay XXXX
Zinfandel XXXX
Cabernet Sauvignon XXX

The winery, constructed of native stone, was built in 1889.

The "new" Mayacamas Vineyards has made some superb wines. One of the biggest Zinfandels ever made was the Mayacamas Late Harvest of 1968, doubtless one of the most intense California red wines I ever tasted. A mouthful of this wine was equivalent to several glasses of a lighter, smaller Zinfandel.

Bob Travers offers this explanation for the Late Harvest: "'Actually, the grapes were picked in the second half of September, which would be early for 1971. But in this vineyard in 1968 the grapes were a rarity of extreme ripeness. So much so, in fact, that the natural alcohol in this wine is 17 percent rather than a normal 12 to 13 percent. The aroma and flavor characteristics are commensurately powerful. Mayacamas 1968 Late Harvest Zinfandel is dry but it is such a big

wine that it tends to overpower most main course dishes." Amen!

The 1968 Cabernet Sauvignon and the 1969 Chardonnay are decided improvements over wines of previous years under a different management. Bob Travers has revived, indeed

Bob and Elinor Travers.

resuscitated, Mayacamas, a winery that had its beginnings in 1889 when it was founded by John Henry Fisher, a San Francisco pickle merchant who had emigrated from Stuttgart. There was a small distillery then as well as facilities to make red and white table wines from vineyard plantings of Zinfandel and Mission grapes. Not much happened to the winery until 1941, when Jack and Mary Taylor, of England and California respectively, acquired the then-empty stone winery, distillery, and declining vineyards. The Taylors proceeded to replant the vineyards to Chardonnay and Cabernet Sauvignon. They changed the name of the winery from Mount Veeder, a local, extinct volcano, to Mayacamas, which natives believe means "the howl of the mountain lion" in the language of indigenous Lokoya Indians.

The Taylors, like the Traverses, were consumers of wines before they were makers of them. They made wines in two brands, Mayacamas for the so-called premium and Lokoya for standard wines made from grapes generally bought in the Napa County area.

The Taylors started their development before the wine boom and so it was not easy to find the capital necessary to expand and make great wines. Some of their wines were quite good, but the full potential of Mayacamas was not realized while the Taylors were in control.

In 1968 Bob and Elinor Travers (with a background of expertise in stock analyses and a year or so of winemaking experience gained while working for Joe Heitz in St. Helena) moved in with their young and growing family and set about making fine wine. They have accomplished this, high in the stillness of the Mayacamas mountains that separate the Napa and Sonoma valleys, with a great deal of luck, pluck, and determination. The wines show what they put into them. Check the most recent bottlings of Cabernet Sauvignon and Chardonnay. Both are big, clean wines with considerable varietal character. Aged in small cooperage, the wines are some-times limited in quantity because in some vintages the Traverses may get only half a ton of grapes from the thin mountainous soil. On the Napa Valley floor, the yield can be as much as four and five tons an acre for some grapes.

The yield may be small but the effort at Mayacamas is great. For the Traverses are part of the new breed of winemaking families who evolved from different backgrounds and professions to the making of wine with love and dedication—and the wines show it.

Forty acres of terraced vineyards grow 2600 feet up on Mount Veeder, an extinct volcano.

MIRASSOU VINEYARDS
Route 3, Box 344
Aborn Road
San Jose, California 95121

Owners:
Norbert C. Mirassou and
Edmund A. Mirassou

Winemaker:
Max Huebner

Vineyards:
1,360 acres

Capacity:
Storage 800,000 gallons
Fermenting 90,000 gallons

Chenin Blanc XXXX
Cabernet Sauvignon XXX
Gewürztraminer XXX
Zinfandel XXX
Champagne au Natural XX
Chardonnay : *Comer*

In continuous operation since 1854 and now operated by the fifth generation of Mirassous, Mirassou Vineyards is truly one of the pioneer family operations of the Santa Clara Valley.

The vineyards were first cultivated on the western slope of Mt. Hamilton by Pierre Pellier, the great-great-grandfather of the present Mirassous. His daughter, Henrietta, married a neighboring vintner, Pierre Mirassou, and so it all began.

Pierre Mirassou's son Peter maintained the vineyards during Prohibition and upon Repeal his sons, Norbert and Edmund, the present elder statesmen of the winery, resumed the family tradition of winemaking, principally varietal table wines and champagnes, which were sold to other wineries. As a matter of fact, some of the most famous wineries of California used to buy from the Mirassous much of the wine carrying their labels. This has changed, because the Mirassous have sought their own identity by bottling their own varietal wines, and the winery has grown and become increasingly successful.

Defeating phylloxera and Prohibition was easy compared to the present-day problem of urban encroachment in the Santa Clara Valley. In 1961 Mirassou Vineyards faced the situation squarely when it pioneered the Monterey County benchlands with the establishment of the 300-acre Mission Ranch at Soledad, California. Today this is recognized as a very sound wine-growing district. The Mirassous expanded still further with the purchase of the 650-acre San Vicente Ranch in Soledad. Much of this expansion can be attributed to the new generation at Mirassou, including Norbert's son, Steve, and son-in-law Don Alexander, and Edmund's sons, Peter, Jim, and Daniel. With this infusion of youth the winery's future seems assured. Steve,

Peter, and Daniel have studied viticulture and enology at Fresno State College. Don and Jim have acquired practical experience from the day-to-day operations at the winery and vineyards.

Most of the Mirassou wines are 100 percent varietals which are made from their own grapes from over 1,000 acres in Monterey County and 360 acres in Santa Clara County. The finest of these wines are Cabernet Sauvignon, Zinfandel, Gewürztraminer, Pinot Chardonnay, and Pinot Noir. They are vintage-dated, the first harvested in 1966 and produced exclusively from Monterey County grapes. The wines seem to confirm the selection of Monterey County as a vineyard site for the ultimate replacement of the Santa Clara County vineyards.

The regular bottlings consist of thirteen wines, mostly varietals and a few generics, including chablis, burgundy, petit rosé,

Winemaker Max Huebner.

Monterey riesling, Chenin Blanc, Gamay beaujolais, Petite Sirah, Pinot Blanc (this will be replaced by white burgundy), sparkling Gamay beaujolais, pink champagne, champagne brut, and champagne au naturel.

The winery courtyard.

Over the years Mirassou has made some of the state's finest and most complex Zinfandels, giving that wine an image and character of its own. One of the first to recognize the qualities of fine Zinfandel, Mirassou has won numerous awards, at both the Los Angeles County Fair and the California State Fair, for its Zinfandel. The Cabernet Sauvignon has improved immeasurably and is taking its place alongside some of the finer Cabernets of the state.

The Pinot Noir is spotty, which may reflect the spottiness of the grape rather than the ability of the winery, and this seems to be the case for the Pinot Chardonnay as well. The Gewürztraminer is without question one of the finest. Year in and year out the Monterey County Gewürztraminer is so

These vineyards date back through five generations of Mirrasous.

brimful of fruitiness that to open the bottle is to release a perfume bouquet that extends across the room.

The champagnes have also improved, so much so that the Champagne au Naturel has become a very clean, good, crisp, sparkling wine that is challenging the big California champagne makers for flavor.

An interesting wine developed principally from Monterey County vineyards is the Chenin Blanc, notably the 1971, which was well known for its delicate fruitiness and was one of the first varietal wines made exclusively from mechanical harvesting and field crushing. The wine is intentionally bottled young in order to preserve the beauty of its fruitiness and is especially pleasing to those who like Chenin Blanc ever so slightly sweet, as it contains 3 percent residual sugar. A good red wine, combining taste and reasonableness in price, is the Petite Sirah, which is generally a fairly full and rich wine with ability to age over an extended period of time. This kind of wine can be coarse when young but exciting if one is willing to wait.

The Mirassou winery is a lively operation, moving with youth and enthusiasm. By no means are all the wines great. as apparently no winery can produce a total line of great wines. The Mirassous are one of the few winemaking families to acknowledge this fact and it is this kind of honesty that reflects itself in the taste of the wines, making the Mirassou line interesting — some wines great, others not.

Mirassou Vineyards may be a winery with a great past, but frankly, the future looks far more interesting.

Storage tanks nestle together beside one of many vineyards.

ROBERT MONDAVI WINERY

P.O. Box 106
Oakville, California 94562

Owners:
Robert Mondavi and Sicks'
Rainier Brewing Company,
Seattle, Washington

Winemakers:
Robert Mondavi and
Michael Mondavi

Vineyards:
400 acres

Capacity:
Storage 700,000 gallons
Fermenting 200,000 gallons

Johannisberg Riesling XXXX
Cabernet Sauvignon XXX
Zinfandel (unfined) XXX
Chardonnay XX
Pinot Noir XX

The dramatic entry to the winery off Highway 29 in the Napa Valley.

Whatever possessed Robert Mondavi to leave the comfort of the successful Mondavi family-owned Charles Krug Winery to found the Robert Mondavi Winery in 1966 is beyond me. Bob must have wanted so bad to make wines in the "Robert Mondavi style," he could taste it, to have taken on the establishment of the giant Robert Mondavi wine complex. He maintains he did it for his son Mike, who has become a wine man in his own right; however, I suspect it was done as much to make his own style wines as it was to provide a "winery base" for Mike.

Financially assisted by the Sicks' Rainier Brewing Co., Bob

Robert Mondavi.

has produced some interesting wines beginning with his Fumé Blanc, made from the Sauvignon Blanc, and patterned after the style of Pouilly-Fumé of France. His whites, Chardonnay, Chenin Blanc, and Johannisberg Riesling, have been quite good considering that they are beginning efforts of the winery.

The reds, Cabernet Sauvignon, Gamay, Pinot Noir, and Zinfandel, are satisfactory but do not measure up to the whites except possibly the Cabernet Sauvignon 1969, which to many was one of the finest Cabernets made in California. I remember twenty years ago when Bob took me on a tour of the Charles Krug Winery he said that one day he was going to make even bigger Cabernets than those being made at Charles Krug—and that

Summer concerts are popular.

Hundreds of new fifty-gallon French oak casks age the wine.

was in the days when some believed there was no demand by the consumer for great big, rich Cabernets. Bob is on his way with his first fine red wine, the 1969 Cabernet Sauvignon.

He has also indulged in some interesting experiments with Zinfandel, which he has made both fined and unfined. The unfined wine appears to be a much more complex, heavier, richer wine. This set a style for Zinfandels that others are also attempting. Hopefully, Bob will try again.

The winery building was designed by Cliff May and although it is as modern as any winery in the state it gives the impression of an earlier California, with its traditional adobe and tile exterior and classic Spanish influence.

Bob believes in the use of European oak casks for aging his wines, and these have given his reds, in particular, considerable character.

A man of indefatigable energy and boundless enthusiasm, a stickler for detail, Bob Mondavi has put together a most interesting winery with some interesting wines to match it.

Flat vineyards and the Mayacamas Mountains create a pleasant panorama from inside the main entrance.

THE NOVITIATE OF LOS GATOS

P.O. Box 128
Los Gatos, California 95030

Owner:
Novitiate of Los Gatos

Winemaker:
Brother Lee Williams, S.J.

Vineyards:
625 acres in Santa Clara, San
Benito, and Stanislaus Counties

Capacity:
Storage 800,000 gallons
Fermenting 80,000 gallons

Muscat Frontignan XXXX
White Riesling XX
Dry Sherry XX

The tasting room is located under a vaulted stone roof in the basement of the winery.

It is most appropriate that a fine religious order of the Society of Jesus is dedicated not only to the maintenance of schools but also to the making of fine wines. Dating back to its founding in 1888, the making of some of California's finest altar wines is an old tradition at the Sacred Heart Novitiate.

Most of the vineyard plantings were imported from France, with a heavy emphasis on Muscat, specifically from Montpellier. Besides the altar wines, a full line of table wines is made, most of which are not vintage-dated, but offered as good, sound, medium-priced wines ready to drink without fuss or aging. Enjoyed in the past have been such wines as Cabernet Sauvignon, Zinfandel, and Pinot Blanc, none complex but all providing good, sound wines with enough flavor to make them interesting.

The dessert wines, however, offer complexities as well as tremendous flavor, particularly the Muscat Frontignan. If the Novitiate made no other wine it would indeed earn its place in fine winemaking by this wine alone. Wines made from Muscat grapes, muscatels, etc., have indeed had a hard time in consumer acceptance — not because the wine has not been good but principally because of its poor public image. In truth, the Muscat Frontignan provides taste thrills that cannot be found in other grapes or wines. Rounding out the dessert line is the popular Black Muscat and one of my particular favorites, the Angelica — a wine noteworthy for uniqueness and taste — as well as such wines as dry sherry, flor sherry, and port.

California's winemaking is indeed enriched by such religious enterprises as the Christian Brothers and the Novitiate of Los Gatos, who bring to winemaking not only the purity of their faith but also undeniable old-world charm, which seems to find its way into the bottle.

OAKVILLE VINEYARDS

Box 87
Oakville, California 94562

Owner:
Oakville Limited Partnership,
W. E. van Loben Sels,
General Partner

Winemaker:
Peter Karl H. Becker

Vineyards:
264 acres

Capacity:
Storage 600,000
Fermenting 125,000 gallons

Cabernet Sauvignon XXX
Sauvignon Blanc XX
Zinfandel X

The winery was established in 1921 by Andrea Bartolucci with the help of his three sons, Louis, Lino, and Henry, but the Oakville winery and vineyard as it is now constituted is a new organization, established in 1969. The new enterprise is a spin-off of Carmel Valley Wine Associates, a brainchild of W. E. van Loben Sels, who has put together a rather interesting combination of vineyards and winery out of the old Bartolucci property at Yountville, California. Under the Bartolucci

1948, although for one purpose or another the winery has been in constant use. It is also interesting to note that in the early 1950s the Bartoluccis began the first large varietal planting of grapes, which find their way into Oakville wines today. The Cabernet Sauvignon, Johannisberg Riesling, and Chenin Blanc are from those earlier plantings. The properties in Oakville were the site of much of the filming of the production *A Most Happy Fella.*

Modern equipment frames the cellar, built in 1892 as the Madonna Winery.

A visitor's first view of Oakville.

aegis, the winery had fallen into a quasi-defunct state. The vineyards however were maintained quite well by Lino Bartolucci, who continues to devote his full time to the operation of the vineyards, along with Kenneth van Loben Sels and Donald Brown, recent graduates in agriculture from California State Polytechnic College.

The Bartolucci brothers did not bottle and market any wines after

Van Loben Sels has found himself an experienced winemaker in Peter Karl Heinz Becker, who spent eleven years with Almadén Vineyards and four years as a producer of his own wines at Michelstadt, Germany, with grapes from vineyards along the Rhine. The first wines of Oakville are indeed interesting, particularly the Cabernet Sauvignon which is one of the bigger Cabernets in California, with a great deal of varietal character, body, and richness in taste. It must be aged for a

longer period of time so that the wine can develop complexity. There is very little of it, but the supply should be substantially increased within the next five years.

The Sauvignon Blanc 1971 is a satisfactory wine if you like the tinge of sweetness that seems to form part of its style. It is not inexpensive, however, selling for $4.50, and is decidedly different from other California Sauvignon Blancs. The Zinfandel of Oakville is pleasant, lighter than most, but has enough varietal character to identify it. The champagne made by the *Methode Champenoise* is not as interesting as other California champagnes. The Chenin Blanc, a wine in good balance, is perhaps the best of the whites produced. It has fruitiness, with just enough acidity to hold the wine together as a pleasant, light, medium dry wine.

A full line of wines is planned by the winery, since it possesses some of the finest vineyards in the Napa Valley, planted to such varieties as Pinot Noir, Zinfandel, Gamay, Petite Sirah, Pinot St. Georges, Carignane, Traminer, Johannisberg Riesling, Cabernet Sauvignon, and Muscat de Frontignan.

Bud van Loben Sels, as he likes to be called, is a fourth-generation Californian who was born in 1915 at the Stanford Winery in Vina, California, and has been active in agriculture for a number of years. He and his wife Jean will be moving into the old Inglenook Ranch home which has become a part of the enterprise, as have some of the old Inglenook vineyards. These fine old vineyards promise that more can be expected from Oakville's wines in the future. Bud is convinced that he has the best vineyards in the Napa Valley. It will be most interesting to test that statement later, in the bottle.

PARDUCCI WINE CELLARS

501 Parducci Road
Ukiah, California 95482

Owners:
Parducci Family

Winemaker:
John Parducci

Vineyards:
200 acres

Capacity:
Storage 490,000 gallons
Fermenting 145,000 gallons

Cabernet Sauvignon XX

Zinfandel X

Flora : Comer

The new Upper Home Ranch, located above the valley in the hilltops.

One of the oldest winemaking establishments in Mendocino County, the Parducci Wine Cellars was established in 1918 at Cloverdale in Sonoma County. The present winery at Ukiah began operation in 1931.

Like so many of the winemaking families of California, the Parduccis come from Italy, in this case Lucca, where the founder, Adolph B. Parducci—although he was born in Santa Clara County—returned to work and learn Italian viticulture.

Today the winery is managed by John Parducci, Adolph's son, while third and fourth generations of Parduccis are preparing to take their place in the family business.

Mendocino County is not the easiest place to grow grapes and make wine but John is particularly proud of his area and states emphatically that he can make wine as good as if not better than anyone anywhere else in the state. He makes his point with some of his Cabernets and Pinot Noirs. The other reds, Gamay and Zinfandel, have also been quite good, all representing the style of Mendocino County, a style which I particularly enjoy in both Pinot Noir and Cabernet

George Parducci, winery treasurer.

Sauvignon, big wines with considerable flavor. If the 1969 Special Selection Cabernet Sauvignon Talmadge, unfiltered and unfined, is any example, John Parducci and his family are going to make some of California's finest, no doubt due in part to the resource material—the Talmadge District Vineyards of the area. The whites such as Chardonnay and Chenin Blanc don't seem to fare as well. French Colombard, a house favorite, and the hybrid Flora do a bit better.

The Parducci family, more than any other, has helped to open up the Mendocino County area to fine winemaking and if they make no other contribution to the wine scene in California they will be remembered for providing the wine drinker with the robust experience of a good Mendocino red wine.

J. PEDRONCELLI WINERY

1220 Canyon Road
Geyserville, California 95441

Owners:
John A. Pedroncelli and
James A. Pedroncelli

Winemaker:
John A. Pedroncelli

Vineyards:
110 acres

Capacity:
Storage 425,000 gallons
Fermenting 60,000 gallons

Cabernet Sauvignon XX
Johannisberg Riesling X
Pinot Noir X

Although this winery dates back to 1927, when it was founded by John Pedroncelli, Sr., it is just beginning to make its mark among wine lovers. Pedroncelli wines with good varietal character, such as Cabernet Sauvignon, Pinot Noir, Chardonnay, and Johannisberg Riesling, are gaining a fairly wide acceptance.

These varietals are vintage-dated and in given years the Cabernet Sauvignon, in particular, is a first-rate wine possessed of a fair amount of finesse and complexity. The whites and the Pinot Noir have not yet matched the Cabernet, but they are on their way to considerable improvement, no doubt assisted by new plantings of those varieties. Aging in small oak casks will also help.

In the past, the J. Pedroncelli wines were usually table generics, red and white, such things as Sonoma red and Sonoma rosé, burgundy, etc., but with the assistance of the founder's two energetic sons, John A. and James A. Pedroncelli, vintage-dated varietals are now the present goal.

The almost poetic comments of the two sons say a lot about their wines. Jim states: "People who come out from the East and settle here are surprised to find that we have so many, many climates. There is one practically every mile; you could be talking to somebody just a few lanes away on a telephone and find yourself asking how the weather is. This makes a huge difference in bringing fruitlike wine grapes to harvest. Each flavor nuance is magnified when the end product is wine. Wine is something that is thought about as it is consumed—more so than a prune, for example. You don't exactly hear people say, 'It's a good prune, not a great prune, but I admire its presumption.' Where we are geographically is a key part of our story and fairly interesting. Dry Creek originates a couple of miles over these foothills. The fog in late summer follows the Russian River up and curves into Dry Creek. It runs into a rise there and begins backing down and burning off. We get the fog, just a lovely amount of it, and we get blue sky and sunshine and we get them sooner than places below, for a balance of chill and warmth and moisture that is quite all our own. We find our wines have a mini-character to them. In essence, that's why we started bottling our own wines. In the early days we sold all our wines in bulk for blending and my dad always felt it was a shame to blend them away, they were so distinctive."

John comments: "The fact that you have to drive up the Redwood Highway and then turn down Canyon Road, then wind over this little rise until you get to our place, is the principal fact about our wines. Our grapes come from here or immediately around here and grapes make wine more than human beings do. I often wish I could take a lot of the people I meet in the tasting room out in the vineyards in September and put a grape in their mouths from this first hill, and then take them just a few miles down the road and give them a grape from the same variety and let them notice the difference. Sometimes I must admit this makes me feel a little useless around the place in my role as winemaker, but I'm afraid it has to be. Jim and I frequently

James Pedroncelli.

refer to nonwinemaking. Everytime you put a wine through a procedure you take something out of it. We're definitely non-procedure types. We tend wine more than we make it. Incidentally, we try to tend it quite elegantly; many of our oak barrels have come all the way from Bordeaux. There is an expression I like when I find myself discussing winemaking. Actually, it refers to how people are supposed to treat other people. The expression is 'with delicacy and kindness.' I'm reaching a bit, I know, but it's how we try to treat our wines."

Lovely, rolling hillside vineyards are planted to Cabernet and Pinot Noir.

MARTIN RAY, INC.
Saratoga, California 95070

Owner:
Martin Ray

Winemakers:
Martin Ray and
Dr. Peter Martin Ray

Vineyards:
100 plus acres

Cabernet Sauvignon XXXX
Blanc de Noir Champagne XXXX
Pinot Noir XXX

Martin Ray, one of the most puzzling characters in California wine, has probably made as great a contribution to the California wine cause as any man since Haraszthy. He has only one problem—he seems to have a way of getting people to hate him. Personally I like him, because on several occasions he has made wine which could challenge for the titles of the finest in Cabernet Sauvignon, Chardonnay, Pinot Noir, and champagne.

Ray believes that he is California's greatest gift to the vine and that he makes the finest wine. (The high prices of his wine will attest to his conviction.) The other half of the problem is that he believes everybody else makes poor wine.

No doubt if Ray were less contentious and more conciliatory he would be today one of California's most respected wine names. He believes—and has proclaimed it loudly from atop his mountain, Mt. Eden—that nobody can make fine wine in California unless it is 100 percent from the varietal named on the label; anything less than that is a compromise and should be banished from the mountain and from the consumer's table. He further believes, perhaps with some reason, that no American is a true wine lover unless he possesses a thousand cases or more in his wine cellar. Although not a possessor of a thousand cases of wine, I am in complete sympathy with the notion.

I am also in complete sympathy with what Martin Ray has tried to do—to set standards which even he himself has had difficulty matching. I doubt, however, that anyone has made finer Pinot Noir or Chardonnay, specifically the 1970 Chardonnay Ecrasant which was offered at fifty dollars per bottle. Whether it is worth it or not is another question. Try it and find out for yourself. Nobody seems to get too uptight when Marquis de Laguiche Montrachet sells for astronomical prices, as does the Musigny Blanc of the Comte de Vogüé.

It is precisely those French wine prices that have spurred Martin Ray on to making fine wines—in his own judgment, of course, better than the French. Martin Ray is an incredible man, having bought his first vineyard from Paul Masson himself and ultimately winding up with the property adjoining, which he deems not only higher in altitude but also in quality.

The wine production at Martin Ray is small but the prices are high—the average price of his wine hovers around the twelve- to fifteen-dollar mark. The wines often come in champagne-bottle shapes and in wood cases almost impossible to open, as they rival solid mahogany. Martin never does anything poorly.

Martin Ray wines throw a great deal of sediment, the whites as well, and are really not wines for the neophyte winetaster. One has to build up to Martin's wine, better yet *save* up, on a number of counts.

He sends out a fine newsletter occasionally which is done by his wife, Eleanor, a former teacher who is as important to the estate as any great lady can be.

Martin obviously does not make friends, for he thinks most other winemakers may be charlatans and this of course has gotten him into a lot of trouble with the industry. But I am unashamedly a fan, for I look at Martin through the bottle and not through the psyche, so I always come out ahead.

Martin is one of the last great rugged independent individuals of our day and there are many stories told about this legendary character, including the day he drove his pick-up truck down the tortuous grade of his hillside to pick up corn, no less, in the vintage of which Martin was extremely interested. The truck began to gather speed and it then became apparent that the brakes had failed. Martin, showing great wisdom, jumped out, fell to the ground bloody but unbowed, and then proceeded to make his way up to the house at the top of the mountain, where he greeted his wife with a "Fetch me a bottle of my wine." This she did, putting a chair on the porch. He sat down and drank the bottle, blood still trickling from his face, and by the time he downed the wine he had regained his strength and his humanity.

Whether the industry is willing to admit it or not, Ray has given a great deal to it, even though he continues to chastise it and show a profound unwillingness to get along with the people around him. This may have caused his undoing, as there seems to be a cloud of litigation affecting his vineyard holdings.

Nonetheless, those who have tasted and enjoyed Martin Ray wines, regardless of the price, are apt to say, as I do, "On occasion I have tasted the finest." If you don't believe me, try some of Martin Ray's Cabernets of the late '40s and early '50s. With all of the faults of Martin's personality his dedication to the making of fine wine always speaks as large as his own mouthings. He should have left the talking to his wines, for indeed they speak eloquently.

Martin Ray among his vines.

RICHERT & SONS

18980 Monterey Highway
Morgan Hill, California 95037

Owner:
Walter S. Richert Family

Winemaker:
Walter S. Richert

Vineyards:
None

Capacity:
Storage 10,000 gallons

Port XXX

Walter Richert greets guests in the winery tasting room.

Walter S. Richert, a man of wit and charm, has been as involved in the California wine industry as a decathlon athlete would be in the Olympics. He has worked at everything, and usually has done quite well — winemaker, chemist, production manager, and marketing developer. When the spirit moves him he writes the *Richert Report*, a chatty, informative, and pleasant discussion about his wines. The Richert winery is small — it owns no vineyards — and bottles some of California's finest dessert wines. Richert's personal love is sherry and in his own words, "I take the relatively ordinary stuff that the vintners produce in the San Joaquin Valley and I transform it into something far more precious." This he has done with the strong conviction that if California wineries don't get all their sherry from the San Joaquin Valley the wine will be worthless.

Richert is particularly proud of a 1972 achievement. The winery offered nine wines, some of them fruit wines, on the commercial market and then submitted all nine of them to the Los Angeles County Fair, where the winery won eight awards. He is willing to forgive the judges their single transgression.

Since the founding of the winery in 1953 both the winery

and the family have expanded, and a trademark symbolizing that expansion has been created, showing four casks representing Richert and his three sons.

A hand-painted sign.

Son Scott should ultimately be a great asset; he will join the winery as a graduate of Fresno State with a degree in enology.

Sherries and ports are the specialties of the house, and on occasion vintage ports are made. I recall vividly the vintage 1947 Tawny Port (tawny ports are not vintaged in Portugal), which was as rich and full a California port as I have ever tasted. Some vintage 1949 Pale Dry Sherry and 1947 Club Sherry also have been made. There has been some heated discussion, however, among wine lovers as to whether these should have been made as vintage wines.

Emphasizing fruit wines is a new wrinkle for Richert, who proudly proclaims that his favorite is apricot. While I am not personally interested in fruit wines, these can be good — fresh and pleasant to the palate. In the long run, however, they do not offer the kind of nuances, complexities, and depths of flavor that are to be found in fine grape wines.

This winery is a prime example of what can be done by a winemaker who does not grow his own grapes. By buying wines, blending, finishing, and maturing them, and taking advantage of the soils of an area that can, without question, make some of the best dessert wines in the world, Richert produces admirable wines.

Antique wine equipment decorates the tasting room porch.

RIDGE VINEYARDS

Cupertino, California 95014

Owner:
Ridge Vineyards, Inc.

Winemakers:
David R. Bennion and
Paul Draper

Vineyards:
45 acres

Capacity:
Storage 50,000 gallons
Fermenting 25,000 gallons

Cabernet Sauvignon XXXX
Zinfandel XXXX
Zinfandel Late Harvest XXX
Ruby Cabernet XX

Winemaker Paul Draper's office is a desk in the corner of the winery.

Standing on a cold and windy day at the top of the Ridge winery vineyards high above the town of Cupertino and Los Altos, I was literally knocked down and swept off the mountain top. When tasting the Ridge wines anywhere, one has the same feeling. I can give a wine no greater compliment. It is interesting to find a style of wine that is so big and assertive that it gives you such a feeling. This may not be a characteristic definable in classic wine terms, but with Ridge wines it's the best I can do.

The Ridge wines always seem to have bold, big, and assertive propensities—the color is so deep that a spill will result in a hole, and a mouthful makes for chewiness beyond belief. This enthusiastic introduction should tell you that I like the wine. I like the style and I like the people who make it.

Wines, whether they be white or red—but particularly red wines—are not for the faint of heart. They have to be seen to be believed and tasted to be convincing. Some call this winery "the House of Zinfandel," for Ridge has created, virtually single-handed, a style and a trend for Zinfandel that has made people sit up, take notice, and see Zinfandel as a unique, interesting, pleasant, and, on occasion, complex wine.

In 1958, the vineyard was purchased by four doctors of philosophy from the Stanford Research Institute for the unidealistic purpose of holding the land for commercial appreciation. There were some grapes on the land and it was felt that the grape crop would at least pay for the real estate taxes and other expenses. The group included David Bennion, H. D. Crane, C. A. Rosen, and H. M. Zeidler. Zeidler has since left and later Richard W. Foster of Los Angeles,

Carl Djerassi, and Alejandro Zaffaroni joined the enterprise.

The gentlemen from Stanford Research, of intellectual curiosity and palate, were intrigued with the idea of making some wine of the 1959 vintage. It was David R. Bennion who was more interested than the others and so he made the wine, approximately fifteen dozen bottles, for his own use. The result was so satisfactory that it gave birth to the whole Ridge winemaking enterprise. Bennion, himself, has been

The upper winery building will not impress unsuspecting visitors.

bitten by the grape to such an extent that he has given up his research career so that he can make wine at Ridge Vineyards.

I tasted with great pleasure and revelation—and now as I look back on it, it should have been with more humility—the wines of those early years, including Bennion's first bottle. The Cabernet of the first batch was incredible! It was a wine that over the years developed immense complexity but was so strong in varietal character and so full as to make other good wines seem poor by comparison. I first tasted it at Scandia Restaurant, Los Angeles, with

Richard Foster, just prior to his becoming a member of Ridge and I shall never forget the day nor the lunch, for they made me realize once and for all that winemaking isn't all laboratory, stainless steel tanks, and modern-day equipment.

There has been some complaint among competing winemakers—and, indeed, some consumers—that Ridge wines

are merely big but not elegant. There may have been a modicum of truth in this assertion, particularly for people who were unwilling to wait for Ridge wine to come around, which in those early days would have taken several lifetimes. To assist Bennion, a talented, young, well-trained winemaker was brought in to help—Paul Draper, who has some Chilean winemaking experience—and the wines in recent years have developed more balance, more finesse. They are unquestionably good, although I hope that the winery will never get away from the wines that can pick you up, knock you down, and sweep you away.

I never found the whites to be as interesting as the reds, although, since the advent of Draper, the Chardonnay and a Riesling Select—something like a Spätlese—have improved immensely and are now beginning to be worth drinking. It is to the reds, however, that I have lost my heart—all the fine Cabernets through the years (such as '63, '65, '68, the grapes of which I had the pleasure of picking with the Wine and Food Society of Hollywood, of which I am a member, and which are called the "Hollywood Cuvée"). Fortunately I have been able to collect these in magnum. This Ridge wine has to be one of the great California Cabernets. Do not liken it, however, to the style to be found in the Napa Valley, for the Ridge Cabernet often reflects a *goût de terroir* of its area, with a very dark, inky color and a lot of tannin. Wine with great substance.

The Zinfandels are as big as the Cabernets, and the Zinfandels come from a variety of areas, depending upon where the grapes were purchased. Ridge, because of its small vineyard acreage, has bought select plantings of Zinfandel from a variety of sources and on the back label, as well as on the front label, the consumer is informed where the grapes for the Zinfandel were grown. It is not uncommon to see such fine wines as 1968 Zinfandel Geyserville, 1968 Zinfandel Montebello Ridge at 1,100 feet, 1968 Zinfandel Geyserville Late Picked— the wine higher in alcohol due to its greater concentration of sugar because of the late picking. Those three wines are perhaps among the finest Zinfandels I have ever tasted. Newer Zinfandel—Occidental 1970— may be even better because it combines bigness with balance and finesse and will probably develop into one of the finest Zinfandels yet. I am inclined to think it should be drunk young, but I'm a minority; the majority of my wine-tasting friends feel it will last indefinitely. Perhaps as I am getting older I prefer more fruit in my wines.

All Ridge Vineyards wines are vintage labeled and unfiltered; and besides the time left on the skins the wines may get some of their bigness from lack of filtering.

One of the most interesting wines made by Ridge is the 1968 Zinfandel Essence from Lodi grapes which, as Bennion puts it, combines the richness, sweetness, and lusciousness of sauterne with a spicy, full-bodied Zinfandel character. It's not easy to find Ridge wines; they are sold principally at the winery and at a few select shops. It's best to buy them as soon as possible, for they are limited in quantity and take years to come around.

Vines have always grown at Ridge winery, even before Prohibition when there were 500 acres. An Italian immigrant by the name of Vincenzo Picchetti

was the first settler on the ridge and in 1880 he established a vineyard and winery on a 1,200-acre tract on the lower slopes. Some of the descendants of Picchetti still live in the area and the name Montebello apparently originated with Picchetti.

Another Italian immigrant, Dr. Osea Perrone, also pioneered at the Montebello ridge on a 1,300-acre tract where he built his ranch house and winery and planted the Montebello vineyards in 1893. After the death of Dr.

1969 the Ridge group purchased it and in 1971 and 1972 stainless steel tanks for fermenting and temporary storage were installed, making the total storage capacity about fifty thousand gallons. The barrels are of French oak and American oak.

An interesting sidelight to the Ridge adventure is the way the French oak barrels were obtained, by importing wines from various important châteaus in France in barrel, and then bottling them at the winery with

Constantly rotated oak barrels age some of California's "biggest" wines.

Perrone, his nephew—same name—cared for the 500 acres, which comprised the peak acreage for the ridge. Ridge now has the lower winery at 2,300 feet and the upper winery at 2,600 feet. Visiting and tasting is usually at the lower winery; more of the winemaking operation takes place at the upper.

The upper winery was the original Montebello Winery, which ceased operation in 1950. In

the label so stating. The Ridge people were interested not only in the wines but particularly in the barrels. This practice has stopped but it was fun during those early days.

The Ridge Vineyards have developed into a rather good commercial project although Charlie Rosen and Hugh Crane still hold jobs at Stanford Research, Richard Foster continues his successful alarm-clock business in Los Angeles, and Carl Djerassi and Alejandro Zaffaroni continue in their commercial enterprises.

A special note about Richard Foster. He is one of my closest friends—although I have tried to be objective about the wines— and as a matter of fact it was I who helped negotiate Richard's membership in Ridge. He had taken my wine course at the UCLA Extension, and because of his great interest in wine we became fast friends. He said something that I shall never forget: that he had been in the time-lock business and although he had done very, very well with it, it had never provided him with any creative satisfaction. He felt that only through wine growing and winemaking could he find this expression of humble, creative, and artful satisfaction. There is probably no one more interested in making fine wine nor anyone more dedicated, although there is much of both in California winemaking. Richard still lives in Los Angeles and in order to give expression to his feelings he must get on a PSA flight most weekends to contribute to the wine growing and winemaking at Ridge. He's indeed a marvelous man, with a fine palate and a tremendous wine soul, who has made life for me even more meaningful, particularly when he served me that 1959 Cabernet Sauvignon that Bennion made "just to satisfy intellectual curiosity." I also had the good fortune to have Dick serve me the 1960 Cabernet Sauvignon, another wine I shall never forget. Indeed, I have been a lucky man.

SAN MARTIN WINERY

P. O. Box 53
San Martin, California 95046

Owner:
Filice Family and Southdown
Corporation, Texas

Winemaker:
Pasquale Lico

Vineyards:
1,096 acres

Capacity:
Storage 2,258,000 gallons
Fermenting 900,000 gallons

Cabernet Ruby XXX
Spumante Moscato XX
Strawberry Fraisette X

The name Filice has been known in the Santa Clara Valley for almost a hundred years. In 1932, Bruno Filice brought into the family an old California winery that had been founded in 1892. After forty years of hard work and good winemaking, the San Martin Winery is one of the largest family-owned wineries in the state with more than a 2,000,000-gallon capacity—considerably up from its 50,000-gallon capacity in 1932.

Inside the sales and tasting room.

Bruno's sons, Frank, Peter, Michael, John, and a son-in-law, Pasquale Lico, have made some of the state's best medium-priced wines from such varieties as Cabernet Sauvignon, Pinot Noir, Pinot Chardonnay, Malvasia, Bianca, Emerald Riesling, Sylvaner, Zinfandel, Grignolino, Ruby Cabernet, Grenache, and French Colombard. This lengthy list of grape varieties attests to the versatility of the winery, which now also makes fruit and berry wines—blackberry, raspberry, and a very interesting wine from apricots called "Aprivette."

Champagnes—brut, extra dry, demi sec, pink, and rouge—are satisfactory. In the medium-price range, they are good buys.

The red and white varietals, not necessarily great bottles, are of very high quality and do not require long periods of aging, except possibly the Cabernet Sauvignon. They have not been vintage-dated and are generally made so that the wine is best

drunk relatively soon after it is purchased.

One of the reds, Ruby Cabernet, a cross between Carignane and Cabernet Sauvignon developed by Dr. Harold Olmo, is one of the best in the state. It is made in a style that makes it a rival of Cabernet Sauvignon for pure palate pleasure. Some of the ruby cabernet bottles of San Martin have been mistaken for Cabernet Sauvignon by enthusiastic enophiles, and often the wine is preferred to the Cabernet.

Of the over 1,000 acres planted in the Santa Clara Valley, 700 are in premium varietal grapes while the balance is in pears, apricots, prunes, cherries, and walnuts. There is no question that San Martin has some of the choicest and most fertile land in the valley.

Considering its inexpensive price, the San Martin line makes for excellent day-to-day wine-

drinking. The aperitif wines such as Dry Sherry, French Vermouth, Italian Vermouth, and Rare Sherry, are also interesting at the

price, as well as good tasting.

The winery prides itself on its 600 awards in various competitions over the years, principally at both the California State Fair and the Los Angeles County Fair judgings. In 1946, at the California State Fair, the first gold medal ever awarded for sweet vermouth was given to San Martin.

A new program that will upgrade the line significantly has begun at the winery, the vintage dating of its varietals, notably the 1968 Cabernet Sauvignon and Pinot Noir.

The most interesting line at San Martin is the Filice line—in which one finds Bruno's children, grandchildren, and assorted in-laws all making a contribution to the winery. San Martin features interesting tasting rooms in San Francisco, San Jose, and on Highway 101 near the winery. They are worth a visit.

San Martin vineyard temporarily withstands the threat of urban encroachment.

The winery recently merged with Southdown Corporation, Texas. Whether this will affect the wines remains to be tasted. If the Filices have anything to do with it, the wines will continue to improve.

SCHRAMSBERG VINEYARDS

Calistoga, California 94515

Owners:
Jack and Jamie Davies
(principal owners)

Winemakers:
Jack L. Davies
Dimitri Tchelistcheff,
Consulting Enologist

Vineyards:
35 acres

Capacity:
Storage 200,000 gallons
Fermenting 14,000 gallons

Blanc de Blancs XXXX
Blanc de Noir XXXX
Cuvée de Gamay XX

In 1957, the Schramsberg winery was designated a historical landmark by the state of California. In 1972, President Richard Nixon designated Schramsberg champagne a historical wine by taking it with him to mainland China and serving it at a state dinner there.

The modern Schramsberg winery has the capacity to produce and age approximately 8,000 cases of champagne. After the China publicity the wine sold instantly. It was a fitting reward for the Herculean efforts of Jack Davies, who took over the winery in 1965. He is a former business executive with Ducommon and one of the most enthusiastic winemakers in California. Davies's goal is to produce the state's finest bottle-fermented sparkling wines. There are many who believe that he

has already reached that goal.

Davies has replanted vineyards in Chardonnay and Pinot Noir, from which he makes the Schramsberg champagne. It is aged on the yeast up to three years. Jack prides himself that his formula for making champagne is the same as that used by the best French producers.

The Davieses have literally brought Schramsberg back from a state of despair and disrepair, although at one time it was one of the state's finest wineries as a result of the efforts of Jacob Schramm, who founded the property in 1862. Schramm established a reputation for so-called fine Schramsberg wines. Schramsberg reportedly was one of the first American wineries to have its wine served and enjoyed in Europe.

Silverado Squatters, by Robert

Louis Stevenson, who had been a visitor at Schramsberg, contains a chapter entitled "Napa Wines" that discusses the visit. Such wines as Red Schramsberger and White Burgundy Schramsberger and Schramsberger Hock were served to Stevenson and his bride, Fanny, who were honeymooning at the beautiful, spacious, mansionlike home in which the Schramms lived then and the Davieses live now.

Schramm died in 1911. A variety of unfortunate circumstances—among them Prohibition—plagued the property for the next four decades. In 1951, the winery was purchased by Douglas Pringle, who also was unsuccessful. In 1965, Davies and his wife, Jamie, took over. They have had spectacular success with it.

Young John Davies and friends stand before the historic limestone caves.

Jack Davies inspects the construction of the new winery.

It is not uncommon these days to find the Davieses' three young sons riding their bicycles through the beautiful, almost hand-hewn tunnels of the winery, which provide the best of aging facilities.

Jack may be the most idealistic man in California winemaking today. He will spare no expense to make his wine the best. Besides using his own grapes, he also has purchased grapes from Draper Vineyards, Zinfandel Associates, Stony Hill Vineyards, and other Napa Valley growers.

His sparkling wines have given California some of its finest, beginning with those of 1966. Schramsberg makes a Blanc de Blancs with Chardonnay and Pinot Blanc grapes that is probably the driest of all California champagnes, with good depth of flavor and character and a beautifully clean crispness to the taste. There is a regular Blanc de Blancs and a reserve, with the reserve providing additional bottle age.

The Cuvée de Gamay, a pink sparkling wine made of Gamay and Pinot Noir grapes, is equally clean. If you tasted it with your eyes closed you would be likely to mistake it for a white sparkling wine. It is unquestionably the best sparkling pink wine produced in California.

The Blanc de Noir is made in very small quantities and is a sparkling California champagne made almost exclusively of the Pinot Noir grape. This wine has considerable varietal character but most important, it is a clean and interesting sparkling wine with an effervescence that can only be described as most sophisticated. The Blanc de Noir may be the finest California sparkling wine I've tasted. An interesting addition is the newly conceived Cremant, a sparkling wine for dessert made from the Flora grape.

One important reason why Jack Davies makes good wines is that he approaches winemaking as a consumer as well as a professional winemaker. And that's a tough combination to beat.

Oh, yes—the Chinese have reordered!

Winemaker Jack Davies.

Champagne riddling racks line the floor of the limestone caves.

SAMUELE SEBASTIANI

389 Fourth Street, East
Sonoma, California 95476

Owner:
August Sebastiani
Winemakers:
August and Sam Sebastiani
Capacity:
Storage 2,000,000 gallons
Fermenting 300,000 gallons

Barbera XXXX
Cabernet Sauvignon XX
Green Hungarian XX
Zinfandel XX
Beaujolais Nouveau : *Comer*

It all began when Samuele Sebastiani arrived in San Francisco in 1893 to tend artichoke and cabbage fields. Later, he moved on to Sonoma County, hopeful of getting into the vineyard and wine business. It was a dream he maintained while he worked in the quarries, hauling cobblestones from Sonoma to help pave San Francisco streets.

In 1904, Sebastiani purchased a portion of the holdings of General Vallejo, who was among the first wine growers of the area. With a 501-gallon redwood tank and some Zinfandel grapes, the Sebastiani winery was begun.

In 1944, August Sebastiani took over modernizing and expanding the winery. August is a born farmer, married to the soil and one of the most interesting characters in the wine business.

the University of Santa Clara. August and Sam represent a continued family operation uninterrupted since 1904; they are one of the few pioneer families still making wine in California.

The Sebastiani family has been largely responsible for the growth of the city of Sonoma, where they have built homes and constructed schools and theaters. They have always shared their bounty with their fellow workers, friends, and neighbors.

In the days of Samuele, much of the wine was sold in bulk. After August took over, new plantings were made, principally varietals, and wines were identified by varietal names and bin numbers. Today there is a movement to vintage dating, which can only enhance the Sebastiani wines. Sebastiani

ripening variety that also does well in the relatively cool climate of Sonoma. Old Sebastiani Barberas age very well, developing some complexity and always maintaining tremendous assertiveness of flavor. When young, the wine sometimes seems coarse, but as it ages the quality and taste take over.

In recent years, the winery has produced some excellent Zinfandel, particularly in 1970,

Sam (left) and August Sebastiani.

and some outstanding Cabernet Sauvignon. The winery has improved its wines, particularly its Gamay and its whites, such as its Green Hungarian, Gewürztraminer, and Sylvaner.

The whites don't have as yet the complexities that the reds are able to develop, but there is no question about their ultimate improvement. The reds continue to get better and better. August and Sam are not afraid to experiment. They are the first California winemakers to make a Gamay Beaujolais Nouveau. The 1972 bottling—harvested by hand in the first week of October and bottled on November 29—was interesting enough to warrant continuing.

Sebastiani makes a full line of wines, including dessert wines, many of them rather pleasant. In 1971, at the Los Angeles County Fair wine judging, the winery took gold medals for its Cabernet Sauvignon, chablis, claret, Green Hungarian, medium sauterne, and medium sherry. Win, lose, or draw, August loves to enter this competition. He almost dares you not to like his wines, and to know his wines is to know him, an interesting gentleman with a deep faith in and love for grapes and wine.

The Sebastiani villa stands on a slight rise of ground above the vineyards.

If you drove to the Sebastiani properties today, you would no doubt find August in coveralls, still working the vines and pushing the barrels around the winery. He is a plain man with great strength of character and a keen, earthy wisdom.

If you are fortunate enough to enjoy August's hospitality, you will find the food bountiful, the wines enjoyable. He is as honest and exciting as the Sonoma Valley, which is today enjoying a rebirth in winemaking, thanks in a large part to the Sebastianis. The third generation of Sebastiani winemakers is young Sam Sebastiani, who was raised in the vineyards and educated at

makes a good number of mountain wines—wines that come from upland or hillside vineyards. Hillside vineyards often are the best.

The winery has been closely identified with Barbera, a wine that is made in a heavier, heartier style. This varietal from Italy may have gotten its California start at Sebastiani. It is an early-

SIMI WINERY

Box 848
Healdsburg, California 95408

Owner:
Russell and Betty Green

Enologist:
Mary Ann Graf

Consulting Enologist:
Andre Tchelistcheff

Vineyards:
325 acres

Capacity:
Storage 500,000 gallons
Fermenting 120,000 gallons

Cabernet Sauvignon XX
Carignane XX
Zinfandel : *Comer*

The Simi brothers founded their winery in 1876, giving it the name "Montepulciano." Although a beautiful name, Montepulciano was difficult for many Americans to pronounce and the winery became known simply as Simi. It has been that ever since.

Like many other pioneer Italian wine people, the Simi brothers made their winery a family operation. They produced a full line of wines until Prohibition and resumed immediately thereafter. For many in the California wine industry, it was difficult to resume the making of fine wines, for many of the vineyards had been destroyed. The Simi brothers obviously had no trouble finding grapes, for their first bottles after Prohibition were excellent. Their 1935 Cabernet Sauvignon, Zinfandel, and burgundy were awarded gold medals at the 1941 California State Fair. Some of these wines are still in stock in their original bottles and are available for purchase at the winery and select retail stores today. The Cabernet and Zinfandel are worthy of drinking today and are good—if expensive—examples of both varieties with considerable bottle age.

A new family is at the helm of Simi at present—the Russell Greens of Los Angeles, who gave up the proverbial rat race and turned their attention to winemaking. Russell, formerly the head of Signal Oil earning a six-figure salary, is spending his time in the best tradition of the gentleman farmer. Being a gentleman farmer is a pleasant notion, but Russell is probably working harder than he ever has in his life and enjoying it more; and to top off the dream, he is turning out some rather good wines.

The Green family is not new

Isabelle Haigh, whose father built Simi in 1876, was born on the property in 1890.

to the area, as they were involved in the development of their own vineyards for twelve years in Alexander Valley, not too far from the Simi facility. Both sets of Green grandparents had chosen the Russian River country as a summer place for their San Francisco-raised families; they both bought lots, one at Rio Nido and one near Healdsburg, in 1910. The entire family has been enjoying the cabins they built there ever since.

Russell's parents moved to southern California, where his father was active in the oil business, but every summer the family returned north to the river, with Dad a weekend commuter. Because of their love of water, the family moved to a fifty-acre ranch, ten miles away, that had some of the best swimming in the Alexander Valley area. A slight bit of investigation convinced them that the prospects for grape plantings were indeed high, and a decision was made to plant grapes, displacing prunes in the area. The Alexander Valley today is full of grape plantings, but in 1958 when Russell came in it was at least 85 percent prunes.

New owner Russ Green relaxes in front of the Barrel Room, which contains many interesting antiques.

The winery at Simi.

Russell believed that the Alexander Valley grapes could make wines the equal of Napa Valley wines. The charts of the University of California at Davis list it as Region III, which means that it is too hot for many top-quality wines and certainly much hotter than the Napa Valley, which many believe is ideal. After a number of wine pilgrimages to the Napa area, Russell didn't believe that the Napa Valley was any cooler, so he went ahead and planted twenty-five acres of varietals. After considerably more investigation into adjacent acreage, he became convinced that the Alexander Valley was just a shade cooler than Oakville, the heart of the Napa Valley Region II.

Russell now makes a full line of wines, some of which are from Simi's past and some of which have had a slight amount of new wine added as a good blend. The advent of the Green generation has helped Simi

immeasurably; now the wines that are being released are good, sound, better than standard, pleasant wines. For instance, the Cabernet Sauvignon is a wine that has satisfactory Cabernet Sauvignon character, certainly enough to make it interesting and to warrant the price of three dollars a bottle. The other wines are generally in a softer style, ready to drink, and are indeed a pleasant surprise to many who are worried about high wine prices. Additionally, Simi makes a Carignane, a tradition at the winery as it is a grape not favored as a varietal wine and generally is used as a filler for other red wines. The Carignane fares very well at Simi, for it makes a relatively soft red wine with good flavor and a pleasant finish. I first tasted the 1935 vintage of this grape and as a result of that particular bottle, which aged extremely well, I

became intrigued with the wine and found that Russell Green's current Carignane is indeed very good. Drinking Carignane— a good one, that is—is almost like rooting for the underdog.

All the other wines, the Zinfandel, Gamay, beaujolais, burgundy, Pinot Chardonnay, Johannisberg Riesling, Gewürztraminer, Chenin Blanc, chablis, rosé of Cabernet Sauvignon, and Grenache rosé, are by no means great or complex, but all have something interesting to say and make a very good value. The day will come when Russell will produce great and complex wines either by finding the time necessary to do it or by limiting the number of wines he produces. There is no question of the interest and dedication on his part. In his own words: "I have not as yet been in the wine business as much as I have actually been in the winery building business." In the past two years he has spent his time building a

new forty-ton-per-hour crushing station to replace the former one-box-at-a-time system, converting the old champagne vault into a well-equipped fermenting room with the refrigeration necessary to control fermenting rates (producing more delicate, fruity wines), and purchasing over 800 French cak barrels to provide a traditional oak-aged character to some of the wines.

In the spring of 1973, Simi began a policy of vintage dating all wines. Russ has preferred not to date any of his wines until all could be dated—excluding the '35s, of course, which were bottled many years ago. The first vintage was the 1971 Pinot Chardonnay, a satisfactory beginning. Later editions will be even better. All whites will bear vintages by the end of 1973; at that time the first vintage reds will appear. The first vintage Cabernet Sauvignon will be released in 1974. Without question, Simi is back!

SOUVERAIN CELLARS, INC.
St. Helena, California 94574

Owner:
The Pillsbury Company

Winemaker:
Phillip Baxter

Vineyards:
30 acres

Capacity:
Storage 200,000 gallons
Fermenting 15,000 gallons

Johannisberg Riesling XXXX
Chardonnay XX
Flora XX

Stainless steel fermentation tanks.

There is a tradition of great quality of winemaking at Souverain Cellars. Lee Stewart came to winemaking in 1943, starting from scratch high above the Silverado Trail on the eastern slopes of the mountains overlooking the Napa Valley.

The winery not only looks over the valley but on a clear day you can see almost to Stony Hill, with which Lee Stewart long had a friendly rivalry over who made the best Chardonnay and Johannisberg Riesling. In a given vintage, wine buffs would glow with interest while enjoying two of California's finest Johannisberg Rieslings—the Stony Hill and the Souverain—each one representing a distinctly different style. The Stony Hill was generally a dryer, crisper wine, while the Souverain was intentionally made with a slight tinge of sweetness to approximate more closely wine of a German rhine style. Two of the finest Johannisberg Rieslings ever produced in the state were made by Stewart in the 1968 and 1969 vintages. Lee Stewart was really making some of his finest wines when he sold his interests and retired.

Lee is a man of indomitable spirit, an excellent winemaker with determined, definite ideas about the style of wine he wanted to make. He came by his winemaking prowess through the wise counsel and gentle hand of Andre Tchelistcheff, who assisted Lee during the early days when he was making the transformation from wine hobbyist to professional winemaker.

From time to time Lee has made some of the state's best Chardonnay and Cabernet Sauvignon, as well as a most interesting sherry called Los Amigos Sherry Sack. It was not only one of Lee's better wines but also his way of carrying on the tradition of Los Amigos Sherry, a vineyard with a proud California history at Mission San Jose, no longer in operation.

Honesty, candor, and forthrightness were notable virtues of Stewart, sometimes carried to a

Phil Baxter stands before the winery.

fault. As chairman of the Los Angeles County Fair wine judgings it was my pleasure to contact Stewart, after a judging a few years ago, about buying one of his award-winning wines. In the course of the conversation he let it be known in no uncertain terms that he was unhappy about the judging. I asked why, inasmuch as his Chardonnay had won a gold medal and his Johannisberg Riesling a silver. He promptly informed me that his Chardonnay didn't deserve it and that the only reason his Johannisberg Riesling did not get a gold medal

was that the judges didn't understand his style. No question—Stewart is as complex as his wines.

The Pillsbury Company now owns a majority interest in Souverain Cellars. Additional capital has helped construct two new wineries, one for Souverain in the Napa Valley, east of Rutherford, with over 200,000 gallons of present storage capacity. The other winery will be named "Ville Fontaine," near Geyserville in Sonoma County, and will represent a $4 million expenditure. It will have 60,000 square feet designed to house a goal of one million cases.

Phillip Baxter is the winemaker at Souverain and William Bonnetti will be the winemaker at Ville Fontaine. Lee Stewart recently returned as chief overseer of both wineries. An interesting aspect of the Pillsbury venture is that no new vineyards are planned; grapes are likely to come from several counties, including Napa, Sonoma, Mendocino, and Lake.

The corporation will have its hands full trying to make wines as good as Souverain's have been. They may—or may not—succeed, and doubtless the first one to tell them in no uncertain terms will be Lee Stewart.

STERLING VINEYARDS
1111 Dunaweal Lane
Calistoga, California 94515
Owner:
Sterling International
Winemaker:
R. W. Forman
Vineyards:
400 acres in Napa Valley,
most of which are centered
in the area of Calistoga
Capacity:
Storage 155,000 gallons
Fermenting 95,000 gallons

Cabernet Sauvignon XX
Zinfandel X
Chardonnay : *Comer*

The new winery looms fortresslike at the north end of the Napa Valley.

A vineyard and winery operation of huge proportions only recently established, Sterling will become one of the largest premium wineries of the state. The new winery building, already a model for other wineries, is a marvel of technological equipment and consummate good taste, although from a distance it appears to be a castle-like fortress, a throwback to old European-style château wineries.

Sterling International, a London-based corporation, operates the winery so as to do as little harm to the wine as possible. The different levels of the winery are built to permit rackings and pumpings to be accomplished through gravity flow. The entire complex is truly a remarkable sight, a multi-million dollar fort developed by three interesting gentlemen—Martin Wakefield, Michael P. W.

One of several aging rooms.

Stone, and Peter Newton. Much is expected of this winery to allay the pressures on other wineries for good varietal wines such as Chardonnay, Gewürztraminer, Sauvignon Blanc, Cabernet Sauvignon, Zinfandel, Chenin Blanc, and a Merlot. The Merlot will be bottled for the first time in California as a 100 percent varietal wine and it will be interesting to taste, for this has not been done before. Merlot is generally used as a blending grape in Bordeaux and increasingly in California. The Cabernet Sauvignon will be blended with a small amount of Merlot as is traditionally done in France.

The wines are crushed and fermented primarily in stainless

steel, although the Chardonnay is fermented in casks. The first, Chardonnay 1969, was a satisfactory beginning but not yet a complex or exciting wine. The 1970 was an improvement, with a better finish and more flavor. The wines are just now coming on the market and most wine drinkers are waiting expectantly, in the hope that the varietals will be great wines that justify the loving effort being made by Sterling International.

The 1969 Cabernet Sauvignon, an interesting wine that needs more flavor and varietal character, shows much promise for the future. Improvement appears evident. The recent bottling of Blanc de Sauvignon 1970

Handmade Swiss bells hang in the bell towers.

proved to be one of Sterling's best wines yet—even, crisp, displaying good flavor and varietal style.

Although the vineyards are planted exclusively to varietals, the intention is to use only the best for Sterling wines. Additional grapes will be bought when necessary. Most of the vineyard sections are on the Napa Valley floor, with a small new planting on the west slope of the Coast range. Interestingly, the vineyards are being mechanically harvested, which should be of significant help in reaching the winery's ambitious goal of 100,000 cases annually.

STONY HILL VINEYARD

P.O. Box 308
St. Helena, California 94574

Owners:
Frederick H. McCrea and
Eleanor W. McCrea

Winemaker:
Bruce Rogers

Vineyards:
36 acres

Capacity:
Storage 5,000 gallons

Chardonnay XXXX
Johannisberg Riesling XXXX
Gewürztraminer XX

Between Diamond Mountain and Spring Mountain, high above the Napa Valley, lies one of the smallest vineyards—yet one of the finest Chardonnay vineyards—in the state of California, sometimes referred to as "America's greatest white wine estate." The whole idea of making wines is a relatively recent enterprise of Frederick H. McCrea, who, with his wife and wine companion, Eleanor, decided upon retirement from McCann-Erickson Advertising Agency in order to attempt to

first three, but the Pinot Blancs he sells to other wineries, including Heitz. The supplying of grapes to other winemakers and vineyardists in the Napa Valley is nothing new to McCrea, as he has a habit of helping wineries and vineyards get started. Stony Hill grapes have been a great boon to the launching of new wine estates by Jack Davies of Schramsberg, Joe Heitz of Heitz Cellars, and Lee Stewart, of Souverain Cellars.

For the McCreas, the Char-

burgundies—Montrachets, Meursaults, Chablis—the wine stands up very well indeed. Caution should be observed in buying a Stony Hill Chardonnay, in that the wine requires three to five years or more of aging in the bottle.

Stony Hill Chardonnay is sometimes deceiving, as it appears when young to be light in character (often a characteristic of white burgundies); but as the wine ages it develops much more character, deepens in color and in flavor, and is

The view from the McCrea home captures the entire Napa Valley.

make fine wine in very limited production.

In 1943 he acquired the Stony Hill property and in 1951 constructed a small but efficient winery. In his earlier days at the winery he made Gewürztraminer, Pinot Blanc, Johannisberg Riesling, and, of course, Chardonnay. Today he makes the

donnays are truly the top of the line and may be the best that California has to offer. The Chardonnays were improving with considerable authority through the late '50s and moved on to some glorious wines, particularly the 1962, 1963, and 1968 vintages. These wines tend to be rich, luscious, soft, full-flavored, and have considerable Chardonnay character. When tasted alongside great white

hardly recognizable from its younger version. Time, here, reaps its own reward. Stony Hill Chardonnays, in my cellar, are best of all when they are five to ten years old.

McCrea was one of the first to use new Limousin oak in the aging of his Chardonnay, and it shows. Sometimes he says he gets too much oak, as he believes he did in 1963. He calls it an "oakie" wine, but it seems to have started the trend among many other California producers of Chardonnay. More oak is used now than ever before and the taste of wine reflects it. The French have always used oak in their white burgundies, so it is very difficult now to tell good California Chardonnay, such as Stony Hill, from good French white Burgundy.

Chardonnays, and particularly those of Stony Hill, when blessed with a great deal of Chardonnay fruit, are considered big, and when mated with oak the balance of the fruit and the oak makes for the best in Chardonnay and one of the finest white-wine experiences in the wine world. There is a different school of thought, however, that prefers Chardonnay with little

The bottling and storage room.

Fred McCrea stands before the doors he carved for the cellar entrance.

or no oak, with only the fruit of the grape showing. Not at Stony Hill. The McCreas are growing older now and there is great hope that the littlest "big" winery in the Napa Valley will continue to make its line of wines and hopefully, someday, bring back the Pinot Blanc. The Pinot Blanc vines have been pulled in favor of the Chardonnay. A luscious sweet wine, Sémillon de Soleil, has been produced in small quantities and will continue to be produced.

For his own consumption, Fred has added an extremely small amount of Pinot Noir, which should make for some interesting red wine from Stony Hill. Still, he should stay with

Chardonnay; there is never enough of that classic.

The wines are sold only through subscription and if you are fortunate enough to make Fred's list you may find yourself with a few bottles of each vintage sometime in October or November. (Total production is approximately 2,000 cases.) Do not expect to find the wines in stores, though occasionally you will find some in restaurants; write to Fred and ask him to put you on the list—with a twinkle in his eye, he may do so.

It is interesting to note that Fred really enjoys the making of wine, perhaps more than the consumption of it. Often friends invite the McCreas for an exclusive Stony Hill dinner, when Fred delights in drinking his own wine. It is quite possible that that is the only way he can get Stony Hill.

SUTTER HOME WINERY

277 St. Helena Highway South
St. Helena, California 94574

Owners:
Mario Trinchero, Louis Trinchero,
Roger Trinchero

Winemaker:
Louis (Bob) Trinchero

Vineyards:
None

Capacity:
Storage 90,000 gallons
Fermenting 12,000 gallons

Sutter Home Winery is not a very well known name, even in the Napa Valley, where it is located. Nevertheless, it has a long and varied history as the oldest winery building still in use as a winery in the valley. It was constructed by John Thomann in 1874 and bought as a winery in 1890 by John Sutter, not related to the Sutter of early California gold rush fame. Just how well John Sutter did with his wines and his winery is shrouded in the past, but the present era for the old winery started in 1946 when it was purchased by Mario and John Trinchero. They decided to concentrate on winemaking only, and bought all their grapes from various Napa Valley growers. They quickly marketed a broader line of wines than almost any other valley winery, and soon were known for their wide selection.

On the death of John Trinchero in 1960, his nephew Louis, known to everyone as Bob, took over as winemaker. The wines began to improve. Bob was aware of the change coming in the California wine industry in the 60s—the striving for excellence rather than just variety and quantity. The Sutter Home line was reduced from over forty wines to six. With this reduction, it was possible to concentrate all the time, effort, and skill it takes to produce fine wines. To that end, Bob Trinchero finally concentrated almost completely on one wine, Zinfandel.

This specialization in Zinfandel is an intriguing one. Few if any wineries have ever done it, with the possible exception of York Brothers at Templeton, California. York Brothers won their fame with Zinfandel before Prohibition.

The Sutter Home Zinfandel was first made in 1968, a warm year. That wine developed the rich, almost portlike character that is typical of such seasons. Much like the style of great wines produced in France, such as the Bordeaux and Burgundies of 1947, the 1968 Sutter Home Zinfandel became popular, and has since become a collector's

A rather unpretentious, barnlike building houses the winery on Highway 29.

item. The 1969 vintage has fared very well in blind tastings of California Zinfandels and it, too, is a big, bold wine. The 1970 Zinfandel is perhaps the biggest of the three, and is an elegant wine, perfumed, of almost perfect balance, extremely characteristic of the area where the grapes were grown. The 1971 vintage is a light version of the 1970, but may develop more in the bottle.

The finding of grapes for a winery without its own vine·· yards is very difficult. A grape scarcity and high prices put an even greater obstacle in Sutter Home's path. In 1968 a grower in Amador County, in the mother lode country of eastern California, was contacted. The Trincheros bought grapes from a single vineyard there known as Deaver Ranch. The twin factors of scarcity and high prices have brought a renaissance of grape awareness to Amador County, and for this Sutter Home can be grateful, because the Amador County Zinfandel grapes produced some of the biggest and most interestingly styled Zinfandels yet made. Other California wineries have followed Sutter Home to Amador County grapes.

The building occupied by Sutter Home is extremely interesting, since it was constructed as a model for wineries in the 1880s. The two-story building has a chalked-deck

upper story, where the fermenters were originally located. Today this floor serves as the barrel-aging room, where Amador County Zinfandel is aged in a variety of oak casks. New French oak from Nevers, Limousin oak casks, and various sizes of American oak casks form the cooperage that has so much to do with Sutter Home Zinfandel's good character.

There are other table wines, as well as vermouth and vinegar, made at Sutter Home, but the Zinfandel is outstanding. The winery is making an intriguing case for the idea that California wineries should look into the concept of making a single wine, as many of the wine estates do in France.

Sutter Home makes an interesting rosé from Amador County Mission grapes. The vines themselves are over 100 years old and still going strong. It is, however, the Sutter Home vinegar that is challenging even the Zinfandel. It is produced by the time-honored Orleans barrel process and is available only in a light red vinegar that has considerable character. For those who might sneer at discussing a fine vinegar here, be aware that a good vinegar is more difficult to make than a good wine.

Sutter Home may, after some false starts as a winery, now come back stronger than ever under the Trinchero reign, with Amador County Zinfandel showing the way.

WEIBEL CHAMPAGNE VINEYARDS

P.O. Box 3398
Mission San Jose, California
94538

Owner:
Weibel, Inc.
Winemaker:
Oscar Hableutzel
Vineyards:
Approximately 100 acres
Capacity:
Storage 1,000,000 gallons
Fermenting 50,000 gallons

Champagne Brut XXXX
Pinot Noir, Estate Bottled XX
Memento Cream of Black
Muscat XX

If you have enjoyed California champagne under a variety of labels that have been unknown to you for one reason or another, don't be surprised if most of them were wines made by Weibel, for Weibel has been virtually everybody's champagne maker, and many hotels' and stores' "private" labels have appeared on Weibel wines. They are among the largest champagne producers of the state and more often than not challenge for the title of best. The Weibels have been making so much champagne that they have become known as California's champagne specialists and have long enjoyed a good reputation for their brut and nature. They have also made

The line is highlighted by the Chardonnay, Johannisberg Riesling, Green Hungarian, and Chenin Blanc, although in recent years they have produced a Pinot Noir, vintage 1966, that is without a doubt the best red wine they have ever made. It is obvious that if they put their minds to it, Weibel can make fine red wine, as well as making good use of their new vineyards and winery at Ukiah in Mendocino County.

A full line of dessert wines, sherries, and ports is made, also quite good and generally quite inexpensive. It includes Governor's Rare Solera Port, Memento Cream of Muscat, and Amberina Cream Flor Sherry, as well as a Cocktail Flor Sherry.

The history of Weibel is interesting, largely because the vineyards are located in Mission San Jose on the site of the old Leland Stanford winery, which has been adjudged a state historical landmark. The vintage of the Leland Stanford winery is 1869.

The Weibels themselves are not new to the making of wine,

Fred Weibel and son, Fred, Jr.

having brought the principles of enology in champagne from Switzerland and France, ultimately choosing California for their application.

The Weibel family also has been responsible for helping many smaller wineries that did not themselves have vineyards to prosper in the business, by providing them with champagnes and wines that could be purchased and refinished by those wineries.

Weibel, Inc., is now a large enterprise, still family operated. No doubt the Weibels have improved on the Leland Stanford site so much that a hundred years from now another historical marker will have to be added alongside the one for Leland Stanford.

The "mother" vineyard stretches toward the winery near Mission San Jose.

Moscato Spumante, a very good sparkling Muscat, and sparkling burgundy.

They also make a line of table wines, of which the whites seem to be better than the reds.

The handsome tasting room.

WENTE BROS.

5565 Telsa Road
Livermore, California 94550

Owners:
Ernest A. Wente and Karl L. Wente

Winemaker:
Karl L. Wente

Vineyards:
1,400 acres

Capacity:
Storage 1,500,000 gallons

Pinot Chardonnay XXX
Pinot Blanc XX
Sauvignon Blanc XX

Years ago when American wine and food societies had to be dragged in kicking and screaming to taste California wines, I petitioned the Wentes for their best white wine for a wine and food society dinner that would show off California wines. The response from the Wentes was out question the Wentes had been making perhaps the finest Chardonnay in the state until the early 1960s. As a matter of fact, there are those who believe that they invented it.

What they did create in America was an insatiable demand for California Chardonnay at a time With a decade of age it was one of the finest California white wines I ever drank and it is a pity that this most consistent of grapes still is not heavily favored—not only at Wente but throughout the state—for with adequate age it is a wine that is the equal of and often times

Karl Wente stands among the intriguing machines of a modern winery.

not Chardonnay, as I had anticipated, but rather a ten-year-old Pinot Blanc. In my naiveté and starry-eyed wine enthusiasm, I felt that Chardonnay would have been a better choice, for with- when Chardonnay was a wine you served only in a darkened room when no one was looking, particularly not a Frenchman. Today the first wine I offer a French wine drinker is Chardonnay. The Wentes have indeed brought Chardonnay a long way.

But back to the Pinot Blanc. superior to Chardonnay.

The Wentes in their wisdom knew this and have been making the finest Pinot Blanc in the state. And why not? The Wente family, under the direction of Carl H. Wente back in 1880, got firsthand winemaking experience from one of the state's greatest winemaking names—second only to Haraszthy himself—Charles Krug. Krug almost single-handedly gave the Napa Valley its great grape-growing image. This is precisely what the Wentes have done for the Livermore Valley, where the first Wente vineyard was acquired in 1883.

If the Wentes were to start today it is doubtful that they would begin with the Sémillon and Sauvignon Blanc grapes. That would be indeed a pity, for the Livermore region seems to have been born to white wine grapes such as Sémillon and Sauvignon Blanc—and of course Chardonnay as well.

The French, through Château d'Yquem and its brilliant owner the Marquis de Lur-Saluces, made a contribution to the Wente viticulture by providing cuttings of Yquem grapes. Whether this has been responsible for Wente's fine grapes can't be known; it is, however, nice to know that there is a touch of Yquem present in Wente's vineyards.

The Wentes are among California's finest wine-growing and winemaking families, dynamically directed now by Karl L. Wente, grandson of Carl. He is assisted by his father, Ernest, and so the Wente dynasty continues unabated.

The dynasty is under heavy fire from urbanization in the Livermore Valley, so it was with great anticipation and some trepidation that the family established new vineyards in the Salinas Valley of Monterey County. The vineyards are approximately ten years old and the wines that have been made from those grapes appear to be solid enough to ensure the survival of Wente quality.

The problem in Livermore is quite serious. The area is blooming with new housing tracts and industrial complexes; only an agricultural preserve will save it, as well as the "Livermore taste." Even though Wente's new-area wines are satisfactory and may even some day be great, I would not want to lose the Livermore to "progress," any more than I would want to lose a Meursault or a Chablis.

There are those wine enthusiasts who say that Wente wines are slipping, particularly the Chardonnay and Sauvignon Blanc. This may come from the challenge of new Chardonnay makers that have sprung up all over the state; for the first time in the state's history Chardonnay is available in a variety of styles that some find more pleasing than Wente's. Wente may not emphasize oak as do some of its competitors, and of course the new vines in Monterey County may not as yet make as complex wines as those made in the Livermore Valley. When Wente wants to make fine wine it can, for it has time, tradition, and experience on its side, as well as a great Chardonnay reputation. The wines are made in much larger quantities than in days gone by, but they are able to stand well against the challenge, and may still be California's finest Sauvignon Blanc and Pinot Blanc.

Other good whites are dry Sémillon and a unique new wine called Le Blanc de Blancs, which is a blend of Chenin Blanc and Ugni Blanc grapes.

Some half-gallon jug wine is made under the old Wente label Valley de Oro. Generally inexpensive and available principally at the winery, the wines are sound, good everyday drinking wines.

The Wentes have also embarked over the years on a program of making red wines such as Gamay Beaujolais, Pinot Noir, burgundy, and rosé. None of these wines, in my judgment, seems to be worth making except possibly the rosé. The Wentes ought to continue to concentrate on the whites in California—Chardonnay, Pinot Blanc, and the rest—something they do extremely well.

The Livermore vineyards are threatened by multiplying housing developments.

An early morning sun defines the entry to the tasting room.

The striking new winery contains a central tasting room and outdoor theatre on the side.

WINDSOR VINEYARDS

P.O. Box 368
Windsor, California 95492

Owner:
Tiburon Vintners, Inc.

Winemakers:
Rodney D. Strong and
James Wolner

Vineyards:
2,700 acres

Capacity:
Storage 2,000,000 gallons
Fermenting 800,000 gallons

When Rodney D. Strong, a former Broadway dancer, started the Windsor Vineyards (also known as Sonoma Vineyards) in 1960, most wine consumers did not take him seriously—indeed, they laughed at the enterprise. By 1964, Windsor wines were sold more for their personalized labels than for any great quality in the wine itself, an interesting marketing idea conceived by Peter Friedman, now president of the corporation. The premise of the winery, at the beginning, was to sell wines to people who wanted to have gifts sent to friends with the label saying "Personally selected by (name of donor of the bottle)."

The wine consumers and the industry have stopped laughing, because Windsor Vineyards has become a most serious enterprise, so much so that in 1970 it became a public corporation. Perhaps the acquisition of over 2,000 acres in vineyards in the Russian River Valley and the establishment of a million-dollar winery complex has made the

difference. I suspect it is more than that.

For some time, until the winery was able to get its own vineyards into production, the wines did not seem to have much character. But things are changing, and changing rapidly, for the better. The beautiful new Windsor Vineyards winery is efficient and

Wine ages in French and American oak.

modern, and is turning out wines that wine consumers now must take seriously for varietal character and quality.

The Windsor wines, marketed through Tiburon Vintners, are sold directly to the consumer by mail order solicitation only. The other label, Sonoma Vineyards, is distributed through retail stores and restaurants.

The enterprising winery, under the leadership of Rodney D. Strong, will certainly make its mark among premium wine producers as more of its vineyards come into production. It will be interesting for both the consumer and the industry to observe how seriously the winery makes its bid for a place at the top—which hasn't been reached yet, but recent bottles indicate that at least the winery is on its way.

I, for one, was among those who...well, if I didn't laugh at least I chuckled. I'm glad to say I'm enjoying drinking my words.

Z D WINES

20735 Burndale Road
Sonoma, California 95476

Owners:
Norman D. deLeuze and
Gino R. Zepponi

Winemaker:
Gino R. Zepponi

Vineyards:
None except for small
Chardonnay plantings not yet
in full production

Capacity:
Storage 2,600 gallons

Another example of home wine-makers turned professional, engineers Gino Zepponi and Norman deLeuze, the Z and D of the winery name, had no grapes to begin with, a normal story for the small wine entrepreneur. They had to rely on others for good varietal grapes, and the Z D complex was fortunate in finding the Winery Lake Vineyards. Pinot Noir, Chardonnay, White Riesling, and Gewürztraminer were made available by Rene diRosa in the Carneros region in the southern Napa Valley, facing San Pablo

Gino is primarily responsible for the winemaking, a naturally evolved right, since his family is second generation Sonoma. He has had extensive tasting experience in the area and has taken many courses in winemaking at the University of California at Davis. Both Zepponi and de-Leuze have, in addition to the winery operation, built a thriving business as consultants on systems devised by them for use by other wineries and implemented under their direction—a happy combination of winemaking and engineering.

The winery building, near Vineburg in Sonoma County, is undistinguished

Bay. Z D winery cooperates closely with diRosa in selecting the most appropriate time to pick the grapes, the next best thing to owning the vineyards yourself.

The winery is a small, air-conditioned building where the wines are fermented in small cooperage. Wines thus far produced by Z D include White Riesling 1969, 1970; Pinot Noir 1969, 1970, 1971; Chardonnay 1971, 1972; Gewürztraminer 1970, 1971. Of the finished wines, the Pinot Noir has stimulated the greatest interest. It is made exclusively from Pinot

Noir grapes from relatively young vines, and as the wine-maker describes it, with a touch of the oak from the nearly two years it has spent aging in fifty-gallon barrels. To the taste, the wine seems light, with just enough character to make it interesting. It is doubtful, however, that it is made to age well over a long period of time. Perhaps it is due to the immature vine, perhaps to the manner and style of making, but it seems a wine meant to be drunk young, enjoyed more for the fruit than any complexity or depth it might develop after bottle aging. The White Rieslings and Gewürz-traminers, though pleasant, need improving.

The labels of Z D are innovative. The 1969 Pinot Noir states that it is a wine "made in Sonoma from grapes grown in the Carneros region of Napa." It is unusual for a winery to state that the wines are made in one area from grapes grown in another. The back label of the same bottle of Pinot Noir is even more interesting. It tells you not only where the grapes were grown, but also the size of the cask in which the wine was aged, the time when the grapes were picked, the sugar content at that time, and the total acidity.

Most Z D wines are sold by mail in California. After some growing pains and necessary expansion, the Z D wines should find their way into full California acceptance, with some interest and demand throughout the rest of the United States.

OTHER WINERIES OF CALIFORNIA

There are many wines and wineries in the state of California that are deserving of mention — and of wine drinkers' tasting and collecting. Some wineries have distribution outside the state, but the majority are limited to California only, some severely so because of their size. Many of the wines discussed may be purchased only at the wineries.

Alex's Winery, Lodi: A unique system of tasting rooms and retail outlets were combined with the Coloma Wine Cellars in 1965. The winery produces the state's only Sake, Mt. Fuji, as well as some satisfactory Cabernet Sauvignon and Johannisberg Riesling, among others.

Bargetto's Santa Cruz Winery, Soquel: This is another of the Italian-origin wineries that have made such a great contribution to the California wine industry. Giuseppe Bargetto, from Piedmont, Italy, set the forces in motion for his sons Phillip and John to found the winery in 1933. The Bargetto family today consists of John's son, Lawrence, and Phillip's two daughters. The family makes wines principally from grapes that are contracted for in the Santa Cruz and Santa Clara areas.

The old and new share the Bertero vineyard.

The crowded Bargetto tasting room.

The most notable of the wines are the varietal reds such as Cabernet Sauvignon, Zinfandel, and Barbera. The whites, Chenin Blanc, Johannisberg Riesling, Sylvaner, and Pinot Blanc, are satisfactory but not quite as interesting as the reds.

There is a considerable quantity of generic wines which can be purchased in gallon and half-gallon containers. They are excellent buys, inexpensive but sound, and with little of the coarseness or harshness that sometimes characterizes wines of this type.

Bear Mountain Winery, DiGiorgio: From land purchased in 1966 from the DiGiorgio family holdings, the relatively new Bear Mountain Winery is located near Bakersfield, California, and is the first Kern County winery to bottle its own line of wines. The first bottlings came in 1969 and consisted of such varietals as as Chenin Blanc, French Colombard, Ruby Cabernet, and Barbera. In 1972, the winery was preparing to make its first sparkling wine. The Bear Mountain wines reach the market under a variety of brand names, including Bear Mountain, Gold Peak, Mountain Gold, and M. Lamont.

Bertero Winery, Gilroy: Also known as the Italian California Wine Company, the Bertero Winery is one more Italian name in California's great long list of Italian wineries, which have formed the strong right arm of the California wine industry.

The winery was formed in 1924, although Alphonse Bertero, the founder, had been growing grapes since 1919. The winery today is going through considerable change and is in the hands of the son, Angelo, and his two sons, who make quite satisfactory Cabernet Sauvignon, Zinfandel, Barbera, Grignolino, Pinot Noir, Chardonnay, and Sémillon. The wines are neither great nor complex although there are flashes of greatness in some of them, but neither are they expensive. They are good, sound table wines made for drinking rather than exciting tasting — the style of wine to be enjoyed without concern that there won't be more just as good next year.

Bisceglia Winery, Mission Bell: An old family winery, begun in 1880 at San Jose, which has operated wineries at St. Helena and Fresno, today makes standard quality wines under the brand names of Paradise and Golden Chalice. At one time, the Bisceglias owned the now

famous Greystone cellar, which was bought at auction for ten thousand dollars during the Depression year of 1931, and later sold it to the Christian Brothers.

Bonesio Winery, Gilroy: Like so many American-Italian wine pioneers, Petro Bonesio, the founder of Bonesio Winery in 1914, learned the winemaking art from his father, Giovanni Bonesio. The elder Bonesio began a wine establishment in the town of Cordono in Piedmont, Italy, in 1847. Petro came to the United States at the turn of the century and was diverted from the grape by the concrete business and farming until 1914. Petro's first winery was constructed in the Rucker district, north of Gilroy. Eventually he moved both winery and family to the present location at El Rancho Solis in the Uvas Valley. El Rancho Solis was built in 1851 from redwood timbers cut and hauled from Mount Madonna, part of the vast cattle and land empire owned by cattle baron Henry Miller.

The winery and vineyard were operated by Petro until Prohibition, when the vineyard was largely replanted to fruit trees; it was again planted to vines after Repeal. Obviously the Bonesio family is interested in farming.

Louis Bonesio is the present operator of the vineyard and winery and has had a complete list of grapes planted: Palomino, Sauvignon Vert, French Colombard, Sauvignon Blanc, Emerald Riesling, and Malvasia Bianca for the whites; for the reds the varieties are Zinfandel, Carignane, Grignolino, Pinot Noir, and Cabernet Sauvignon. Rosés are made from the Mission and Grenache grapes.

The winery emphasizes good, sound, inexpensive table wines, made for early drinking and simple everyday meals. There are some older choice Estate Bottled varietals which are more interesting to drink and these are marketed as select bottlings with the Santa Clara Valley as the appellation of origin.

The visitor's entrance at the Bonesio Winery.

There are also some curiosity wine items in the Bonesio line, such as Red Grenache, Mataro Catawba, and Malvasia Nera. These are worth trying as interesting, esoteric examples of what can be done with these grapes.

The Bonesio family is yet another Italian family that has made its mark in the Santa Clara Valley, not only for its wines but also for its pure wine vinegar, marketed as Luigi's Pride in red or white.

Cadenasso Winery, Fairfield: Three Cadenasso wines are of interest—Grignolino, Pinot Noir, and Zinfandel. Grey Riesling, some dessert wines, and vermouth are also made, but none have the character of the Cadenasso reds.

The vineyards are located in the Fairfield area and at Cordelia in Solano County—hence the brand name Solano Vineyards, as well as Cadenasso.

The Cadenasso Winery is not young. Like other Italian wineries, it probably began somewhere in Italy prior to its founding in California in 1906 by Giovanni Cadenasso.

The winery has had several locations, beginning with the Rutherford Ranch in Green Valley.

California Growers Winery, Cutler: Eighteen separate growers formed this cooperative winery, led by Robert Setrakian, president, one of the most intelligent and knowledgeable leaders in the wine industry. The winery emphasizes dessert wines and brandy. With the great table wine demand, the winery is producing a wide range of varietals and it may be a little too early to ascertain whether, at some time in the future, these varietals will

A garden of half-gallon jugs grows before Cadenasso's winery.

become exciting wines. At the moment, the wines represent a satisfactory beginning, as well as a promising departure from the high-quality "standard" wines the group has been making up to now. It also makes one of the state's most interesting brandies. Look for the wine under the new Setrakian label and the established California Growers name.

California Wine Association (Antonio Perelli-Minetti), Lodi: This is another giant, with roots going back to 1894, when sixty-four California wineries grouped themselves together under one banner. Today, only one is left—Perelli-Minetti—which now owns a variety of the labels, such as Ambassador, Eleven Cellars, Greystone, and two well-known brandies—A. R. Morrow and Aristocrat—plus some 200 other wine and brandy brands of the past.

Some most pleasant sparkling wines have come under the banner of Ambassador, while the best of the table wines have been made under the Eleven Cellars label. Noteworthy in the Eleven Cellars is its Cabernet Sauvignon. Much of it is made with Cabernet Sauvignon grapes

from the Napa Valley and when this is the case, a stripper indicating it appears on the neck of the bottle. The California Wine Association offers a wide variety of wines at moderate prices, and even though it is terribly large, some individualistic wines have been made.

Caymus Vineyards, Rutherford: Charles Wagner is an old hand at growing grapes and supplying them to wineries. Now he has built his own winery, named after a Spanish land grant, and intends to make Estate Bottled wines of his own. His seventy acres are planted principally to Pinot Noir, Cabernet Sauvignon, and Johannisberg Riesling.

His first bottlings were most satisfactory, particularly a Pinot Noir Blanc de Noir 1972, a white wine made from Pinot Noir grapes. It is an interesting, well-balanced, and rich wine. Charlie's other entry is a 1972 Johannisberg Riesling that is crisp, full, and pleasantly styled.

Château Montelena, Calistoga:
This winery, one of the most picturesque in Calistoga, in the north end of Napa Valley at the foot of Mt. Helena, is enjoying a comeback of the first magnitude. It was built in 1882 under the direction of a French architect, who constructed a castellated facade that has often been compared to Château Lafite. That may be stretching it, but the winery and its premises are nevertheless unique, and include a three-acre lake with two Chinese-style teahouses and a large, authentic junk from Hong Kong, each added to the winery by a Chinese resident in 1947. Only in California.

Today, the winery and vineyard operation is directed by Montelena Associates, a group consisting of James L. Barrett, a southern California attorney, Ernest W. Hahn, a construction magnate, Lee Paschich, a business executive, and Mike Gergich, a winemaker. The vineyards have been planted principally to Cabernet Sauvignon and Zinfandel.

Early tastings of the Cabernet and Zinfandel provided good, interesting examples of the varieties. In fact, the wines have everything going for them except a long record of past performance in the glass. Zeal and attitude are evident in this new enterprise, but the real question is whether or not it will provide great wine. Time is the only answer.

Columbia Cellars, Columbia: An extremely small family operation, owned by Spencer Hoffman, whose best wines are dessert wines, particularly Columbian Gold. Distribution is at the winery only.

D'Agostini Winery, Plymouth:
Located on the upper Shenandoah Valley of Amador County, the vineyards originally were laid out by Adam Uhlinger in 1856. The D'Agostinis bought them in 1911 and began producing wines in the original cellars, the oldest winery in Amador County. Today the cellars are a California State Historical Monument. The aging cellars

The appealingly bizarre facade of Château Montelena.

are cave-type, dug into the mountainside.

The wine is bottled in half gallons and fifths with screw caps. It can be described as "Italian grandfather-style wine" —big, good, and generally reasonably priced. There is one Estate Bottled wine, Zinfandel, and it is generally a good one, characteristic of the area. The so-called reserve burgundy in half gallons and fifths is made principally from Zinfandel, Carignane, and even some Mission. The claret is made from Mission, Carignane, and Zinfandel, while the sauterne is made from Chasselas. It is stock, everyday wines like these that are helping many wine drinkers avoid the high wine prices created by the industry boom.

Delicato Cellars, Manteca:
Located on a frontage road off Highway 99 in the San Joaquin Valley, this million-gallon winery has been providing table wines for retail sale and bulk wines for other wineries since 1935. The winery was founded by brothers-

in-law Sebastinano (Sam) Luppino and Gaspare (Jasper) Indelicato. Today, Jasper's three sons operate the winery and sell table wines and champagne under the labels Sam-Jasper, Delicato, and Delicato Private Stock. Most of their wine is available at the winery or at stores in the Stockton area.

Diamond Creek Vineyards, Calistoga: One of the tiniest mountain vineyards in the Napa County area is owned by a transplanted southern Californian, Albert Brounstein, and is located atop Diamond Mountain. This winery is restricting itself exclusively to Cabernet Sauvignon, several vintages of which are now in the barrel. It is still too early to determine greatness, although first tastes from the barrel will reflect the youthfulness of the vines and a measure of promise for the future.

Mr. D'Agnostini displays his Zinfandel.

L. Foppiano Wine Company, Healdsburg: Much of the wine history of Sonoma County is tied to the old world, particularly to Italy. The Foppiano family contributed richly to the Sonoma story when John Foppiano left his home in Genoa in 1874 to seek his fortune in the gold fields of California.

The family is proud of John because of his fortitude in walking across the thirty-seven miles of jungle and swamp that was the Isthmus of Panama before the construction of the canal. He remained in the gold field areas around Jackson and Sonora for approximately three years—although the family recalls that they never saw any of the gold.

In 1896 John bought the Smith Winery, the site of the present Foppiano Winery. In 1910 Louis A. Foppiano, the oldest son of a family of ten children, bought the winery from his father.

The Foppianos battled against two nearly lethal blows during the twentieth century, *Phylloxera vastatrix* and Prohibition. They won both fights. During Prohibition the family survived by maintaining the ranch and shipping fresh grapefruit to Eastern markets. In 1924 Louis died, and Matilda, his young widow, with her son, Louis Joseph, and two daughters, Rosalind and Norma, continued to work the ranch and finally, after Repeal, rebuilt and enlarged the winery.

Louis Joseph was born in 1910 in the house that is now used for the winery offices. He has continued the winemaking tradition of the Foppianos not only by making wine but also by providing a son, Louis M. Foppiano, who is presently the manager of the winery.

A full line of wines is produced, including Petite Sirah, burgundy, Zinfandel, chablis, rosé, Cabernet Sauvignon;

Gamay Beaujolais, Grey Riesling, and mountain red, white, and rosé wines.

These are not great wines, but are quite good considering the cost. The Petite Sirah and the Zinfandel have shown the greatest amount of varietal character.

Franzia Brothers Winery, Ripon: One of the largest wineries and vineyard holdings in California is Franzia Brothers Winery, which was founded in 1906 as a grape-shipping business by Giuseppe Franzia and expanded into a winery in 1933. Giuseppe had five sons, all of whom helped build the winery. Today, the winery is a rather large, publicly held company. Two of the sons, Joseph J. Franzia and John G. Franzia, Sr., are principal officers of the company and are still operating it.

The Franzia Brothers Winery, today as in the past, has made some of the state's finest so-called standard quality wines at prices that are certainly popular. These are by no means great or complex wines but are sound, good, satisfactory, pleasant for everyday use. Notable are some of the red wines which are blends from the San Joaquin Valley, where the winery is located, and from the Napa Valley, and some of the wines are so labeled. A full line of wines is produced from its thirteen vineyard properties at various locations within a few miles of the winery.

E & J Gallo Winery, Modesto: It is one thing to talk about great wines of California and it is yet another to talk about great wineries of California. Obviously, not all great wineries make great wines. A great winery can be one that is extremely modern, possessed with great technical skill and know-how and resource material such as vineyards, and yet not make wines of great style, character, or interest. There are many great California wineries that make popular-priced wines, which, in the long run, tend to make the American public more wine conscious.

Perhaps the greatest of these

Gibson's winery has an industrialized appearance.

is the E & J Gallo Winery, representing two brothers who have become the most famous wine names in America, as well as being the largest, most influential wine force in the country. Perhaps more Americans have had a glass of Gallo than any other wine.

The Gallos weren't always large, however; it was in 1933 in the city of Modesto that the two Gallos began their grape empire, with barely enough money to lease a warehouse for their first vintage. Today, the Gallos have their own bottle-manufacturing plant, sell in excess of 20 million cases a year, and are among the most copied winemakers and merchandisers in the world.

The Gallos don't stick to just traditional types of wine, as they apparently feel that the American market enjoys new "innovative" types, such as Thunderbird—a flavored wine—Ripple, Boone's Farm fruit wines, and Pink Chablis.

More wine writers have proclaimed the "best value" status of Gallo Hearty Burgundy than

any other wine and so consumers have come to rely on Gallo as a good glass of wine to drink whenever they want one, wherever they need one, at a price that is more than reasonable. The wines, of course, are standard wines, made well, uniformly, and with great quality control, so that any time you buy a bottle you are likely to get the same flavor. Now the real question is whether you like this type of wine and this approach.

The answer is that these wines are good for the money, that they are not necessarily complex, interesting, great—terminology one uses for wines of great varietal character. The Gallo wines should be put in their proper perspective, as indeed sound, satisfactory, everyday wine, at low cost. You will have to move up in dollar expenditure in order to find the greater and better wines.

There is talk that Gallo is moving into the premium field of wine. If that is the case, a great winery will become even greater. Make no mistake about it, there is great technical skill at Gallo. If you don't believe it, just ask some of the French and German winemaking visitors. As for the wine, I enjoy it simply because I put it into proper perspective.

Gibson Wine Company, Elk Grove: The Gibson Wine Company has earned a place in California wine history because of its belief in and production of wines made from fruits other than grapes. In 1972 its raspberry wine, under the brand name of Vinesse, was submitted for judging and given a gold medal. The judges, perhaps a bit snobbish when it comes to fruit wines, took this one very seriously because it was one of the few they had encountered that had complexity—a most unusual feat for this type of wine.

Although the founder of Gibson Wine Company, Robert Gibson, a former stockbroker, died in 1960, complexity in his wines would not have surprised him. He was a firm believer in making wines of this style and built perhaps one of the largest wineries specializing in berry and fruit wines, with large plants in California and in Covington, Kentucky, where wine in bulk from California is bottled.

The company also produces wine at the Elk Grove Gibson Winery under the names of Gibson's Old Fashioned Brand, Gibson's Premium Select, and the Vinesse line.

Gold Hill Winery, Coloma: John Hempt has begun a new winery in the heart of historic California gold country, adopting the brand name "Gold Hill." There are only eight acres of vineyards, but all wines are Estate Bottled and include Chenin Blanc, Johannisberg Riesling, and Cabernet Sauvignon. The wines, first introduced in 1972, are fair.

Grand Cru Vineyard, Glen Ellen: A result of the revival in winemaking is the many old wineries being reactivated in the famous vineyard regions of California. In Sonoma County, Allen Ferrera and Robert Magnani purchased the old Lamoine Winery, which dates back to 1886, renamed it Grand Cru Vineyard, and are restoring it to productivity.

Harbor Winery, Sacramento: Charles H. Myers is a home winemaker who, when he isn't teaching English at Sacramento City College, is making wine for his own consumption and for those few who have so much enjoyed what they have bought that they are now encouraging him to expand production.

Charles has been making wine since 1955 and has been relying on the expertise of friendly vineyard owners to supply him with top quality varietals. He has been making any wine that he feels is worth making, consistent with the availability of good grapes, but has concentrated on Amador County's Zinfandel and Napa Valley's Chardonnay.

A "grape nut" of the first order, Charles is ever ready to drink, taste, and make wine. While very limited in quantity, his Chardonnays have been fruity, with less emphasis on wood, and of considerable varietal character. Production for 1972 for instance was some 1,200 cases of Chardonnay and 250 cases of Zinfandel. Also interesting is a small amount of

dessert wine pressed from Mission grapes that have been allowed to overripen and become very sweet. A limited bottling of flor-style Palomino sherry is also available. Charles has become a professional winemaker, something every amateur wine drinker wants to do, and he has done it well.

Husch Vineyards, Philo: A very young—and small—winery, bonded in 1971, Husch Vineyards is a model of what many young Californians consider the

Pruning a vine in the bleakness of winter.

American dream. Tony Husch and his wife Gretchen arrived in the Anderson Valley in 1968, not to make wine, but to escape the clamor of the city. Recognizing the land boom in grapes, they planted their twenty acres in Chardonnay, Gewürztraminer, and Cabernet Sauvignon. The first wines were offered in 1972, limited in supply and high in price. At Jurgensen's in Beverly Hills, the Cabernet was fetching nine dollars a bottle in the spring of 1973. In time, it may indeed be worth the price.

Italian Swiss Colony, Asti: Much of what has been said for Gallo wines can also be said for

Italian Swiss Colony, which makes wines in large quantity, much of it standard, but good for the money. I've enjoyed many a bottle labeled Zinfandel by Italian Swiss Colony and enjoyed it much more when I realized how little it cost.

The history of Italian Swiss Colony is older than that of Gallo. It was founded as a unique Italian-Swiss agricultural colony in 1881, with the altruistic purpose of assisting Italian and Swiss immigrants over the hump of getting settled in the New

World. The colony's land was named Asti, after a town in the Piedmont area of Italy. The Pietro Rossi family brought Italian Swiss Colony back to the forefront of wines in California following Prohibition. Since World War II, Italian Swiss Colony has had several owners and is presently owned by United Vintners, a division of Heublein, Inc.

The winery attempts premium wines in limited editions under the labels Private Stock and Gold Medal Reserve. Some of them, indeed, are quite good. Again, with the cost in mind, they demonstrate what a winery can do when large facilities and a modern, efficient plant are turned loose on special batches of wine.

Kenwood Vineyards, Kenwood: This winery is another example of a young group of entreprenuers taking an old, established property and reviving it under a new name. Martin and Michael Lee, along with John Sheela, brought the Pagani Brothers Winery, in Sonoma County, and changed its name to Kenwood Vineyards. Where the Paganis sold only half-gallon and gallon jugs of their wines, Kenwood is bottling in standard fifths, and the owners have established distribution of their wines to stores throughout California.

Landis Vineyard, Fresno: Dr. Albert Landis and Dale Landis, father and son, are the founders and present operators of Landis Vineyards and have formed a happy partnership in the production of table wines—Zinfandel, Ruby Cabernet, Grenache rosé, and Barbera. The grapes for these wines are still under cultivation and of course it is too early to determine whether the wines will be interesting, since the San Joaquin Valley does not have a reputation for great complex varietals. The winery has developed a good line of dessert wines more in keeping with the San Joaquin Valley capabilities. Sherry was the first wine on the market, cream and dry, purchased in bulk and aged in small oak casks for a minimum of three years before selling. These wines were quite good and will, over the years, make the Landis Vineyard, though small, important. The sherry is stored in an air-conditioned winery and is baked rather than made by submerged flor techniques.

Elmo and Jim Martini display awards of the winery.

Dr. Landis has been a practicing dentist in the Fresno area since 1936 and has made wine for his own family for more than twenty years. Dale, who is a student of enology both in the vineyard and at Fresno State University, has been the principal winemaker of Landis Vineyard since it became a bonded winery in 1967. Some of the grapes come from vineyards maintained by classmates at Fresno State University and supervised by Vincent Petrucci, a most formidable academic force for the good of viticulture at the school. By its nature Landis will always be a small operation, small in distribution. Its dessert wines are worth the considerable effort necessary to obtain them.

Lockeford Winery Corporation, Lodi: The Lockeford Winery, one of the few remaining cooperatives, was constructed in 1946 to handle production of local growers in the Lodi area. It was originally built to produce bulk dessert wines and brandy in the so-called European tradition.

As of 1967, the winery was producing twenty-three wines — dry, dessert, and sparkling — which were made by the Charmat process. All the wines were bottled on the premises and less than 15 percent of the wine was sold in bulk.

In January of 1972 Lockeford Winery Corporation became LFD Vintner Corporation and, along with the new ownership, new techniques have been added for the improvement of the wines.

The wines to date have been sound, inexpensive, and easy to drink, with no requirement for bottle age. They are the kind of wines that are likely to be on one's table for everyday use. The dessert wines, however, continue to remain superior to the drys.

Martini & Prati Winery, Santa Rosa: Elmo Martini and Edward Prati produce bulk table wines, sparkling wines, and an expensive line of vermouth in their old two million-gallon winery, which dates from 1881. Descendants of old Sonoma County wine-growing families, they sell their product under two labels — Martini & Prati and Fountain Grove.

Justin Miller Winery, Rutherford: F. J. Miller, a transplanted Englishman, has become quite controversial as a result of his patented "Millerway" process for the production of sparkling wines. The essence of the new method is to make the effervescence last for days, even after a bottle is open, provided the wine is not shaken, a tremendous asset for those who want to open a fifth of sparkling wine and not finish it at one sitting.

Essentially, his system is to insert carbon dioxide into the wine while it is quiescent, as opposed to the common method of artificial carbonation which utilizes more violent agitation.

The wine that the Millerway system produces has a different, perhaps uncharacteristic, flavor from that found in French champagnes or California sparkling wines that approach the flavor characteristics of French champagnes. Millerway is an interesting technical concept which,

as of this moment, cannot be used for wines labeled "sparkling wine" because of the prohibition of such labeling on carbonated wines. Make no mistake about it, however, his wines are most interesting and, perhaps through litigation, the Millerway process may be more widely adopted.

Nepenthe Cellars, Portola Valley: A relatively new winery in San Mateo County, Nepenthe Cellars was constructed beneath the home of George and Yvonne Burtness in 1967. At present they are making fair varietals, such as Cabernet Sauvignon, Zinfandel, Chardonnay, and White Riesling which, in time are likely to improve.

Nicasio Vineyard, Soquel: Dan Wheeler's tiny winery is making some fairly interesting wine under the label of "Nicasio — Wine by Wheeler." Cabernet Sauvignon and Zinfandel are interesting reds. His whites, Chardonnay and Johannisberg Riesling, are equally interesting. Don't expect to find these in a store around the corner.

Nichelini Vineyards, St. Helena: Built in 1890 by Switzerland's Anton Nichelini, the place where today Jim and Rosemarie Nichelini entertain visitors every weekend is a hilltop winery. An enjoyable place to visit, the winery produces such types as burgundy, Cabernet Sauvignon, Gamay, Zinfandel, chablis, Chenin Blanc, Sauvignon Vert, dry sherry, and port. The reds are preferable to the whites and are rated good, not great.

Pedrizetti Winery, Morgan Hill: This is a small, family-owned winery with fair wines. Primarily it has specialized in jug wines such as Grenache rosé and Zinfandel rosé. Lately, the trend has been to the so-called classic varietals of which the Barbera and Zinfandel are good values.

The Lockeford Winery tasting room.

Pesenti Winery, Templeton:
Tucked into the still not very well-known wine area of Templeton is perhaps one of the smallest family wine operations still going, the Pesenti Winery. It was founded in 1934 with the intention that the wines would be sold only locally. The generic table wines, of which there is a full line, are inexpensive—and rightly so for they are obviously not great wines. The varietal line, including Cabernet Sauvignon, Zinfandel, and Zinfandel rosé, is much the better of the line, and it too is not very expensive.

The Pesenti wines are of interest to the wine drinker as a good but not the best example of the kinds of wine that can be made from grapes in this area. The Templeton, San Luis Obispo County, wine plantings have expanded so much that in a few years there will be a plethora of grapes and wines. Although viticulture and enology professors in California have made some suggestions as to what can best be grown in the area, not enough wine of any one type has been made there for a wine consumer to draw any conclusions as to what is best to buy. Pesenti will help you make that judgment.

Pirrone Wine Cellars, Salida:
Built in 1936 by Frank Pirrone and now run by his son Alfred and his wife, this substantial winery has increased its capacity to a million gallons and has recently added a tasting room. While most of its wine is sold in bulk to other wineries, selected bottles, sometimes with grapes from other areas, are sold at the winery only.

Ruby Hill Vineyard Company, Pleasanton: Always a magnificent winery and estate, Ruby Hill is making very little wine these days. Some sauternes and a burgundy still carry the Ruby Hill label but the rest of the vineyard production has been sold to other wineries. Ernest Ferrario has reached an age at which he wants to—and does —take it a little easier.

Ruby Hill was founded by Joseph Crellen in 1887. He was succeeded by his brother, C. L. Crellen. Ernest Ferrario, who was born near Lake Como, Italy, bought the ranch in 1921. Ferrario had always had an interest in wine, but it was the high price brought by grapes during Prohibition that induced him to buy Ruby Hill. Wine grapes were at a premium for home winemaking. Ferrario also made wine for medicinal and sacramental purposes.

Recently, Ruby Hill was purchased by the Southern Pacific Land Company, an arm of Southern Pacific Railway. Under this new management, the winery has the potential of being a great estate once again.

San Antonio Winery, Los Angeles: This is a Los Angeles winery, established in 1917 and located only a stone's throw from the downtown civic center, that has the ability to distribute its wines in its own tasting rooms all over the county. It has been able to acquire grapes—some from as far away as Napa Valley —with which to make some promising wine. Until now, the winery has made mostly standard wines, but is attempting to upgrade the line, and some of the varietals, such as the Pinot Noir and beaujolais, have won awards at Los Angeles County Fairs. In addition to the regular table wine, the winery has specialized in flavored wines and it has made some of the state's finest.

Santa Barbara Winery, Santa Barbara: Established in 1962 by architect Pierre Lafond, Santa Barbara Winery is currently turning out fairly good wines in a district that may, in time, become one of California's more important new grape growing regions. Before Prohibition, Santa Barbara and southern San Luis Obispo County were important wine producing areas. However, in only the last dozen years has serious attention again been concentrated

Spring Mountain's immaculate winery-residence.

on these regions. During the growing season the area's climate is cooled by ocean fog and seasonal winds, ranking it as a Region I classification, according to the University of California, and one of the best for premium table wine and champagne grapes. The wines, considered standard now, may eventually rate with California's best.

Spring Mountain Vineyards, St. Helena: Doubtless Michael Robbins, owner and creator of Spring Mountain Vineyards, consumes almost as much of his wine as he sells, for Mike is another one of the hobbyists who have gone into winemaking and done it quite well. Mike enjoys the wine business, and he has been in it in one way or another for some time, including an abortive attempt and fascination with Mayacamas in its early days. His operation is small but it is good.

He has taken an old Victorian house, part residence and part winery, on the western slopes of the Napa Valley at St. Helena and has proceeded to surprise people with the goodness of some of his initial offerings, particularly his Chardonnays, a Cabernet Sauvignon Marriage, and a Sauvignon Blanc which was made for him. The quantity was modest, the quality was high, and there is no doubt that his wines will show even more complexity as time passes.

Winemaking does not come easy for Mike, as he works in Los Angeles and on weekends hops on a plane to his residence-winery to assist his staff of one or two in the growing of the grape and the making of the wine. On Mondays he returns refreshed, eagerly waiting for the five days to pass so he can make the return journey home.

Mike is learning very well how to make wine despite his legal and engineering background, and like many others who have come to the Napa Valley has had help from the community in the form of grape supply and winemaking counsel. This is a trademark of most wine-growing areas in California and lends further credence to the notion that there is more to the making of wine than just enology and viticulture. It would have been indeed interesting to see what Mike would have done had he started after Prohibition.

Joseph Swan Vineyards, Trenton: A small newcomer to the world of winemaking, more by way of hobby than by profession, Swan Vineyards is located in Trenton village in Sonoma County. It was begun in 1967 with some Chardonnay planted in the Sierras at 5,000 feet. It's a risky business to go that high but Swan claims that no frost damage has as yet occurred. As a veteran Western Airlines pilot, he adjusts extremely well to height.

The emphasis at Swan will be on high quality Pinot Noir, Zinfandel, Cabernet, and Merlot.

Production thus far has been limited mostly to Zinfandels from purchased grapes from the Dry Creek area. Swan says that he'd rather make mistakes with other people's grapes rather than with his own, and that kind of

philosophy speaks well for the future. His first commercial wine, a 1969 Zinfandel, has shown considerable good taste and promise, particularly since it has been aged in cooperage which is small—under 60 gallons. The plan is to continue to age in small French barrels.

Swan Vineyards, like many others that are beginning, offers great hope for the future.

Thomas Vineyards, Cucamonga: Thomas Vineyards lays claim to being the oldest winery in the state. The records show it was begun on March 3, 1839, when Tiburcio Tapia was given the Cucamonga land grant by Juan Alvarado, then governor of Mexico. Tapia built an adobe home, planted a vineyard, and started California's first winery.

Today the winery is owned by Joseph Filippi, long known in the area as a vintner. The Filippi family came from Venice, Italy, to the Cucamonga Valley, which was in 1922 very well known as a winemaking area, and today they own approximately 300 acres of vineyards of which the Thomas Vineyards are a part.

Smog is a problem in this area today. It has affected the quality of the grape as well as the yield. The area has never been well known for table wines. Thomas Vineyards makes some varietals such as Cabernet

Sauvignon, but the grapes for it no doubt come from north coast counties. What Thomas Vineyards does well these days is a whole line of dessert wines including Angelica, supposedly named for Los Angeles, tokays, sherries, and Malvasias and under its Old Rancho brand a number of satisfactory dry table wines—claret, Zinfandel, chablis —that can be purchased in gallon and half-gallon quantities.

There is also a line of very good red and white wine vinegar and an interesting garlic-flavored vinegar. The fruit wines—blackberry, cherry, strawberry, loganberry, and raspberry—are gaining favor and are quite good. The winery continues to be of great interest, not only because it is a historical landmark close to the great metropolitan center of Los Angeles, but because, from a wine standpoint, it continues to turn out interesting dessert wines and vinegars.

Trentadue Winery, Geyserville: Trentadue Winery is a family winery operation, to many the epitome of winery operations. Although new, this is the kind of winery—run by a family dedicated to winemaking and earning a livelihood from it—that was the foundation of the California wine industry.

With his three children, Annette, Victor, and Lisa, and

wife, Evelyn, Leo Trentadue has planted a variety of grapes: Zinfandel, Cabernet Sauvignon, Gamay, Carignane, Chenin Blanc, Sémillon, French Colombard Sauvignon, Merlot, and Chardonnay. It is an ambitious program, and only time and tasting will tell whether the winery can make wines to match the ambition.

If the wines prove to be good, then buy heavily because the supply will be limited. Leo Trentadue is striking a blow for a quality wine future at reasonable prices.

Valley of the Moon Winery, Glen Ellen: The Valley of the Moon Winery is a pleasant, country like collection of buildings located on Sonoma Creek under the enormous and inviting branches of an ancient oak. Visitors are always welcome and the Val-Moon label offers them a wide range of generic table wines to taste and buy.

Nicholas G. Verry, Inc., Parlier: An older winery, the Verry family winery emphasizes retsina, the resin-flavored wine that is popular among the Greeks. They also make a light white wine they call Philery.

Conrad Viano Winery, Martinez: Clement Viano, a graduate of viticulture at Davis, is in charge of a winery producing a reasonably good selection of generics, such as burgundy, sauterne, and rosé. The better wines come under the Viano Private Stock label, such as the varietals Cabernet Sauvignon and Barbera, which tend to be more interesting than the chablis and Grey Riesling.

Villa Armando Winery, Pleasanton: A rather recent rejuvenation of the old Frank Garatti property first established in 1902, the Villa Armando Winery is run by an ex-Brooklyn wine merchant named Anthony Scotto. The wines are improving, both in distribution and taste, with more interesting reds than whites, particularly for such varietals as Barbera and Zinfandel.

Thomas Vineyards was established in 1839.

Woodside Vineyards, Woodside:
Not too long ago Roy Brady, the editor of *Wine World* magazine, a man whose palate is perhaps one of the finest in the country, served me a glass of Chenin Blanc without showing me the label. I mistook the wine for a bigger variety, as it was a bigger, more complex, more interesting wine than one would normally expect to find in a Chenin Blanc. For many, many years Chenin Blanc was a grape used as a filler either for generics or to complete a more famous varietal, such as Chardonnay.

The wine was Woodside's Chenin Blanc, which I have now enjoyed in a variety of vintages. It is a most extraordinary wine— as are on occasion Woodside's Chardonnay and Cabernet Sauvignon, which is sold under an old label and vineyard name, La Questa, dating back to about 1883 and originally made by Emmet Rixford. The only problem with the wine, as is true with so many small vineyards, is that the production is so small that one can hope to get only a bottle rather than a case.

Small wineries of this kind form the backbone of California's claim to making superb, complex wines. Consumers can look to these wines as an art form and should not be discouraged because they cannot find them, but rather feel encouraged that this style of wine is being made, for it acts as a standard for larger wineries to follow. To lose wineries of this type would be to lose much of the greatness in California wine.

Robert Mullen did not drink much, if any, wine before embarking as an amateur in winemaking in 1960, when, with the help of friends, he began with a small enterprise. Today, his tiny winery is located underneath his home at Woodside. He grows grapes, makes and drinks wine, and is a great asset to the consumer because of the excellence of his wine. It would indeed be a pleasure if I could get him to

consume a little less of it in order to sell me a little more of it.

York Mountain Winery, Templeton:
American wine drinkers, even California ones, are probably unaware of the existence of winemaking in the area of San Luis Obispo and of the York Mountain Winery. The winery is located in a remote area situated in the Santa Lucia mountains nestled nicely between Highway 101 and the Pacific Ocean. The Hearst Castle is not too far away and, along with a visit to York, makes a pleasant jaunt.

The wines of northern California, and earlier the wines of southern California, have long been popular with American wine drinkers; but connoisseurs have somehow overlooked the centrally placed county of San Luis Obispo. It comes as a shock to many that Andrew York began making wines in San Luis Obispo County at Templeton in 1882. Oddly enough, York first moved to the Napa Valley and then made his way to Templeton to grow apples and grapevines. When the grape yield proved to be greater and easier to sell, York turned to winemaking and built a small winery, which still stands on the property. (The winery is historically interesting, for the original deed to the land dates back to 1875 and was signed by President U. S. Grant.) By 1900 more land was purchased and planted to Zinfandel, and the winery became famous among wine lovers as producing some of California's most impressive Zinfandel.

York's claim to winemaking fame has always been the production of Zinfandel in a style decidedly different from that found in either northern or southern California; it is reflected in the Zinfandels produced by the winery of the 1940s and earlier— wines of bigness, complexity, and good varietal character. The

wines were very inexpensive and often could be bought by the wine drinker in bulk. There are old-timers who can recall with great reverence going to York and buying their Zinfandel supply in barrels. Some even returned later with the same barrels for refills. It was a convenient way to buy and drink wine, a method mourned in its absence.

In the heyday of the York Mountain Winery, the farm laborers and oil workers in nearby communities were supplied with the rich, zesty, fruity Zinfandels of York in barrels, and it may well be that this sustenance sparked great technical and agricultural progress in San Luis Obispo County and in a development not

Polly Mullen and helpers label Woodside bottles in the kitchen.

too far away, Bakersfield.

After Andrew York's death in 1913, sons Walter and Silas took over the winemaking chores, which in turn they relinquished to the next generation, Wilfred and Howard York. It was really Wilfred, however, who continued the York tradition and who in the late 1950s and early 1960s provided many historical tales of the area and enjoyed bringing out some of California's best Zinfandels for visitors.

During the period of the '60s, the winery began to suffer from lack of care of the vineyards as well as from deer foraging among the vines. The York chapter was closed by the sale of the winery

to Max Goldman, a winemaker who is attempting to bring back the glory of York with a variety of new plantings such as Cabernet Sauvignon, French Colombard, Chardonnay, Pinot Noir, and perhaps a sparkling wine. When the wines are available, good or not, it will indeed be a pleasure to see the York label, for nothing can spoil the memory of York's great Zinfandels of the past.

Yverdon Vineyard, Spring Mountain: Another in the budding young operations to be found in the prime districts of California is Yverdon Vineyard. The property of a father and son combination, Fred and Russell Aves, the winery is located high atop Spring Mountain, overlooking the Napa Valley.

The Aves, of Los Angeles, have constructed an impressive new winery which features the first hillside caves dug in Napa County during this century. Their first wine was a satisfactory, but not great, Johannisberg Riesling. Other varietals will follow but, like so many new operations, the winery will take time to produce its best efforts. Being small, however, should help considerably.

Page 169
A high morning sun forecasts a warm summer's day in a Napa Valley vineyard.

Page 170/171
On a golden afternoon, high above a summer coastal fog, a Hughes helicopter provides a young couple access to a very private picnic on a grassy Pacific bluff (overleaf).

The *Vitis labrusca* is truly an all-American vine. Undoubtedly, it was what Leif Ericson found when he named the land he discovered "Vinland" eight centuries ago. Certainly it was what the first colonists in Massachusetts and Virginia used to make the first American wines and what later wine pioneers such as William Penn and Lord Delaware used in major plantings.

The *Vitis labrusca* thrives on the East Coast of North America, surviving the inconsistencies of weather. It produces wines from varieties called Catawba, Concord, Niagara, Delaware, and Ives.

Wines of the *Vitis labrusca* species have a heavy taste and aroma, attributable in part to the ester, methyl anthranilate. It is not an easy wine for an outsider to appreciate fully, and too many so-called connoisseurs have been unwilling to regard it with an unprejudiced palate.

I am certain that if I had been born in the New York wine district, I would have come to know and understand the beauty, flavor, and complexities of the native wines. I plead guilty to not having looked carefully at the wines of the *Vitis labrusca*. It is a sin I share with others.

The important thing about New York wines —and the wines of other American regions outside California—is that they shouldn't be compared to the wines of California and Europe. They should be compared only among themselves. If this rule were followed, American wine drinkers would take another long drink of *Vitis labrusca* wines. They might even feel the way Longfellow did

Only a day away from harvest, French hybrid Seyve-Villard 5276 grapes glow radiantly at Bully Hill.

when he wrote:

Very good in its way
Is the Verzenay
Or the Sillery, soft and creamy;
But Catawba wine
Has a taste more divine,
More dulcet, delicious and dreamy.

One man has come to the rescue of the anti-labruscans, and more than any other Eastern wine pioneer he has helped to improve New York wines to such an extent that international wine connoisseurs no longer are turning down their glasses. The man is Dr. Konstantin Frank, who should be dubbed the "Haraszthy of New York." He has brought enthusiasm, depth of knowledge, and missionary zeal to his vine planting, grape growing, and winemaking.

Before Frank became established in New York, only New York champagnes had acceptance in most American cellars. Frank has added the *Vitis vinifera* names of Chardonnay, Cabernet Sauvignon, Johannisberg Riesling, Späetlese, Gewürztraminer, and Pinot Noir. Not only has he placed these wines in American cellars but he actually has created such a demand for them that some are collectors' items.

A great deal of Frank's success can be attributed to Charles Fournier, who took a chance hiring the older immigrant in 1951. Frank was involved in viticulture and agriculture in Austria and Bavaria, before he came to America at age fifty-two in 1951.

Fournier, the head of Gold Seal, gave Frank the opportunity, and the knowledge that Frank had gained while in charge of a vineyard in the Ukraine before World War II

The Pleasant Valley Wine Company at Hammondsport, New York State's first bonded winery (overleaf).

4

proved invaluable. Frank was confident that the weather of New York did not have to be a handicap. In fact, he reasoned, the cold would help. He grafted vinifera varieties onto native roots and a new concept was born.

Frank labored for over a decade, grafting more than a quarter of a million European buds onto American roots. His bold moves should have an important influence on the future of wines produced in New York. His efforts have resulted in about sixty varieties of European grapes that have been grown successfully on American rootstocks. When Frank sees a plant that differs from the others in the row—perhaps because it reproduced early—he propagates it as a separate strain.

Unquestionably, Frank has been the leading innovator in the upgrading of the New York industry. But the list of modern-day pioneers who brought their intelligence and dedication to the New York scene is endless. The list includes such notables as Gilbert C. Smith, cooperative extension specialist; Seaton C. Mendall, vineyard consultant, Taylor Wine Company; John Einset, Keith Kimball, and John Watson of the New York Agricultural Experiment Station, Geneva, New York; the New York State Fruit Testing Cooperative Association, Geneva, New York; John Brahm III, vineyard superintendent, Widmer Wine Cellars, Naples, New York; Vincent D'Ingianni, vineyardist, Dundee, New York; Jurgen Leonholdt, director of grower relations, Pleasant Valley Wine Company; LaVerne Schoeffler, vineyard manager, Gold Seal Vineyard; Harland Tyler, vineyard manager, Taylor Wine Company; Willard B. Robinson and colleagues, Department of Food Science at Geneva, New York.

Like so many grapes, the French hybrids were originated in France to combine the best of both worlds—the good wine of vinifera with the strength and hardiness to resist disease. As good grapes should, they require planting on deep, well-drained soils. Gilbert C. Smith, cooperative extension specialist, points out that one of the assets of the French hybrid varieties is their ability to produce a commercial crop from secondary or tertiary buds when the primary shoots are killed by frost.

In the New York story, which ultimately affects Midwest and other Eastern areas, two other grape growers have played leading roles. M. Louis Seibel, a leading French hybridizer, made over 30,000 crosses of vinifera and native American vines. Only a small amount of these were successful, but he has been most successful in producing phylloxera-resistant crosses for France and successful varieties for New York. Seibel's efforts made certain that the imported varieties that came to Eastern areas always were hardy varieties.

Phillip Wagner was the first and leading importer of French hybrids to New York and the East Coast. Wagner, who once was editor of the *Baltimore Sun* and later purchased Boordy Vineyards, was responsible for testing and propagating French hybrids so that others could follow and do as well as they have.

Wagner maintained an experimental vineyard. His efforts can be compared to an agricultural station and are not unlike the work done at the University of California at Davis in the Department of Viticulture and Enology.

In Gilbert C. Smith's bulletin on French

The Greyton Taylor Wine Museum, at Bully Hill, has an intriguing collection of old wine equipment.

hybrid grapes, an interesting list of French hybrid grapes in commercial production in the Finger Lakes district is listed with appropriate commentary, perhaps a bible not only for the grape grower but also for the student and consumer of New York hybrid wines. The list follows, with comments from Mr. Smith's Extension Bulletin:

White Wine Varieties

Ravat 51 (Vignoles) — A mid-season golden colored grape with medium size, thin-skinned berries in medium size, compact clusters; makes a fine white wine, similar to Pinot Chardonnay.

Seibel 5279 (Aurora) — Most widely planted of the French hybrids in New York; a very early white-to-pinkish grape with large medium-loose to compact clusters; produces an excellent, delicate white table wine; delicious grape for eating.

Seibel 9110 (Verdelet) — A mid-season variety with beautiful gold berries in large clusters; a good dessert grape; produces a delicate white wine.

Seibel 10868 — A mid-season white to pink variety with large compact clusters; produces a Chablis type table wine.

Seibel 13047 — An early, white thin skinned grape with long and compact clusters; produces a good quality, neutral white wine; good table grape.

Seyve-Villard 5-276 (Seyval) — A mid-season white grape with large and compact clusters; produces a superior white wine.

Red Wine Varieties

Baco Noir (Baco No. 1) — An early mid-season variety with medium clusters of small black berries; used in red table wines.

Maréchal Foch (Kuhlmann 188-2) — An early, small clustered black grape with small berries; produces an excellent red wine.

Landot 244 (Landal) — A mid-season blue grape with medium-loose clusters; produces a fruity wine of deep color.

Leon Millot (Kuhlmann 194-2) — An early blue variety with small berries in medium-loose clusters; produces a good wine similar to Foch.

Seibel 1000 (Rosette) — A late mid-season blue variety with medium to small bunches; used for rosé wines.

Seibel 5898 (Rougeon) — A mid-season blue grape with medium, compact, attractive clusters; makes a blending wine with good red color.

Seibel 7053 (Chancellor) — A mid-season blue variety grown in France for red wine.

Seibel 8357 (Colobel) — A late mid-season blue grape considered a "teinturier" because of the intense color of the wine produced from it.

Seibel 9549 (DeChaunac) — An early mid-season blue grape with medium to large loose open clusters; berries color early in season; wine samples have received high ratings.

Seibel 10878 (Chelois) — A mid-season blue grape, used for Claret type wine.

Seibel 13053 (Cascade) — An early blue grape with medium to large, loose clusters; berries start to color earlier in the season than most varieties; produces a superior rosé wine.

Seyve-Villard 5-247 — Ripens late mid-season; long, loose to compact clusters; berries blue; not popular for wine production.

Bubbling like bewitched cauldrons, carefully supervised batches of wine ferment in the experimental laboratory at Taylor Wine Company.

New York, like California, can boast of wineries in many different areas of the state. Of its thirty-nine wineries, twelve are located in the Finger Lakes district, a summer vacation and resort mecca.

In 1839, in the garden of his Hammondsport, New York, church, the Reverend William Bostwick planted cuttings of New York native labrusca vine shoots. The Episcopal minister could not realize it, but his vines prophesied the future of the tiny village, and its surrounding area, on the south tip of Keuka Lake. For it was at Hammondsport that winemaking was to grow into a major industry in New York State, beginning in the period following the Civil War.

Today, still remote and engagingly rural, the Finger Lakes district comfortably promotes the coexistence of some of the largest and smallest wineries in New York, although the competitiveness and differences in philosophy between the men who own and manage them is excitingly energetic and healthy.

Page 181
Dr. Konstantin Frank, the outspoken and controversial genius who proved the creditability of Vitis vinifera wines in New York State, samples a bottle of his Gerwürztraminer at his home in Hammondsport, October, 1972.
Pages 182/183
The lovely and serene beauty of Keuka Lake, and its surrounding countryside, camouflages the industrious work of the many wineries located in the area.
Page 184
On the Pennsylvania shore of Lake Erie, the new Penn-Shore Winery suffers through a January snow storm, typical of the winter weather Eastern vineyards must tolerate.

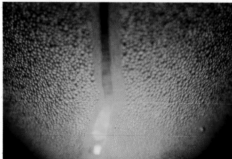

BOORDY VINEYARDS

76 Seneca Street
Dundee, New York

Owner:
Seneca Foods Corporation

Winemaker:
Ray Knafo

The story of Boordy Vineyards is in fact the story of Phillip Wagner, a legend in his own lifetime. He was among the first, if not *the* first, to specialize in the growing of French hybrids. Together with Jocelyn, his wife, Phillip Wagner—on his home property in Riderwood, Maryland, just north of Baltimore—established vineyards in 1943 to grow French hybrids. These were grapes which the Wagners themselves brought from France; they introduced them commercially and showed the way for the rest of the industry to follow in the growing of wines of European character under the difficult conditions of New York's soil and climate.

Mr. Wagner was so successful that he published a book, still splendidly authoritative, called *American Wines and Winemaking*, for even home winemakers to use. He established a strong reputation as a nurseryman and has been propagating the French hybrids for over twenty-five years.

There is no doubt that hybrids have been his life's work, together with the making of some unique, quite good wines produced and bottled under the Boordy Vineyards label, which he originated and which is now owned by Seneca Foods.

The first Boordy Vineyards winery, of course, was in Maryland, where the original vineyards and winery remain. A winery is located in Penn Yan, New York, and interestingly, another winery is located all the way across the country in the Yakima Valley at Prosser, Washington. According to Mr. Wagner, there is no intermixture of the production of these three regional wineries, the place of origin being indicated in each case on the label.

The eastern wineries produce wines from French hybrids while the western winery uses both French hybrids and vinifera. At Yakima Valley the emphasis is more on the brand name and on the region than on the grape variety; the wines are blends because the feeling is that better wines can be made that way. As time passes, however, there will be some varietals produced, including Cabernet Sauvignon, Pinot Noir, Sémillon, and Chenin Blanc.

Although Phillip Wagner has made an enormous contribution to New York wines and his name is internationally known, he and his wife have been an integral part of the Wagners' nursery business.

The Boordy Vineyards wines have improved steadily in almost all respects—taste, aftertaste, aroma, cleanness. They are bottled under Boordy Rosé Wine, Boordy Red, Boordy White,

Phillip Wagner checks an aging wine.

and Boordy Blümchen labels. Boordy Blümchen is an interesting wine patterned after the Muskateller of Europe. The most interesting, however, is the red, which, still to this day, does not present itself as a complex, great wine but when tasted in the context of eastern hybrid background is excellent and does hint at its apparent goal to be thought of as a wine similar to a French burgundy. Perhaps "hint" is a rather strong word, but pay no mind—the wine is sound for what it is: a New York State hybrid, certainly one of the better ones.

The present combination of Seneca Foods and Wagner know-how will be something most interesting to watch and taste over the next decade. The hybrids can only improve and indeed the Yakima Valley wines may yet prove to be the most interesting.

The Seneca Foods Corporation has taken over Boordy Vineyards and is responsible for the thrust into the new area at Prosser, Washington, in the heart of the Yakima Valley. It is Seneca's belief that the latitude of Washington approximates some of the better wine areas of France and Germany. Of course, it remains to be seen if the wine—as the company states—"will be more similar to the French than other American wines." The first examples were Boordy Vineyards Yakima Valley White 1971, a blend of Sémillon and Chardonnay grapes; Boordy Vineyards Yakima Valley Rosé, dominated by the Grenache grape; and Boordy Vineyards Yakima Valley Red 1971 (the label does not reveal the names of any of the grapes therein).

The wines at Yakima are made by Andy Tudor, a former California winemaker at Fontana Winery near San Bernardino, California. Andy Tudor joined with L. Jerome Walcott, Jr., vice-president of Seneca Foods Corporation, in a most honest statement that has given the portent for the future: "When we have enough produce we will go to the varietal wines but we need more experience, we need to know which grapes will grow best here, yield best and those

Jocelyn Wagner.

that will produce an acceptable wine. It will take—who knows, ten years, twenty years. But we have faith and we are beginning."

The winery building at Bully Hill.

BULLY HILL VINEYARDS, INC.

R.F.D. #2 Bully Hill
Hammondsport, New York 14840

Owner:
Walter S. Taylor

Winemaker:
Hermann Wiemer

Walter S. Taylor is a complex man who not only loves to have fine wines made under his aegis but also loves to write and talk about them—one of the finest triple-threat men in New York's thriving wine industry.

He is a man who possesses, as do so many wine people, a generous dash of missionary zeal, which he needs to sell New York State wines in California. To compete with the California vintners on their own home ground is not a simple task, particularly if there is any labrusca character in your wines. Walter takes pride that his wines do not reflect labrusca character. The wines, when tasted blind, are difficult to pinpoint as to origin, and I for one would not guess that most of Bully Hill's wines come from New York.

Walter is president of the Bully Hill Vineyards in the Finger Lakes region of New York; he is a member of an old wine-making family whose familial roots and vine plantings of native New York grapes, Ives and Delaware, date back to 1880. He established the Bully Hill Vineyards in 1970 and in short order has become a vintner to be reckoned with, for his vineyard represents some interesting advances for New York State wines, implemented by the vineyardist and winemaker of Bully Hill, Hermann J. Wiemer. Wiemer is experimenting with new French-American

Walter Taylor poses with the portrait he painted of his father, Greyton Taylor.

grape varieties—Baco Noir, Chelois Noir, Colobel Noir, Cascade Noir, Rougeon Noir, Leon Millot, Ives Noir, and Maréchal Foch—for red wines. For white wines the grapes are Seyval Blanc, Aurora, and Diamond. These grapes are hybrids, a cross of grape varieties, a technique pursued on both sides of the continent by authorities in viticulture.

Taylor prefers the hybrids to popular California grapes such as Cabernet Sauvignon and Chardonnay, and he believes varieties developed in his vineyards produce fine wines on

New York soil. He is convinced that New York wines have not been fully exploited or understood and that in time there will be great New York wines challenging France, Germany, and California. Taylor admits that his winery has used Cabernets and Chardonnays in New York, but with the hybrid grapes a new era in New York winemaking is being launched.

He takes further pride in stating that Bully Hill wines do not have any California wine or European wine in them, even though New York State law allows a wine to be labeled as New York wine even if as much as 25% of the wine comes from California. The five wines tasted – also offered in California by Bully Hill – were Rosé 1971, Vintage White 1971, Aurora Blanc 1971, Vineyard Red 1971, and Baco Noir 1970. They range in price from $3.50 to $3.75 a bottle.

Although I did not find the wines to be in a superb, complex class, it was obvious that they were moving in the right direction. The Baco Noir 1970 and a few earlier editions were obviously the best and could very easily obtain superb and complex status before long. I found that the wine left good flavor lingering on the palate, and, with additional aging, complexity might not be too far away. The Rosé was a clean wine, somewhat typical of a California rosé, which is quite a feat in itself. The Vintage White had a slight character of *Vitis labrusca* and this may be a result of what the late André Simon suggested, that the taste of the wine may represent the taste of the soil, *goût de terroir*, rather than the taste of the grape itself—an interesting concept and perhaps an accurate one. The Vintage White did have 5 percent Delaware grape in it, which may account of course for the labrusca accent.

The Aurora Blanc 1971 had a tinge of sweetness, perhaps because the grape was picked late. The Vintage Red 1971 was the least interesting of the four, although other tasters seemed to find the wine much better than I did, and it is the one which in blind tasting seemed to receive a fair amount of acclaim. It is a wine that could be enjoyed as an everyday wine with simple foods.

None of the wines had much, if any, of the so-called foxy taste long associated with New York wines and this particularly pleases Taylor and justifies his faith in the hybrid grapes.

Incidentally, Taylor explains that there is controversy on the meaning of foxiness. Some New York growers use it to denote the musky odor and flavor peculiar to *Vitis labrusca* grapes. Another theory is that the term came from an old verb "to fox," which meant "to intoxicate." Whatever the term may mean, foxiness is not a prime characteristic of Bully Hill wine.

Bully Hill is a unique vineyard in a unique growing region. It is 1,000 feet above Keuka Lake. The soil is extremely poor— shale, clay, and solid rock. The slope of the property goes to the south and east, and it couldn't be better for a vineyard if it were wholly man-designed. The grapes produced there are high in sugar, which doesn't hurt one bit. If New York State still is on tap as a major wine-producing area it is not due to the lack of effort on the part of Walter Taylor.

Walter S. Taylor is the son of Greyton Taylor, an heir of Taylor Wine Company. Walter, though, makes it clear that

neither he nor any member of the Taylor family has any responsibilities for the management or the winemaking of the present Taylor Wine Company or its subsidiary, Great Western.

In 1969, Taylor was executive vice-president of the Taylor Wine Company's Great Western division. He then spoke out on a subject about which he felt deeply—New York State's wines and New York State's winemaking laws. Of particular concern to him was the New York State law that allows water or California wine to be added to New York pressings, which may still be labeled as New York wine. Taylor's father, the late Greyton H. Taylor, agreed with him and encouraged him to leave Taylor Wine and to do things his own way. Together they brought back the Bully Hill farm where the original Taylor winery and vineyards were started in 1883.

A new winery was started after the old buildings were torn down, with only 500 cases produced the first year. Some 240,000 bottles were produced in 1972. The ultimate goal is 480,000 bottles a year.

No question, young Walter is the maverick of the New York State wine industry who professes grandeur for his wines and New York State's wines. He is also careful to point out that he uses no California wine to reduce the acidity of the New York grape. Neither water nor sugar is added; he claims new methods in technology make this unnecessary.

He also refuses to use the ion exchange method of clarifying his estate-bottled wines because he feels that nutrients, such as vitamin B and minerals, are lost. The ion exchange method also leaves some 400 milligrams of salt in each bottle. By leaving in the natural sediment Taylor feels the natural

taste is protected. The salt content of his wines is only twenty-one milligrams per bottle, particularly important to people on a salt-free diet.

Bully Hill also vintage-dates its bottles and Walter insists that every bottle contain grapes 100 percent from the year indicated. Just reading all the material Walter is quite willing to send to you, either in connection with his Greyton H. Taylor Wine Museum or his wines, you feel— after tasting his wines—you want to stand up and cheer for the maverick vintner.

1961

GOLD SEAL
NEW YORK STATE WINE
Johannisberger Riesling
Natur Spätlese

GOLD SEAL VINEYARDS, INC.
Hammondsport, New York 14840

Owner:
Gold Seal Vineyards, Inc.
Winemaker:
Didierre Bretonniere
Vineyards:
500 acres
Capacity:
Storage 3,000,000 gallons
Fermenting 1,500,000 gallons

Gabled roofs and steeples identify the Gold Seal winery, founded in 1865.

Gold Seal Vineyards can lay special claim for much of what has happened to the betterment of New York State wines, particularly in this last generation. It allowed the Konstantin Frank experiments and it has had as president Charles Fournier, who was once the manager of Veuve Clicquot-Ponsardin in France. Fournier has taken special pains to make some of New York's finest champagnes, including at one time a Fournier "Nature" made without dosage.

In the early '60s, experiments by Frank with viniferas of Chardonnay and Johannisberg Riesling developed wines that were extraordinary and to this day rank as one of the state's—indeed, one of America's—greater wine achievements.

Gold Seal is not a new vineyard. It was founded in 1865 on the shores of Keuka Lake in the heart of the Finger Lakes district. It was then known as the Urbana Wine Company, making wine under the name of Gold Seal. Champagne, throughout the generations, has been its forte. It still makes remarkably good champagne, the best of which is the Charles Fournier Blanc de Blanc. In addition it makes a full line of wines, some of which are marketed under the Henry Marchand label and include Château Chablis Blanc, Château Rosé Sec, and Château Rouge.

A most interesting generic bottle, chablis, is labeled C. F. [for Charles Fournier] Chablis Nature, a generally clean, crisp wine. The other generics, rhine, sauterne, rosé, and burgundy,

An underground storage tunnel.

are not as interesting. The Gold Seal native wines such as Catawba White, Catawba Pink, Catawba Red, Concord Red, Carousel Pink, and Carousel Red are good examples of native types, as are the Gold Seal dessert wines.

There is a claim that the chablis nature is made from Pinot Chardonnay grapes grown in New York State and this is undoubtedly true. The wine is reminiscent of the "experiment wines" made in the early '60s by Konstantin Frank with Chardonnay grapes, together with Johannisberg Riesling and Gewürztraminer; these were indeed some of the best New York wines I have yet experienced. They were well made and as the years have passed they have developed complexity, an experiment others no doubt are

unable to duplicate. The Gold Seal people are to be complimented for having developed those wines but it must have been very difficult to get a volume in commercial production, for they are not now being made. If they were, those wines could well compare with wines from vinifera areas of the world —sad indeed that they are not produced.

The earlier Chardonnay and Johannisberg Riesling are in my cellar, a decade old, and are still remarkable wines. Gold Seal

Some of the Gold Sea wines.

is most deserving of honors for having grown and made them. The winery would be well advised to pursue the efforts necessary to duplicate them, for they are the best that have ever been produced at Gold Seal, with the possible exception of the champagnes of Charles Fournier.

Today the company makes wines from its own vineyards, 500 acres under cultivation, which accounts only for about 20 percent of the grapes actually used by the winery, the balance coming from over 150 independent growers. There is persistent effort to grow viniferas such as Pinot Noir, Johannisberg Riesling, Pinot Chardonnay, and Cabernet Sauvignon, as well as such bybrids as Seibel 5279, Seibel 1000, Baco, and Foch.

The over 100-year career of Gold Seal can, for my taste, be poured into the vinifera bottles made by Frank. I wish that the winery could be encouraged not only to make native and hybrid varieties but also to push a little farther down the vinifera trail.

PLEASANT VALLEY WINE COMPANY

Hammondsport, New York 14840

Owner:
Taylor Wine Company, Inc.

Winemaker:
Stephen D. Coon

Capacity:
Storage 5,000,000 gallons
Fermenting 3,500,000 gallons

Like other New York State wineries of the Finger Lakes region, Great Western—the brand name for Pleasant Valley— is an old company with its beginnings in 1860. The winery's great claim to winemaking fame lies principally in its sparkling wines, with its best reserved for its brut and, in an ascending order of sweetness, Special Reserve and Extra Dry. These are bottle-fermented champagnes which have their origins in Pleasant Valley's history as wines that performed very well in European competitions: in 1873 in Vienna, 1889 in Paris, 1897 in Brussels, and 1900 in Paris. It is only relevant to report this now to point out that connoisseurs of those early days liked the Pleasant Valley champagne and referred to it as a great champagne of the western world; hence the name "Great Western."

There is a complete line of wines today and I prefer— oddly, for a Californian—the Catawba. It was the first wine made by Pleasant Valley and apparently they have learned how to do it well. The winery has also done a good job with hybrids, and the Baco Noir burgundy on occasion can be rather satisfactory but does not seem to develop the complexity of the Baco Noir of some of the other New York producers.

Another wine that has fared very well is Great Western's Chelois, a sometimes interesting, full-bodied red wine which is advertised as being reminiscent of a Bordeaux. I don't find it so. The Chelois grape at Pleasant Valley makes for a distinctive, interesting, but not necessarily exciting wine. It is made reasonably well here and makes for good everyday drinking at a reasonable price, perhaps one of the winery's better buys.

On the whole, the champagne at Great Western is the thing!

The Pleasant Valley Wine Co.

An ornate chandelier amidst casks.

Modern equipment.

TAYLOR WINE CO., INC.

Hammondsport, New York 14840

Owner:
Taylor Wine Co., Inc.
Winemaker:
James Ferguson
Capacity:
15,000,000 gallons fermenting

The corporate offices of Taylor Wine Company stand solidly above New York State's largest winery complex.

Today the Taylor Wine Company is one of the largest producers of so-called premium wine in America, putting out in excess of three million cases of wine a year—a far cry from its humble origins when the winery was founded by Walter and Addie Taylor on a seven-acre vineyard on Bully Hill in April of 1880. Actually, some of the vines have an even earlier origin: they were planted by the Reverend William Boswich, rector of St. James Episcopal Church, in his rectory garden in 1829. The geography and the climate at Keuka Lake and the soil areas close by were ideal for grape growing, attracting the Taylors, who started with the native American varieties of Delaware, Catawba, Duchess, Elvira, Niagara, Concord, and Ives. It

wasn't long before the Taylors were shipping sound red and white table wines from those varieties by the barrel to New York City, where they were bottled.

For many years the business prospered, with the Taylor family reflecting the ideals of sound winemaking practices that were the forerunner of many others in the New York wine industry. The Taylors were among the leaders in the introduction of French-American hybrids, which has become such a successful part of winemaking in the Finger Lakes region. Keeping up with the times, they have also led the way in the introduction of mechanical harvesting, so much so that 80 percent of their grapes are now machine-picked.

The history of Taylor wines reads almost like the history of New York State winemaking, beginning small and growing to production of enormous propor-

tions. The company today corks 26,000 bottles daily.

When Walter Taylor's reign was over it gave way to three sons—Fred, Clarence, and Greyton—who made the business grow, so that by 1913 the acreage of vineyards at Bully Hill was insufficient and grapes had to be purchased from other growers in the region. That practice is still followed today and varieties of grapes are supplied by more than 340 growers, many of whom pride themselves on being third-generation suppliers.

When Prohibition began in 1919, Taylor Wine moved its operation from Bully Hill into the Columbia Wine Building, constructed in 1886, adjacent to the Pleasant Valley Wine Company. At that time there were more than a dozen wineries in the Hammondsport area, but regrettably only a few lasted until America saw the light with repeal.

It is to their credit that the Taylors survived Prohibition by doing the very same thing that some of the California wineries were doing: selling table grape juice and sacramental wines. Some of the winery's concentrated grape juice was sold in barrels for legal conversion into wine at home.

The Columbia Wine Building, expanded to meet modern

Immense redwood vats, holding as much as one hundred thousand gallons.

needs, remains the hub of Taylor wine activities. Expansion continues at this moment.

Things were not always rosy, however, after Prohibition, and progress thereafter was painstakingly slow. Recovery was made largely through the Taylors' premium bottle-fermented champagne, which is virtually the core of the winery's business. There are more than 12 million bottles aging in storage at any given time. By any standards, that is a lot of champagne.

Taylor is so heavily involved in champagne making that a new champagne-processing building, now complete, will increase its production capacity by 50 percent.

In 1955, the Taylors changed their status from partnership to a privately held corporation, in which the family was still principally involved. At the end of 1961, Taylor acquired Pleasant Valley Wine, which had been operating as a division of Great Western Producers, Inc. Then, to put the capper on the Taylor story, in 1962, Taylor made a public stock offering and now runs the two businesses—Pleasant Valley and Taylor—as distinct wineries, indeed competitors, each operating as an independent unit.

The Taylors are very little in evidence these days at Taylor

Wine Company—indeed, Walter Taylor loves to say that the real Taylors are over at Bully Hill. Nevertheless, the Taylors earned their proper place in New York winemaking history with the Taylor Wine Company and a new era, of course, has begun with Taylor as a corporate entity.

A full line of wines is made, with the champagnes—to my taste—being the best. Most notable is the brut champagne, which has good flavor and crispness and is pleasantly dry;

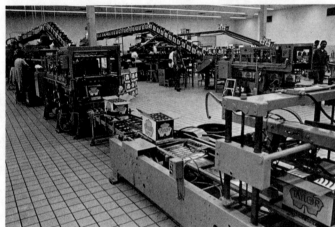

A partial view of Taylor's labeling and packing facility.

even though there is a hint of labrusca in the wine, it is not unpleasant. The other sparkling wines, dry champagne which is not as dry as the brut, pink champagne, Cold Duck, and sparkling burgundy, are satisfactory although not in the class of the brut.

The table wines are not labeled varietally and are generics; it is to the credit of the company that among the better bottles are the simply and truthfully labeled Taylor Lake Country White, Taylor Lake Country Pink, and Taylor Lake Country Red. These wines are neither great nor complex, but they are sound, reasonably good, and within their price range they are very good examples of New York State wine.

A good line of dessert wines, including some in jug-type containers, are certainly in different style from European or California counterparts. Tawny port, sherry, muscatel, etc., are quite satisfactory but cannot be compared

if your tastes run along European styles, for in these you will find the New York State soil asserting itself. Indeed, some of the wines are made with classic New York grapes such as Catawba, and they are truthfully good examples of what classic native New York grapes can do.

The French-American hybrids are to be found in the table wines except for the Lake Country Pink, which shows the Catawba grape to good advantage, as does the Lake Country White, which shows the Niagara.

The Taylor Company and the Pleasant Valley Company produce a full range of wines—red, white, sweet, dry, and sparkling. They also finish and bottle muscatels bought in California. Their wines are blended and standardized so as not to vary appreciably from one year to another, and except for the champagnes are sealed with metal caps; bark corks are not used in still wines.

For such a large enterprise, greatness and complexity in its wines is perhaps difficult, just as it is for some of the larger winemaking enterprises in California. The Taylors did establish a reputation for quality, dependability, and consistency. To those ends the Taylor Company in its corporate form is continuing.

VINIFERA WINE CELLARS

R.F.D. 2
Hammondsport, New York 14840

Owner and Winemaker:
Dr. Konstantin Frank

Vineyards:
78 acres

Capacity:
Storage 100,000 gallons
Fermenting 60,000 gallons

Vinifera is a label on the threshold of greatness, a monument to the tenacity and patience of Dr. Konstantin Frank.

In a relatively short period of time (barely six years), Frank has put together wines of such magnitude that even the most notable of experts finds it impossible to rate them much behind the finest German wines. I served his Johannisberg Riesling Spätlese blind to one of California's most notable winemakers and wine drinkers, Joe Heitz, and, without hesitation, he said it was a German moselle. I watched with glee, pride, and a little fear as I unveiled the label. Then my friend and I laughed together, for the joke really was on both of us to discover that New York wines from the tutelage of Konstantin Frank are so superb. "It's almost too bad," my winemaking friend said, after I unveiled the label, "that William Penn, Thomas Jefferson, Lord Delaware, and John Smith aren't around to taste an east coast wine like this."

Those men were among the early wine pioneers. For the most part, they failed in attempts to make good wines from the native *Vitis labrusca*, and they did not succeed at transplanting the European strains of *Vitis vinifera*.

Frank has succeeded at doing both. He has taken the foxiness (the unique "earth" taste associated with eastern wines) out of his grapes and, mostly, he has proved once and for all that the vinifera can prosper in an eastern seaboard setting. One of his wines—a Spätlese Riesling Nature that is made without sugar—has a great depth of flavor, and another even greater effort, a Trockenbeeren Auslese Riesling, sells for $45 a bottle. Try it before you say that the price is too high.

Frank has many other wines of high quality and lower cost. The pride of winemaking is so evident in his wines that it's discouraging to think that Frank, a robust worker at age seventy-four, is not a man of thirty just starting out. When he is gone, who will follow? It seems logical that the vinifera grapes should become an integral force throughout eastern and western America, but many of the other winemakers in those areas argue that the cost is high and the yield low. I hope this attitude will change as wine drinkers become accustomed to the magnificent vinifera wines.

If Frank and his associates

Dr. Frank talks about his collection of vines.

The Vinifera Wine Cellars home and winery.

can make their wines in larger quantities, I am certain that they can give California wines a run for their money in America. It doesn't appear, however, that volume production in New York is possible. The late André Simon said that great doubt exists amoung New York grape growers as to whether the famous-name grapes such as Cabernet Sauvignon, Johannisberg Riesling, Chardonnay, and Pinot Noir can produce wines in large quantity that are free of foxiness.

Who knows? Konstantin Frank may change all that, too. The vinifera wines he has produced have been great surprises. Perhaps he has time for more.

Four professors from Cornell University—N. B. Hoffman, Harry Kerr, Albert W. Laubengayer, and Elmer S. Phillips—said it best in a film narrated by Phillips:

"One secret to Dr. Frank's

success lies in his selection of special rootstocks that produce a more hardy plant that grows well in the Finger Lakes region. In late winter or early spring, mature wood from a vine that can tolerate the climate, diseases, and other factors is cut about one foot long. To this is grafted a shorter section from a desired vinifera plant. Diameters must be the same and the junction of both must be perfect. After appropriate cultural practices, roots grow in one section and leaf structure in the other. After this happens and spring arrives, the grafted plant is set out in a nursery where constant observation determines the plant's future. When success is assured over several years of observation, the plants are again multiplied by grafting and moved to the larger working field. In several years, the plants mature and with the care necessary for vinifera plants, present a vigor in early September that forecasts a successful harvest in a few weeks."

Besides working with Pinot Chardonnay, Gamay Beaujolais,

Pinot Noir, Cabernet Sauvignon, Johannisberg Riesling, and Gewürztraminer, Frank has experimented with a number of unusual European varieties, among them (the quotes are those of the Cornell professors):

Fetjaska—"The Hungarian grape variety produced in Ukraine and Moldavia."

Kabasis—"One of the best wine varieties from Bessarabia which produces a high quality rosé wine."

Mzuny—"The top grape variety native to the Georgian Caucasus. Its wine is equal to the best German and French whites."

Sereksia Rosodja—"That is native to the Ukraine and makes the.very best Russian wine."

Sereksia Tschornay—"Makes the highest quality Ukrainian pink wine."

Muscat Bely—"A new table-grape variety high-producing Turkestan grape with a desirable

balance of sugar and acid."

Taify—"A big-producing black grape of high quality."

Husaine—"A red-colored variety with an extremely pleasant pulp, well balanced with sugar and acid."

Tschaosh—"The leading table grape from the Caucasus with big berries and a delicate taste."

Cardinal—"The origin of this grape is Fresno, California, from a cross of two vinifera varieties."

Ziza Kapri—"One of the best grapes from southern Asia that may be used fresh, dried, or as a wine producer. Eaten fresh, it's a favorite of Moslems."

Kara Burni—"Native to Bulgaria, this has big berries that keep and transport with ease and the taste is excellent."

I have my fingers crossed for Dr. Frank, a pioneer who ranks with Agoston Haraszthy in the history and development of American wine. Konstantin Frank was born in the Ukraine in 1899, but there is something wonderfully significant about the date. It was on July 4.

WIDMER'S WINE CELLARS

West Avenue & Toby Street
Naples, New York 14512

Owner:
R. T. French Company
Winemaker:
Edwin Haynes
Vineyards:
500 acres
Capacity:
Storage 2,500,000 gallons
Fermenting 600,000 gallons

The building roofs at Widmer are stocked high with barrels of aging sherry.

John Jacob Widmer, who found the Finger Lakes region of New York to his liking for winemaking, established Widmer's Wine Cellars. Perhaps his coming from Switzerland had something to do with his attraction to this area, aside from the fact that the soil and the climate seemed appropriate for wines.

Widmer did not come entirely on his own but at the insistence of his brother, who preceded him in the area. He planted his first vineyard in the spring of 1883; to this day it is fruit-bearing.

The first customers of Widmer's were Swiss residents in Rochester, New York, and Peterson, New Jersey. The first wines must have been satisfactory, though they were sold in kegs rather than in bottles, for the demand for the wine increased and in 1891 Widmer began to ship wine in bottles.

Up to the time of Prohibition the vineyards and winery expanded under the direction of John Jacob Widmer. Later three sons, Paul, Frank, and William, took over. This was during Prohibition and not the best possible time to assume responsibility for a vineyard and winery operation. John Jacob Widmer continued in the business until his death in 1930. Although his

final days were spent during the period of Prohibition, the winery continued to operate by producing unfermented grape juice, fruit and wine jellies, syrups, and kindred nonalcoholic products. Like many other wineries trying to stay alive, Widmer's also produced sacramental wine.

In 1941, Widmer acquired the Maxfield Wine Cellars and began to utilize the facilities for Widmer's wines. The company survived a disastrous fire in 1943 which destroyed most of the production facilities but miraculously left the wines in storage untouched.

The winery today is no longer owned by the Widmers but by a name familiar in another industry, the R. T. French Company of Rochester, New York. Widmer's Wine Cellars is a rather large winemaking enterprise, bottling 4,000 cases of wine per day not including 500 cases of sparkling wine. There is here, as at some of the other New York wineries, a complete line of wines, including dessert wines, champagnes, red and white varietals, and generics.

The most interesting of the wines are the varietals, particu-

larly the whites such as the Delaware, Vergennes and Elvira, all of which seem to be fairly clean, distinct in flavor, and with a pleasant finish. The Moore's Diamond did not show as well as the others, nor did the reds labeled as Isabella, Burgundy, Claret, Widmerheimer Red, and Seibel-Rosé.

The dessert wines showed reasonably well although some were labruscan in character, but there was one wine that caught my particular fancy, and that is the Widmer New York State Sweet Catawba, a wine with some charm. Although it takes a bit of getting used to, it is well worth the effort.

Widmer also makes a unique unbaked sherry, aged on the winery roof in barrels fully exposed to the hot summers and bitter New York winters for at least four years, or sometimes eight years, before bottling. Widmer has also succeeded in growing Riesling grapes and producing several Auslesen vintages.

Soon there will be a line of Widmer California wines—the winery will offer "the best of both worlds." An area in the Alexander Valley in Napa County has been purchased and planted to top varietals.

OTHER WINERIES OF NEW YORK

There are many wines and wineries in the state of New York that are deserving of mention—and of wine drinkers' tasting and collecting.

Benmarl Wine Company, Marlboro: Projected is an interesting "new-old" winery in New York's Hudson River Valley, founded by artist Mark Miller and his family. The name Benmarl is derived from ben—early Gaelic for hill—and marl—a word describing the slaty soil. Planned plantings are Chardonnay, Pinot Noir, Cabernet Sauvignon, White Riesling, and a variety of French—American hybrids. The wines will be vintage-dated and estate bottled; as yet they have not been tasted by the writer, as only two vintages have been made.

Over 100 years ago, the wine-growing area in this region was of considerable importance and the decline, thereafter, was probably due more to political or economic causes than for any poor quality of either grape or wine. The goal will be, by 1978, to produce 50,000 gallons.

Canandaigua Industries Company, Inc., Canandaigua: If being the largest means being the best, then this winery would command a lofty position, for it claims to be the third largest vintner in the nation. Suffice it to say, being the largest does not necessarily mean it is the best.

Canandaigua, however, makes a large range of wines under a variety of brands such as the old label Virginia Dare, Richards and Richard, and Wild Irish Rose. It has been making wines in the Finger Lakes region since 1945. Spurred on to becoming larger, it has acquired wineries in the South, such as Richards Wine Cellars in Petersburg, Virginia, and Tenner Brothers in South Carolina, as well as the Hammondsport Wine Company in New York.

From a sales standpoint, its most successful product is a fortified dessert wine which carries the label Wild Irish Rose.

The most interesting thing Canandaigua is doing is to resuscitate the Virginia Dare label with a white Scuppernong wine, a unique and most American grape that is, even more uniquely, grown in Virginia from the so-called mother vineyard; indeed, the label refers to "The Mother Vineyard Company." The Scuppernong is to my liking for its own unique taste. Like many other American native varieties, it takes a bit of getting used to but is worth the effort.

High Tor Vineyards, New City: From atop High Tor, a mountain made famous by Maxwell Anderson's prizewinning play, another playwright, Everett Crosby, in 1954 introduced the first New York State wines made entirely from French hybrid grapes.

The winery consists of seventy-eight acres and produces three wines, a red, a white, and a rosé, all under the brand of Rockland.

In 1971, Crosby sold High Tor to Richard Voight, owner of the Peppermill Restaurants in Connecticut. Voight has hired an Episcopal priest, Father Thomas Lee Hayes, as his winemaker but Everett Crosby continues in the position of consultant to the winery.

Monarch Wine Company, Brooklyn: It would be difficult to comment on New York wines without including Monarch's Manischewitz wines and champagnes. Many Americans have grown up with the taste and liking for wines made from the Concord grape. Sometimes these wines are referred to as "kosher" wines because they are made under religious supervision and are used for religious ritual and holy day celebration.

These wines do not particularly require aging, are generally sweetened, and can be found in a range of sweetness from Concord, the most popular, to medium dry and dry Concord. No doubt they are fun wines to drink and are a favorite among many but they hardly make good companions at the table; they are best served slightly chilled as an aperitif or an after-dinner wine.

Niagara Falls Wine Cellar, Lewiston: In 1972, Richard P. Vine and Edward Moulton opened a small winery on the east side of the Niagara River along an escarpment ridge that perhaps thousands of years ago was the shore line of Lake Ontario. Vine, with eleven years' experience behind him at the Pleasant Valley Winery, is the winemaker and expects to produce in Niagara County some of the best wines yet made in New York State. His claim is that the rich gravel soil is ideal for highest quality wine growing.

O-Neh-Da Vineyard, Conesus: This winery has made wine since 1872, with particular emphasis on altar wines, which are produced under the supervision of the Divine Word Missionaries, a Roman Catholic religious order of priests and brothers. This is the only Church-owned winery outside of California. The winery is located on the shores of Lake Hemlock, one of the westernmost Finger Lakes (O-Neh-Da is Indian for "hemlock"). The winery today is owned by the Barry Wine Company and consists of a hundred acres producing about 500 cases of wine per day, with emphasis on native varieties such as Delaware, Iona, Niagara, Catawba, and some semiexperimental acres of White Rieslings and Gewürztraminer. O-Neh-Da is under the direction of Leo Goering, the winemaker, who came from Geisenheim, Germany, in 1919. The winery was founded in 1872 by the first Roman Catholic Bishop of Rochester specifically for the making of wine valid and licit for Mass and also so that the wines could be easily available to the priests of the Rochester diocese. After Prohibition the winery and about a thousand of the surrounding acres were sold to the Society of the Divine Word. The order continued the operation and began to plant new vineyards and to modernize the winery. They also established a seminary on the surrounding land.

Most of the production is sold to the clergy for religious purposes, which not only includes the wine previously mentioned but also haute sauterne, cream sherry (from Niagara), burgundy, and port from Concords, Clinton, and Foch.

The winery today is owned by K. W. Cribari and A. B. Cribari, all part of the Barry Wine Corporation. These gentlemen have been in the winemaking business for three generations.

In 1887 Walter Taylor planted this Bully Hill vineyard.

WINERIES IN OTHER REGIONS

BAJA CALIFORNIA

Bodegas de Santo Tomas, Ensenada, B.C : Perhaps the greatest thing that has ever happened to winemaking in Mexico,

Dimitri Tchelistcheff at Santo Tomas.

notwithstanding Father Juan de Ugarte and the mission era, is the transplanted Napa Valleyite Dimitri Tchelistcheff, who is the winemaker at Bodegas de Santo Tomas. The winery, known as Mision de Santo Tomas, has always made a full line of wines but now excellent examples of what a talented enologist can do are beginning to come, such as the Santo Tomas Chenin Blanc —a wine with good acid

balance, character, and a clean aftertaste—and the Barbera—a wine with considerable varietal character but reflecting a little bit of the heaviness of grapes from an overly hot summer. The wines represented the first efforts—first plantings by the young winemaker—and probably are the best wines made in Baja and perhaps in Mexico.

Tchelistcheff expects his planting of varietals to make good Pinot Noir, Chardonnay, Cabernet, and Grenache. He is the son of Andre Tchelistcheff of Beaulieu, and he has brought to Santo Tomas the same kind of missionary zeal that it once had (pardon the pun) and indeed the same kind that his father brought to Beaulieu in the making of fine varietals.

Dimitri has great faith in the Santo Tomas region, for he says, "Actually the climate of our valleys here at Baja is almost identical to the climate of the upper Napa Valley around Calistoga. We have the same cool early morning fogs and it's hotter than hell in the summer. This is what gives us such a tremendous edge over the other vineyards of Mexico."

I did not find the other wines particularly interesting, for they were still from old vines not yet replaced by Tchelistcheff. Give him time, and give yourself the opportunity to taste some of the dessert wines. Especially try the Santo Tomas Cordon Azul Champagne, which is made principally from the Chenin Blanc grape. The more interesting version is the dry, as opposed to the demi-sec.

Dimitri will make fine—indeed, great—wines in Baja and he will join the trio of Oregon, Washington State, and Baja in taking on California wines. Perhaps in due course the West Coast will become—if it is not already—one of the most important wine areas in the world.

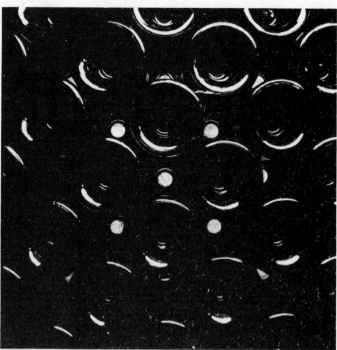

Wine gathers additional age in the bottle.

MICHIGAN

Bronte Champagne and Wines Company, Keller: If *Warner Vineyards,* Frontenac, and *St. Julien* of Paw Paw have anything to say about it, wines in Michigan may replace motor cars for eminence in the state. Michigan is now the third largest producer of wines in the United States, following California and New York.

Although the industry is old, there are many changes being wrought in Michigan's wines and vineyards, principally due to the planting of French-American hybrids that are adapted to Michigan climate, such as Baco Noir, Aurora, Marechal Foch, etc. Don't misunderstand—the area produces very fine Catawba, Delaware, and Concord, but the direction is toward the hybrids.

Members of the Michigan Wine Institute are really moving forward; for the first time they are imposing a tax on themselves to establish a research project for the growing of French-American hybrids. The movement forward will not happen overnight, as there are 16,000 acres of grapes of which 14,500 acres are of the Concord, used principally for fruit juice. But there are good, dedicated people moving Michigan in the right direction: Robert Wosniak, secretary-treasurer of Bronte; Dr. T. W. Wosniak, its founder; James J. Warner and J. K. Warner of the new Warner Vineyards label; and Nathan Stackhouse, an import from the University of California at Davis, a graduate in enology, whose father-in-law is Charles Welch of Guild Wineries & Distilleries, San Francisco.

The emphasis is obviously beginning to move toward wines and not just the growing of grapes used principally for juice for companies such as Welch, A. Merch Company—a subsidiary of Smuckers—and the Paw Paw Grape Juice Company at Paw Paw, Michigan.

There are others pushing

5

forward, such as the winemaker at Bronte, Angelo Spinazze, who was among the first to work with French–American hybrids in Michigan. Bronte Winery can lay some dubious claim to fame for having conceived the takeoff of Cold Duck around 1964.

Going a bit further with viniferas, particularly Chardonnay, is *Tabor Hill Vineyard Wine Cellar,* in Baroda, Michigan, a small but individualistic enterprise making less than 10,000 gallons of wine. As regards the Chardonnay, as with so many other experiments time and taste will tell.

An interesting note: In *Wines and Vines,* a most informative wine trade publication in California, owned and edited by Philip Hiaring, Mr. Stackhouse is quoted as saying that he prefers making wine in Michigan to making it in California. Mr. Hiaring points out that Mr. Stackhouse is in charge of the wine and commercial juice operations at Michigan Wineries at Paw Paw and says, "Michigan is far better than California for growing grapes. In many respects the weather there [in California] is too good, so warm the grapes mature too fast and even the poor vines prosper."

An interesting observation, somewhat supported by other wine people in the East, but as always there is the bottle that can be tasted to support or refute the observation.

MISSOURI
Mt. Pleasant Vineyards is a small but thriving winery in, of all places, Augusta, Missouri— vineyards of twelve acres owned by Lucian W. Dressel and Eva B. Dressel. You are not likely to believe it, but it is true: this winery was founded in 1860 on the north side of the Missouri River just thirty miles west of St. Louis. Wines from the vineyard were shown and honored at the Columbian Exhibition in 1893 and the St. Louis World's Fair of 1904.

As with many wineries, Prohibition literally killed it. Not until the Dressels came along was the winery revived.

The Mantey winery and vineyard.

The Dressels are amateurs who started out with a love for wine and have indeed become professionals who pattern their winemaking along Alsatian lines. There is no stainless steel, only white oak barrels.

The plantings now are new French–American hybrids together with some *Vitis vinifera*, Johannisberg Riesling, Gewürztraminer, Pinot Noir, Chardonnay. Viniferas will indeed be exciting, but you may have to go all the

Norman Mantey, owner of Mon Ami.

way to visit Mt. Pleasant Vineyards in order to find out.

OHIO
Mantey Vineyards, Inc., Sandusky: A winery of a forty-acre vineyard producing 400 cases per day, owned by Paul Mantey who operates the cellar by himself and makes fourteen different wines, including a dry Catawba. The Mantey name is old in Ohio, dating back to 1880, when the growing of grapes and production of wine was a thriving enterprise on the south shore of Lake Erie. The emphasis was on Catawba, with considerable consumption of it in Pittsburgh and Chicago; the business grew from a few thousand gallons to fifty thousand. The winery today sells principally to distributors and retailers rather than directly to the consumer, with emphasis still on Catawba.

Norman Mantey, Paul's brother, operates the *Mon Ami Champagne Company* which was purchased in 1956 with concentration on sparkling wines; including sparkling Seibel, sparkling burgundy, champagne extra dry, and a full line of table wines. There is an interesting wine made from a seldom used varietal grape, the Agawam; Mon Ami's best wine is probably the Delaware and of course has its location at the most appropriate place— Catawba Island in Ohio.

Both wineries owned by the brothers compete for each other's business in the state of Ohio only. Both enterprises have shown the ravages of time as Mon Ami owns no vineyards and Mantey's vineyards have recently been bisected by a federal expressway.

Meier's Wine Cellars, Inc., Cincinnati: Nicholas Longworth can assuredly lay claim to the title of "Father of Viticulture" of Ohio and can take his place alongside Haraszthy of California and Frank of New York, for obviously he was the prince of Catawba and the great prophet for Ohio wines when he wrote in 1847 about sparkling Catawba, "My own impression is that in skillful hands our Catawba will make a wine superior in flavor and aroma to the best French champagne imported. The aroma of the Catawba grape continues in the wine in all its stages. I made the first champagne five years since. It was produced by chance and induced me to erect a building for the manufacture and to send to France for a manufacturer; I shall be content, if we can always make as fine a wine by design as was then made by accident."

Fine wine for its type is again coming out of Ohio and certainly not by accident.

The history of Ohio's wines and the history of Meier's are for all intents and purposes one and the same. Ohio's wines were first planted in the 1820s by Nicholas

Longworth, a lawyer and a politician. He first turned to the grape as a result of the discoveries in South Carolina in 1802 of native American grapes, the old familiar Scuppernong and the Muscadine. But it was Catawba that Longworth chose, for that seemed to do fairly well in the severities of the Ohio climate. He may have been the producer of America's first sparkling wine, the Sparkling Catawba that others refer to—much too kindly—as America's first champagne.

Catawba is still the principal wine and grape of Ohio, and good Catawba it is.

André Simon, one of the world's great wine lovers, spotted the luscious sweetness of the Catawba but deplored that much of this product was labeled "Sauterne" so that Americans would buy it. He was right, for Catawba has its own virtues as any good palate will recognize.

At the time of the Civil War, Ohio was making 35 percent of the country's wines, for which

most of the credit should go to Nicholas Longworth and to John C. Meier, who began his operations in Silverton, near Cincinnati, at about the same time as Longworth.

Meier's principal vineyard today is on Isle St. George, where the winery has had vineyards since 1844. The whole island is the property of Meier's and grapes are ferried across to Sandusky by boats which carry thirty-five tons of grapes for the five-hour round trip. Approximately 350 acres are under cultivation here, the bulk of which is Catawba, with the balance Concord and French–American-hybrids such as Baco No. 1 and some Seibels.

The winemaker at Meier's, Galo MacLean, with a European and Chilean background, believes that the future lies with the French–American hybrid grapes. He has made the statement: "For the European winemaker to try to live with labrusca is almost impossible. It's just too far away. You can't tell whether

it's good or bad. Wine should be mutual with food but the trouble with labrusca is you cannot taste the food you eat because it overpowers everything." A strong statement from an obviously honest winemaker.

He has given expression to his beliefs by persuading Henry Sonneman, managing director and wine-master of Meier's, to plant French–American hybrids along the banks of the Ohio River in the area of New Richmond. It is an experimental vineyard entitled Château Jacque-Jan, named after his two children, Jack and Janet. The wines bear the label of Château Jacque-Jan, with white wine called chablis made from Seibel and Seyve-Villard, and the reds, labeled Ohio Valley Red Table Wine, made from Baco Noir and Chelois.

MacLean best describes his wines as fairly honest red and an excellent white.

It is this kind of people who are Meier's, still a family-owned winery, and who will bring Ohio

A guide lectures an interested tour group.

back to pre-Civil War eminence. An intriguing thought, provided we are willing to take the Catawba seriously.

Steuk Wine Company, Sandusky: Steuk is a small vineyard, operating with only four acres and bottling a hundred cases per day of table wine, champagnes, and other sparkling wines. The brand is Wilhelm Steuk and it claims to be the oldest winery in the United States still owned and operated by the founding family. That family included, in the 1850s, two great-grandfathers of the present owners, who commenced the grape-growing and wine-making operations. They were Lewis Harms and William Leopold Steuk. The company may make some of the country's finest Catawba wines, sweet, sparkling and dry; they are worth the serious and interesting effort to understand and appreciate the Catawba.

Tarula Farms, Clarksville: There are over thirty wineries in Ohio, none of the others as large as Meier's, and one of the oldest—Engels and Krudwig of Sandusky, perhaps the oldest Ohio winery, founded in 1863—is in liquidation, with all wine-making equipment and inventories disposed of. There are, however, some smaller new wineries, including Tarula Farms, of which a Yale University graduate in chemistry is owner, manager, winemaker, and probably everything else. Wistar Marting claims to have taught himself winemaking from textbooks suggested by the staff at the University of California Department of Enology, Davis, California.

In 1965, he switched the

The rock encrusted earth at Catawba Island, Ohio.

emphasis of his farming from corn to grapes, with assistance by the Ohio Experiment Station at Ripley. At the moment, he expects to make between 20,000 and 25,000 gallons—the largest production to date since his beginning in 1965—and he has twenty-five to twenty-seven acres in grapes onto which he has introduced French–American hybrids. He claims to make an acceptable non-labrusca table wine similar to many of the standard French wines and California wines. The main pro-

duction is a dry red, a dry white, and a rosé (slightly sweetened), each being a blend of French–American hybrids. Mr. Marting claims that there is a revival taking place along the Ohio side of the Ohio River that will eventually restore the area to its once-claimed reputation as the "Rhineland of America."

When Marting applied for his vintner's license in 1965 it was the first issued by the Cincinnati office of the Treasury Department to a winegrower since the days of Prohibition.

OREGON
Until recently, no one spoke of Oregon wines, even in whispers. It is not enough to say that there were efforts, going back to the 1830s, to grow the grape and make the wine in Oregon, for undoubtedly in almost all states —perhaps in all places in the world—at some time or another somebody wants to grow grapes, to make a wine for hospitality or to worship his god.

Obviously no great wine has yet been made in the region but it is coming, and perhaps coming fast, out of the Umpqua Valley of Douglas County, Oregon.

Doubtless there have been persistent, stubborn, dogged attempts to make wine in Oregon, including a visit in 1920 by F. T. Bioletti, head of the Department of Enology at the University of California at Davis, who suggested Grants Pass, Oregon, at a most inappropriate time—Prohibition. In between Grants Pass and Eugene there is the Umpqua Valley, which seems to be doing very, very well these days with the help, nurturing, and counsel of Richard Sommer of *Hillcrest Vineyard* and Paul Bjelland of *Bjelland Vineyards*. Both are growing vinifera as are growers of such grapes as Riesling, Gewürztraminer, Sauvignon Blanc, Sémillon, Chardonnay for the whites; for the reds the emphasis is on Cabernet Sauvignon, Zinfandel, Pinot Noir.

In tasting the Oregon wines I have found that I prefer the whites to the reds with the Cabernets not yet making it in great character or complexity; they seem not to be in balance. That should come, however. The whites—and most notably the Johannisberg Riesling—are the most revealing and obviously the best, and perhaps should be emphasized.

Champagne bottles rest securely in a riddling rack.

It is interesting to note that both gentlemen are from California. Richard Sommer was educated at the University of California at Davis in agronomy. He planted his land as early as 1961 and has been moving along at a steady pace with considerable progress. The latecomer, Paul Bjelland, who worked as an educational administrator in Los Angeles, has some twenty-eight acres of the 200 he owns under cultivation and he is moving well in friendly pursuit of Sommer. The whole Oregon wine scene consists of under ten wineries, of which Hillcrest and Bjelland are without doubt the most interesting. Both these gentlemen are serious about their vinifera efforts and it is only a matter of time before the whites will have considerable complexity. However, I am not so optimistic about the reds because of the coolness in and around the Roseburg-Umpqua Valley area—cooler than the Napa Valley. But perhaps with

the same doggedness of earlier Oregonian pioneers in wine, such as the Von Pessls brothers, Adam Doerner, Jess Applegate, and now Sommer and Bjelland, the reds indeed may catch up with the whites. If so, then California had better look out. Some of those pioneers, as in other states, have used California as a yardstick—so far as to say that they can make better wine than found in California. As it is always—we shall taste.

PENNSYLVANIA

Penn-Shore Vineyards, Inc., North East, Pennsylvania, is a new enterprise with 125 acres, featuring such brands as Penn-Shore Champagne, Penn-Shore Extra Dry, and Penn-Shore Table Wines. Catawba is the star but now the winery is in the process of marketing varietals and blends of European wine grapes including Pinot Chardonnay, which should be most interesting. Seyval Blanc is another star. The winery and vineyard are

in Erie County, which has some tradition for grapes—located by, as the winery claims, the tempering influence of Lake Erie.

WASHINGTON STATE

Ste. Michelle Vineyards, Seattle, Washington. An interesting experiment is taking place in the Yakima Valley in the state of Washington, where the American Winegrowers Co., doing business as Ste. Michelle Vineyards, is attempting to produce varietal wines from the Sémillon, Cabernet Sauvignon, Pinot Noir, Grenache and Johannisberg Riesling grapes. Some are selections from California and Ste. Michelle's technical adviser to winemaker Howard Somers is the grandmaster himself, Andre Tchelistcheff of Beaulieu Vineyards.

The Cabernet Sauvignon is aged in new American oak casks while the Pinot Noir is aged in Limousin oak. The white and rosé wines are aged in stainless steel. The whites get one year of bottle aging and the reds two.

These wines are not easy to make; they grow in an area in which the vines are barely able to survive, but the experiment is proving quite successful, particularly for the white wines, which are indeed good. The Johannisberg Riesling and the Sémillon are perhaps the best, with the reds not doing as well —but that, of course, can change. The vineyards were established after a merger of the National Wine Company and Pommerelle Companies to form the American Winegrowers, whose oldest vineyard, the Sémillon, was established as early as 1939. Later plantings were made as certified root stock became available. The vines are grown on their own roots and the cultivation, as in

Russia, must be layered with dirt after pruning to prevent damage from freezing.

These first wines would, in a blind tasting of the Johannisberg Riesling and the Sémillon, be mistaken for wines from California or possibly France. Quite a compliment!

If Ste. Michelle is any indication, the wine picture looks good for Washington State, especially when the wineries get the hang of making better reds and a good Chardonnay. And when Seneca, with its Boordy venture (see page 185), gets further along, it will be a most interesting wine era, with Washington State, as well as Oregon, challenging California.

Stainless steel and wooden tanks share the floor at Penn-Shore.

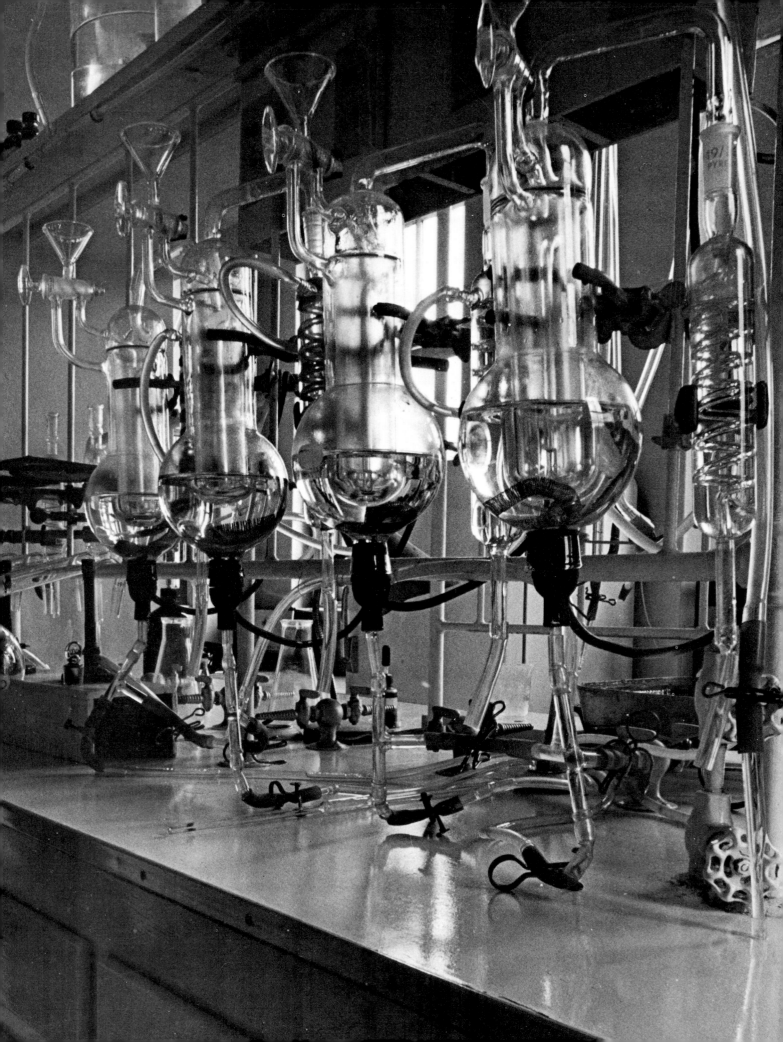

What tomorrow will bring in American wine is up to us, the collective society of tasters, drinkers, appreciators. The art of wine appreciation is like anything else in our modern society. If we take it for granted, it will take us for granted; mediocrity will be the result.

The fact is that the wines of America represent the best of both worlds right now. They have roots in families that go back generations. They have a special tradition that few—if any—modern industries can match. They also are intertwined with twentieth-century technology—with modernization and efficiency and the science of American enology.

The results have been astonishing. From an industry that produced "Model-T" wines barely three decades ago have come incredibly interesting wines. Many of them have literally challenged the world's best.

But for all my enthusiasm, I can't help but retain a latent feeling of gloom. I worry about the American wine audience. It is so new, so young, so interested in just tasting and drinking and not in appreciating. There aren't enough people around who will stand up for better wine.

If the consumer does not speak out, if the wine industry goes on unchecked, uncontrolled, and unknowing, we will all be drinking Chevrolets and Fords, perhaps at reasonable prices (although I doubt that), but certainly without any reasonable hope of complexity, depth of flavor, or lingering finish in our wines.

There is no question that the middle range of American wines has gotten better. As the sciences of viticulture and enology have expanded, so has the bottle of genuinely bad American wine.

The real question is whether we will forget how to make great wines—either through ignorance or through lack of interest, time, and money. Great wines are not made by the clock. They are made by interested and dedicated people who are wine drinkers themselves and who worry constantly, as Andre Tchelistcheff of Beaulieu says, "about the way their children turn out." The love of fine wine has to go that deep and that love must be felt by both the vintner and the buyer. At this point, I do not know who is more important.

Really, it is a choice: wine for everybody at a reasonable price, or wines that run the spectrum from average to good to great. Naturally, I would like to see everyone drinking wine and spending little money to do it. But at the same time I also would like to see everyone appreciating wine. I question whether that's possible with a mass production.

What disturbs me is the General Motors approach to winemaking. Does General Motors turn out handcrafted cars? No, because that just doesn't happen on an assembly line. General Motors turns out very nice, very ordinary cars. For the most part, they all look alike.

My reaction to wine is this: When it is great, I want to go and shake the winemaker's hand. When it is bad, I want to commiserate with him. And I want people to know that a middle-level winery is not likely

The laboratory at The Christian Brothers winery at St. Helena suggests the importance of modern technology in the winemaking art.

6

to be as good as a higher-level winery. It has to do with grapes, with time, with money.

Good or bad, wine still leaves us with the ability to enjoy something simply because it is good and not because we need to like it. We are getting into an era, however, when we are beginning to enjoy wine simply because it costs a lot of money and we can't afford not to like it. I reject that kind of thinking. Wine was meant to be enjoyed, to be drunk out of nothing but love for the taste.

As big business infiltrates the wine industry, I worry for the future of the little man and the family vineyards. I really think that great wines have to be made small and kept small. Handcrafting is vital. If we are to sustain that, we must be willing to pay for it. Don't expect to see any more inexpensive wines from small wineries. We will have to recognize that to keep them going, we must pay the price. And why shouldn't it be that way? I think a great California wine should command the same price as a great French wine; likewise, a great New York wine should be selling for a price equal to the finest German wines.

The demand for land has put a terrible squeeze on the wine industry. When I began taking an interest in wine twenty years ago, it was easy to buy land in the Napa Valley for under $1,000 an acre. Now it costs a minimum of $5,000 and maybe as high as $10,000. And that acre won't have grapes on it. It costs at least $2,000 to clear it and get it planted and another $1,000 to put in a sprinkler system. The start-up costs, then, run between $10,000 and $15,000 per acre, and the prospective vintner has yet to see a grape — and won't for five years. That's how tough it is. We're in a position today in which a future wine grower must be either a noble, rich man or a big corporation with unlimited financial backing and the foresight to see that once past the initial investment, wine is a very profitable business.

For example, consider the Livermore Valley. To survive as a wine-producing area, it must have some help. The government has to zone, or the property will be taxed to death. The winery will die, after which comes subdivision and development. Concannon, Wente Brothers, and formerly Cresta Blanca, which now is a Mendocino County winery, are feeling the pressure of developers and highway people.

That kind of thing has virtually ruined the Santa Clara Valley, and now the Napa area is being threatened in the same way. Freeway builders want to slit its throat, right down the middle. The best land in California for growing fine wine grapes would soon be gone.

It happened in France not too long ago, too. In Burgundy the bidders actually tried to put a freeway right through the middle of a couple of important vineyards. You could hear the screaming all around the world, and in the end, they put the freeway over the vineyards, not through them.

The hope in the Napa Valley is the Agricultural Preserve, which limits land subdivision to twenty acres or more. Nobody is going to build a subdivision under those conditions.

The wine industry — and particularly the small vintner — also is heavily dependent on the retention of a strong family structure. A winery such as Heitz will live on — or should — if Joe Heitz's children take it over and carry on the same tradition. But if the kids decide they want to do something else

An ancient oak has been carefully bypassed in the rigid symmetry of Paul Masson's Pinnacles vineyard.

Page 206
Approaching a landing at Ontario Airport, a commercial jet glides over the vineyards of Brookside Winery at Guasti, California.

Page 207
Spurred by the current high prices commanded by wine grapes, new ground is being ruthlessly cleared for the planting of vines. In Sonoma County, an old orchard of black walnut trees is uprooted in favor of Vitis vinifera.

Pages 208/209
The ruggedly beautiful Pinnacles National Monument, in California's Salinas Valley, overlooks the most important new premium wine growing district in North America. Pioneered by Paul Masson, Mirrasou and Wente Brothers, it is predicted that a hundred thousand acres of vineyards will be planted in the area by the year 2000. One of the state's smallest wineries, Chalone, is located on a mountain top adjacent to the Pinnacles, and can be seen at the top right center of the photograph (overleaf).

—and who says they won't—then one day Joe Heitz will have to sell, and chances are all that love and care will be a thing of the past. The big money boys would take over then, and if they were vintners and not just developers, there's nothing to stop them from diluting the quality they just got with the mass they may already have.

The presence of big money is always a threat to the wine industry. Even if you have had the most noble of ideals as a part of a long winemaking tradition, it is difficult—if not impossible—to turn down the giant corporate dollar. Suppose you have struggled hard all your life—you love what you are doing but there hasn't been much reward for it—and now all of a sudden some people with a lot of money come around. It is an opportunity for you to have financial security, and most likely, you take it. You would be foolish not to. We have seen a lot of that already—the Beringers sold out and so did the people who owned Beaulieu and Inglenook. The only major family wineries left in the Napa Valley are the Mondavis (at Charles Krug) and the Martinis. Martini is a rather large operation, but they make very fine wines and they are still owned by one family. What happens if people like that decide to sell? For a long time some thought that the villains of the wine industry were the production giants. Not so, for those people are not the villains at all. The real crime, you see, would be in creating any more oversized bulk producers. In the 1970s, our undoing may come from those conglomerates who care little about quality, and whose sole desire is to make money—and wine—fast.

Take the Nestlé people who purchased Beringer and wanted to market perfection. There isn't much question that Nestlé's produces some of the world's finest chocolate —maybe the best—but chocolate can be produced on an assembly line. You want chocolate to taste good but you want it all to taste alike. Nestlé's came to Beringer and I suspect they felt they could make great wine in much the same way, and one day they might. They bought the finest equipment, the best stainless steel tanks, and they have a good winemaker. But at first they had problems; their first wines have not tasted very good. Making wine is not like making chocolate.

The encouraging thing in the case of Nestlé's and Beringer is that there were honest admissions that the wine could have been better. For that reason, I think it's too early to be too critical of an operation such as Beringer. I don't think—I don't expect, anyway—that truly great wines will come easily to them, but admitting that the wine was not all it might have been was a big step in the right direction. I'd like to see Beringer and other major operations like it make two kinds of wine. They could make a truly great wine and at the same time produce good volume wines.

The question really is whether a big winery is capable of making a great wine. The difference between great and good in the semantics of the wine drinker is very large. To make a great wine involves major changes in winemaking philosophy—even to do it on a limited basis. Many bulk wineries insist that what they're doing really is great; they dismiss people like me as idiots —and they may be right!

Paul Masson currently is a good example of a major winery attempting to do something better. With their new holdings in the Pinnacles area, Paul Masson wines have improved, although it's a little early to tell just how far they'll go. The new area is 10,000 acres and it's supposed to be prime growing land. But as encouraging as the Paul Masson holdings are, there is a discouraging side. The fact is they are going to continue to make their wines—from the Pinnacles or any other area—in large quantities. When you make wine for the masses it is difficult to have great wine. Up to now, Paul Masson wines have been somewhere between adequate and satisfactory. It appears as if the new wines will be good ones —possibly great, with greater effort and at considerably higher prices. We're going to see more and more of that kind of wine-making—until we have more of that style of wine than we know what to do with.

It is important that you understand that I am not condemning Paul Masson—or any producer like them—for the wines they produce. I drink their wines all the time; they make very good everyday table wine. The real wine appreciator, you see, is an odd lot. The art appreciator who buys great art doesn't also buy average art; the auto lover who drives a great car doesn't also buy an ordinary one. But the wine drinker does. Having a spectrum of quality available is the thing.

Paul Masson is not the only vintner with extensive new plantings in the areas south of San Francisco. Almadén and Wente Brothers also have made major plantings, and other new vineyards have sprung up all over Monterey County.

Almadén's vineyards in the Paicines area are a magnificent setup, covering over 5,000 acres. Again, everything is first rate.

Whether the wine can reach the "great" status remains to be seen. Chalone is nearby and it makes a magnificent wine, but in such a small quantity that it's almost impossible to buy anywhere. Because of the deliberate pace with which vines grow and mature, we probably won't know for sure about either the Pinnacles or Paicines wine for another twenty years. The newer plantings of Mendocino County fall into that category too.

Another area that is potentially exciting is the area that was the launching pad for California's entry into the world wine market: Baja California in Mexico. Many parts of the Baja have climates similar to those of northern California, and as the wine market mushrooms, this could be a region to watch. Baja's most notable wine-maker at the moment is Dimitri Tchelistcheff, the son of one of California's most storied winemakers—Andre Tchelistcheff. Dimitri learned the techniques of his father, studied at UC Davis, and has brought that knowledge to the Mission de Santo Tomas. Ironically, it is not far from where Father Juan de Ugarte made the first West Coast plantings in 1701. He has planted his own varieties in the Baja—Cabernet Sauvignon, Zinfandel, Pinot Noir, Chardonnay and Chenin Blanc —and they are doing quite well. In time, Santo Tomas could be a premier winery.

I have confidence in young Tchelistcheff because he has that first prerequisite of the winemaker; Like his father, he loves wine. This may seem like pointing out the obvious, but believe me, it isn't. There are too many people—too many supposed craftsmen— who don't love wine, and their product shows it.

T hat's the very problem that's hindering some wine technicians, university trained or otherwise. The great scientists at UC Davis have done superb things — they've made the wine industry a viable one — but a few of the scientists rarely drink wine because they simply aren't exposed to it. Being a scientist is only half of what you need; you also need to be a wine lover. Davis has an abundant supply of scientists and wine lovers. I wish the industry would pay them more heed. But I would also like to see the scientists be more creative, and more critical, to produce for lasting progress.

A few years ago someone brought a scientist friend of mine a great bottle of old sauterne and asked for his opinion of the wine. He replied that it had a certain percentage of acid, a certain percentage of sugar, a certain percentage of this and that; he had it all broken down. It was an interesting analysis. But at no point did he answer that it was good or bad or great or mediocre — because, you know what? He hadn't *tasted* it!

In the end, it comes down to the consumer. He may not know how to make wine or what has gone into its makeup, but his experience tells him enough so that he can taste a wine and know whether it's great or inferior. I think the American consumer who is enthusiastic and experienced in tasting is probably the most knowledgeable consumer in the world, simply because he's probably been exposed to more of the world's fine wines.

I wish more wine technicians and scientists had this tasting experience. (A few do, but most don't.) With that as a balance to their superior technical ability, there would

be no limit to the heights that American wine could reach.

There are good schools of enology and viticulture in this country, but the University of California at Davis — which is northeast of San Francisco, near Sacramento — is clearly the greatest and most innovative, perhaps the best in the world. The Davis operation is truly impressive. They have every possible variety of wine catalogued in bottles in their cellars. It's a monumental achievement and especially invaluable if you are a beginning wine grower. Additionally, Davis has produced a tremendous amount of research. They have elevated the art of winemaking — not only in California but all around the world — but I wonder whether more could be done to elevate the art of wine.

The research of recent years has led to numerous things — to fermenting in stainless steel and even aging in stainless steel; to the importing of French oak to California for use in aging Chardonnay; to hybridizing; to clonal selection (which actually means the "best grape" selection, bringing together the best of the vines and producing a thoroughbred); to a better understanding of malolactic fermentation. A malolactic is a sort of secondary fermentation, one that doesn't necessarily make a better wine, only a more palatable one. This is one of the important reasons why California wines are usually reliable and seldom bad or spoiled. A great deal of fermenting now — and I suspect it will increase in the future — is done under cool conditions. Jackets are put on the stainless steel tanks; the cool, almost cold, conditions return more flavor in white wines, and the fermentation goes much more smoothly. It is very expensive to get the

continued page 226

Twin stainless steel fermenting tanks mirror the blue, cloud-filled sky.

A composition in red and white wines.

The development of a vineyard is a relatively simple task of cultivation. It has been proven that grape vines grow in almost every area of the world, and under the most primitive of conditions.

In fact, it is the belief of many of Europe's most prominent wine producers, that the more difficult a vine's struggle, the better wine it will produce. This philosophy is most apparent in the German river valleys, where the finest white wines in the world are made.

In America, and especially in California, weather and soil pose few problems to the wine grower. Grapes of all varieties have been planted and found to flourish. What is interesting, is to try to detect the subtle taste variations that the soil and climate of different regions impose on the character of a particular wine.

It is this subtlety that makes our domestic wines interesting and appealing. When we begin to discern the qualities of the various wine producing areas, and the gentle nuances they bring to the taste of their wine, then Americans will have found that sense of appreciation that, at present, differentiates us from the French, Germans and Italians, who know the characteristics of their wine producing regions better than they do the the labels of the bottles.

Page 215
Land for a new vineyard, foreground, awaits staking and planting in the Napa Valley.
Page 216
The essential elements of a new vineyard: earth, redwood stakes to support the young shoots, and man's constant attention.
Page 217
Framed by the branches of neighboring trees, a young vineyard flourishes under a warm Sonoma sun.
Pages 218/219
A February fog crowns the mountains that protect Napa Valley vineyards from the damp Pacific coast winter climate.
Pages 220/221
Hovering like some ominous creature out of a science fiction film, a helicopter dusts a vineyard.
Pages 222/223
The efficiently designed machinery of the harvest gives further evidence of the strides made in the processing of grapes.
Pages 224/225
Caught in an unseasonal rain shower, ripened Cabernet Sauvignon await harvest in a Napa Valley vineyard, September, 1972.

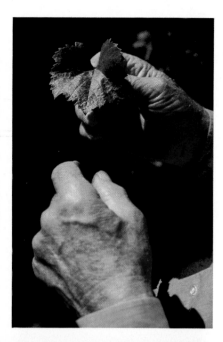

CONVEYOR BIN & SCREW   **MUST PUMP**   **CRUSHER & STEMMER**

STEM SCREW CONVEYOR   **EMERGENCY STOP**

equipment and create those ideal conditions. But it pays long-range rewards in quality.

We have learned a great deal about wines in the past few years, and we will learn more as research progresses. Reflecting on the past, it is almost certain that because of uncontrolled conditions and lack of knowledge, most early wines—certainly nineteenth-century wines—were bad ones. Winemakers simply didn't know how to control the bacteria; or, rather, the bacteria controlled them. In the making of wine, there are certain bacteria you want and certain bacteria you don't want. That's why most modern wineries are so clean, so sterile. The antiseptic conditions protect the investment in the grape.

There has been some experiment—but not a lot—with cuttings and rootstock of European varieties in California over the years. This may be one way to upgrade American wines, but our various governments' concern for imported plants makes it unlikely. When you bring in cuttings or rootstock, you have to put them in a nursery for four or five years when they can be kept under observation. This is an incredible process. A few vines come in, but not enough to matter. Most of our cuttings and rootstock come from our own plants—which, of course, trace their origins back to the varieties of Europe. Interestingly, our rootstock is considered among the finest anywhere.

Meanwhile, work goes on here—at Davis and elsewhere—on crossbred varietals. Professor Harold Olmo of UC Davis and Louis Martini of Napa Valley have perfected the science of clonal selection on various selections of grapes. New varieties—such as Flora, Emerald Riesling, and Ruby Caber-

net—either have made an impact on the California industry or soon will. It is possible that the day will come when there will be a reduction in the number of varietals planted. We may, in fact, concentrate on the noble varietals—the Cabernets and the Chardonnays—and ignore other less popular grapes that produce interesting wines.

I am not against specialization—most of the great wines of France are produced under those kinds of conditions—but at the same time I would hate to see good wines phased out simply because another wine happens to be the most popular of its time. Most of the new vineyards and new plantings have concentrated on Cabernet and Chardonnay, but I strongly suspect that wineries will, if anything, end up making more, not fewer, varieties in the future. The reason why is that various grapes take various lengths of time to produce wine—some very quickly, some very elaborately. That spectrum appeals to the American businessman. Not only that, but because of the length of time a vine takes to mature, it's just not economically practical to obtain a property and then strip it of what it contains and plant, say, Cabernet. That could take at least five years.

Although I don't believe in total specialization, I do feel strongly about vintners producing wines they should not be producing. Certain areas are favorable to certain grapes—the five-region setup in California is a loose definition of what should go where—but a lot of vintners pay no attention. Trying to put together a line of twenty to forty different wines is an impossible task—at least from a quality standpoint. It seems like a terrible compromise. Some vintners do things better than others with one particular grape—and vice versa. If everyone concentrated on producing what was best for him—and I would hope that would be more than just one wine—then you would see some truly fine vintages. One way to encourage the vintner to do just that is to let him know when you are pleased or not.

Regardless of what does or does not happen with specialization, there must be a firm check and balance put on the winemaker regarding the composition of his wine. The law says if you call the wine Chardonnay you must have 51 percent Chardonnay grape in it. Even that's not very much, but tell me who's making sure he puts 51 percent in it? What there really should be are competent boards of tasters in each county to observe and taste the wine continually. The good taster would know, and he could say, "Hey, you can't put that out as Chardonnay. There's not enough Chardonnay character in it. If you're going to market it, you've got to call it something besides Chardonnay."

The California winemakers are very quick to respond to that kind of statement by saying, "Well, that's *my* style of Chardonnay. That's my soil." They don't have that problem in Burgundy. We know what a French burgundy is supposed to taste like. Nobody purports to make a burgundy in Bordeaux. But we'll make a wine called "Chardonnay" in fourteen different counties and produce fourteen different types of Chardonnay. The big wineries, in particular, recoil at the suggestion of local tasting boards. I don't care. I know that California—and perhaps New York, too—is capable of making wine that would make your head swim. We could make such great wines that we could take them over to France and even the French would love them. We have a lot of things going for us—knowledge, soil, climate—everything you need.

The tasting boards could make determinations and restrictions about where to grow specific varietals. They could determine how they are grown, such as not having the rows of grapes too close together (you get better grapes if you have distance between the rows). They could restrict young vines not qualifying as Chardonnay until they've reached a certain stage of maturity. They could classify yield—only so much tonnage could be called Chardonnay and the rest would be called something else because only so much of any crop can be good.

You can't stretch a wine or an area; you can't drain it and milk it. All of these controls and restrictions are a part of the winemaking process in certain areas in France. That's what chateaus like Lafite and Latour are all about. They've been growing principally Cabernet Sauvignon grapes there for 200 years.

It's always difficult to say something is not good because there are always people —the winemaker and all of his followers— who think what they're making and drinking *is* good. I've been around some southern California winemakers who have said, "I don't like those northern wines. They've got too much acid in them. A red burgundy should be sweet." Rubbish. In the first place, the southern winemaker shouldn't be concerning himself with burgundies. He should be making great dessert wines, because he can!

Some of that attitude relates to what you're used to drinking. I suppose that if I had been weaned on sauterne and beef, I'd probably have gotten used to it and probably would like it. So maybe some guy does prefer some sweetness in his burgundy. I don't question that man's taste or his right to that taste. But I won't give up trying to make him see my side of it.

I also don't want to change the style of the winemaker. It reflects on him and on his craft, and winemakers have a tendency to make wines that match the mood of the day. At one time, the wines of Bordeaux were lighter and sweeter; then there was a period of heavy tannin and it took twenty years for the wines to come around. With the demand what it is, the current California style for some is the fast style—the no style.

At the same time, from a few select wineries Californians are finding and drinking bigger and bolder red wines. The Cabernet Sauvignons, Zinfandels and Petite Sirahs of recent years are much bigger in taste, higher in alcohol content, deeper in color, and with a stronger, more lingering finish than ever before.

Grapes selected from a certain area, with a high concentration of sugar or from mature vines, generally produce a bigger wine. Deeper color is produced by leaving the wine on the skins longer. Wine made for longer bottle life also is left on the skins longer. A balance between the flavor of oak and fruit is another facet of style. The predominance of oak or fruit is controlled by the time the wine ages in barrels.

Some wines being produced today may outlive us all. They need many years of bottle aging to develop the nuances and complexities of a well-made old wine. But many wine drinkers are not waiting for these wines to mature and are drinking big wines for the sake of bigness. And bigness in a wine does not necessarily mean greatness.

If the style is only bigness, the wine is one-dimensional in character. Complexities, nuances, and depth of flavor are the things to look for, but these can be achieved only after long bottle aging.

There are many reasons for style changes in wine. Consumers may prefer to drink big, fruity wines young, while another earlier generation might have dismissed the same wine as immature or raw. Today's wine drinkers are generally affluent and they can afford big, fruity wines in the five-dollar to ten-dollar range. Space for wine storage in today's smaller homes is reduced so the consumer cannot lay down wines for years unless he builds special private-storage facilities. Not many people can afford that. On the other hand, the real question is whether we can afford to sacrifice our prime wines to the demands of the moment.

A tasting board—or a governing board, call it what you like—also could attempt to keep some kind of check on the helter-skelter growing of grapes and the ensuing shipping of those grapes to different areas for incorporation in different wines. Almost every grape can be used to make something else. I've seen somebody make something called Zinfandel Blanc out of Zinfandel grapes. And the winemaker doing that might be located in the Napa Valley and the Zinfandel grapes he worked with might have come from the Sonoma Valley. I do not believe this is deception. However, I do not believe the consumer understands this. At one time, not a few Cabernet Sauvignons in California were simply labeled "Claret." Cabernets weren't popular then.

Another restriction that needs to be amended is the one that prohibits a small

A glass of Chalone's 1969 Chardonnay rests invitingly on a fifty-gallon cask at the winery.

Giant redwood aging casks line the cellars at The Christian Brothers.

winemaker from sending his wines across state lines. A wine drinker in Omaha, for example, cannot order directly from the California winery. In most states, California wine must pass from an exporter to a wholesaler to a distributor to a retailer. The cost for that is high; it is not worth it financially for the smaller producer. It is sad to think that you can send a gun through the mail but not a great bottle of wine. How can an out-of-state resident have any impact on California winemakers if he hasn't had a chance to taste their wines? Sadly, the man in Omaha can obtain the very best of European wines, but can't obtain the quality wines of his own country.

The one thing the guy in Omaha does have is a solid base in the tasting of American wines. If he's bought all the American wines available, chances are he's had a lot of mediocre to good table wines. When—and if ever—he gets to the very good and the excellent, he'll appreciate them. One of my pet peeves among wine drinkers is the guy who starts at the wrong end of the spectrum, who likes to think of himself as an instant connoisseur. In the long run, those people are going to hurt the style of wine; they're going to destroy what they purport to love.

In any case, we have not made it easy for the middle-income American who wishes to drink above-average wines. Money will buy anything, of course, but not everyone has an unlimited bank account. It used to be that the fine American wine—from California or New York—was a much better bargain than the European wine. Now there's really no difference. Who knows? The cost of American wines—the great ones—eventually may be higher than the superb wines of Europe. After all, if you want to buy a bottle of '59 Chateau Latour, chances are you can find one; but try to buy a bottle of Chalone from any year. You can't. The quantities made are just that small, and they sell so quickly there's seldom even a public offering. That isn't going to change because Chalone isn't likely to get bigger.

The big wineries *are* going to get bigger, simply because they are able to meet the supply and demand. If people want junk wines, the vintners will oblige. Through all the great popularity of Cold Duck, a lot of people I know said that it was good for the future of wine drinking, that it would bring people into the fold and then they'd work their way up. I don't agree. There's no logic that tells me that the guy who eats regularly at McDonald's is going to evolve into a man who patronizes fine French restaurants.

Another personal pleasure that's fast vanishing is the taster-vintner social relationship. It used to be you could drop in at most wineries, however big or small, and share a glass of wine with the winemaker. Now the small wineries can no longer afford tastings or tasting rooms. The larger ones can offer considerable hospitality, but it is seldom spontaneous, and often your only contact with the winery is through a trained guide who may just as well be showing you the inside of a vegetable-canning factory. The tremendous influx of people to the wineries has led to these situations. In the future, even the larger wineries may be banding together to sponsor public tasting rooms.

Maybe we have created a monster. There is so much pressure on the winemaker now that he no longer is the same accessible man he used to be. A decade ago, you'd drop by a winery and they'd be delighted to see you; they were happy someone cared. Now the tourists arrive in buses. Beaulieu is building a reception center and still offers tour guides. It's the same at Inglenook and Beringer and a lot of others. There's no way to talk with the guy who's doing it. For the most part, the result can be largely impersonal wines.

It seems logical that the solution to the problems—the real ones and the potential ones—should lie in the French method. But that doesn't always work, either. The French have greater family dynasties and are generally wealthier and more entrenched. Not only that, but wine is an integral part of the French economy. If the entire California and New York wine industries were destroyed, who would yell? It wouldn't mean a thing except to a few fanatics like me.

But if Americans really take to wine—really care about it—it has a chance. Attitudes can change. We must learn that demand should not be allowed to pull down the industry, to dilute and stretch the wine. Rather, the winemaker must be encouraged to resist such demands and continue to make complex, exciting wines. If he doesn't, he tampers with my heritage, *our* heritage. And to me, that's what wine is all about.

On the following pages are maps of the most well known and widely traveled wine districts of California and New York. The major wineries of each area have been indicated. All wineries discussed in this book are listed under their proper regions, with page numbers identified for easy reference.

Also in this section you will find information on California and New York wine labels, with clues on how to interpret the required legal language that is most frequently used to write the labels and describe the wine.

Beginning on page 244, the important characteristics of American wines are described in detail. These descriptions have been developed by the Wine Institute as a guide for judges whose responsibility it is to officiate at wine judging competitions. They provide the consumer with an accurate description of what to expect from an individual wine type.

An attractive Californian samples a wine at the colorful Sebastiani Vineyards tasting room in Sonoma.

7

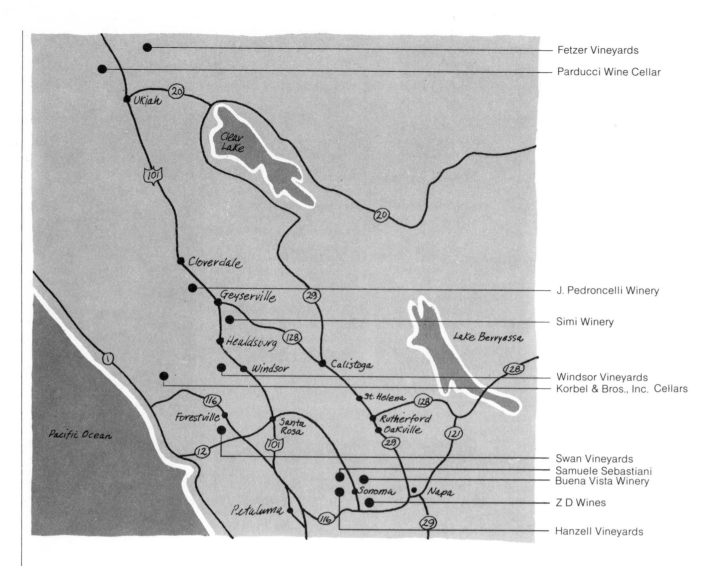

— Fetzer Vineyards

— Parducci Wine Cellar

Ukiah (20)

Clear Lake

(101)

Cloverdale

Geyserville (29) —————— J. Pedroncelli Winery

(128) —————— Simi Winery

Healdsburg

Lake Berryessa

(1)

Windsor *Calistoga* (128) —————— Windsor Vineyards
—————— Korbel & Bros., Inc. Cellars

(116) *St. Helena* (128)

Pacific Ocean *Forestville* *Santa Rosa* *Rutherford Oakville* (121)

(12) (101) (29)

—————— Swan Vineyards
—————— Samuele Sebastiani
—————— Buena Vista Winery

Sonoma *Napa*

—————— Z D Wines

Petaluma (116)

(29) —————— Hanzell Vineyards

SONOMA TO THE PACIFIC

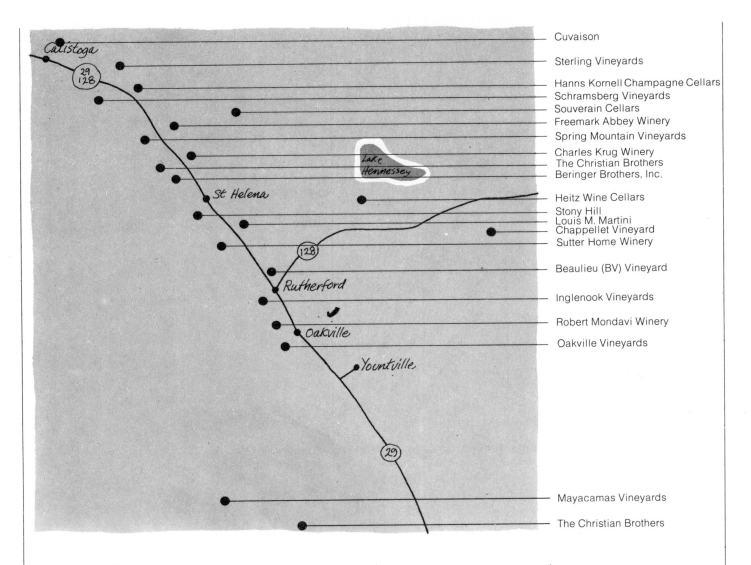

Calistoga
29
128
St Helena
Lake Hennessey
128
Rutherford
Oakville
Yountville
29

Cuvaison
Sterling Vineyards
Hanns Kornell Champagne Cellars
Schramsberg Vineyards
Souverain Cellars
Freemark Abbey Winery
Spring Mountain Vineyards
Charles Krug Winery
The Christian Brothers
Beringer Brothers, Inc.
Heitz Wine Cellars
Stony Hill
Louis M. Martini
Chappellet Vineyard
Sutter Home Winery
Beaulieu (BV) Vineyard
Inglenook Vineyards
Robert Mondavi Winery
Oakville Vineyards
Mayacamas Vineyards
The Christian Brothers

THE NAPA VALLEY

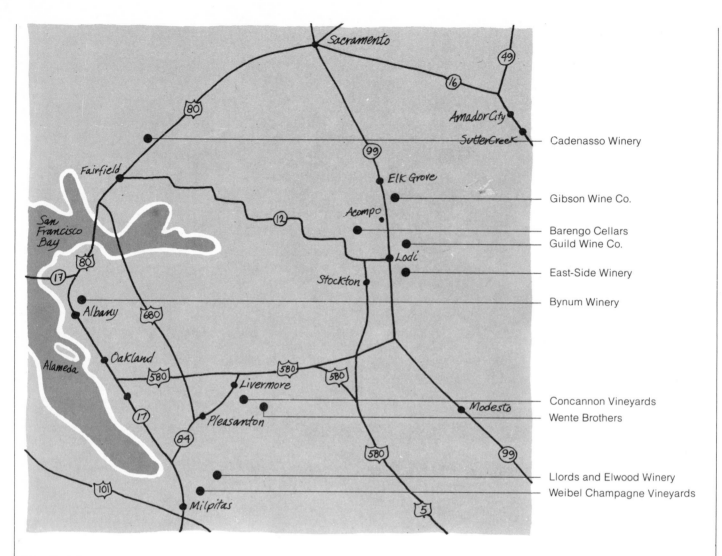

Cadenasso Winery

Gibson Wine Co.

Barengo Cellars
Guild Wine Co.

East-Side Winery

Bynum Winery

Concannon Vineyards
Wente Brothers

Llords and Elwood Winery
Weibel Champagne Vineyards

SAN FRANCISCO BAY EAST TO THE FOOTHILLS

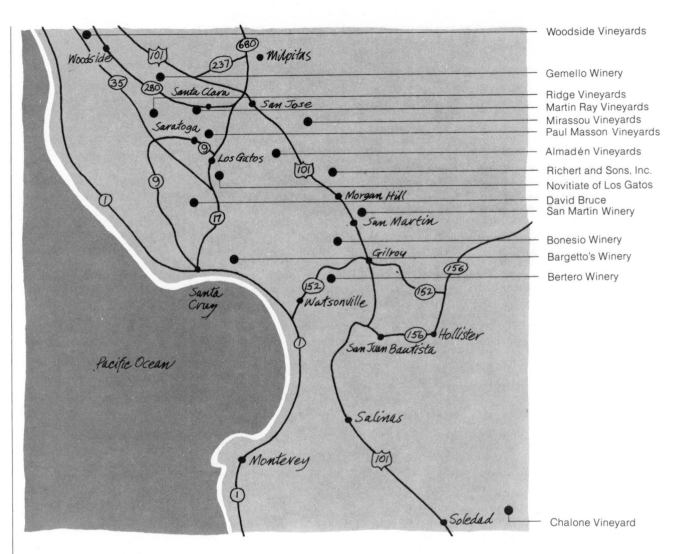

Woodside Vineyards

Gemello Winery

Ridge Vineyards
Martin Ray Vineyards
Mirassou Vineyards
Paul Masson Vineyards

Almadén Vineyards

Richert and Sons, Inc.

Novitiate of Los Gatos

David Bruce
San Martin Winery

Bonesio Winery

Bargetto's Winery

Bertero Winery

Chalone Vineyard

SANTA CLARA AND THE CENTRAL COAST COUNTIES

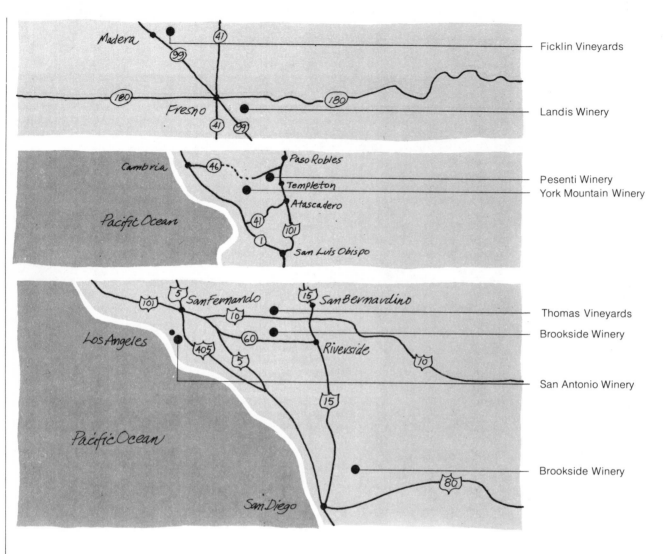

Ficklin Vineyards

Landis Winery

Pesenti Winery
York Mountain Winery

Thomas Vineyards

Brookside Winery

San Antonio Winery

Brookside Winery

SOUTH TO THE BORDER

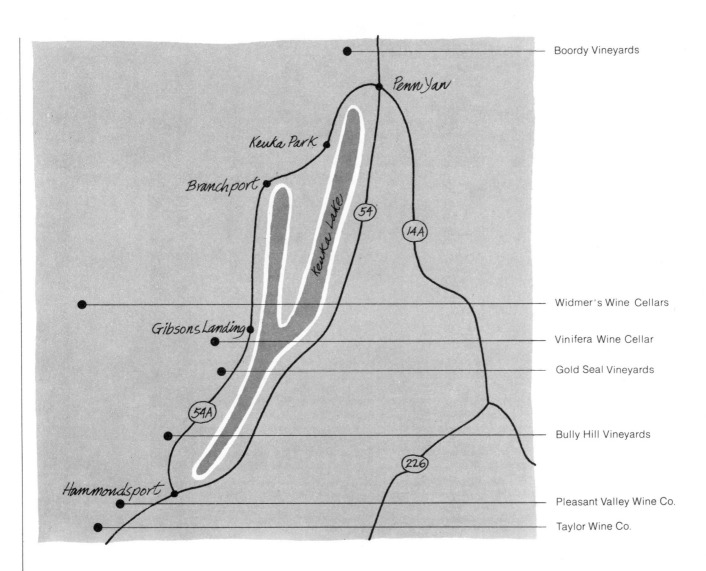

Boordy Vineyards

Penn Yan

Keuka Park

Branchport

54

14A

Keuka Lake

Widmer's Wine Cellars

Vinifera Wine Cellar

Gibsons Landing

Gold Seal Vineyards

54A

Bully Hill Vineyards

226

Hammondsport

Pleasant Valley Wine Co.

Taylor Wine Co.

NEW YORK STATE

Geographic Origin
If a county name appears on a label, the law requires that at least 75 percent of the grapes used to make the wine must have been grown in that designated district. Because of recent expansion of many California wineries to other areas, the rulings on appellation have been broadened. If a winery in one county owns vineyards in another county, it can use the appellation of that district on its label as long as the fermentation and finishing of the wine is done in the state. Some Napa wineries are seeking regulations to prevent wineries outside the county from using the Napa district name on their labels, even though the vintners are using Napa grapes to make the wine. European winemakers have argued for generations over the legal definitions of their district names. The disputes in California — and America — have just begun.

Estate Bottled
This wording indicates that the winery actually has made 100 percent of the wine. Originally, it also meant that all the grapes used to make the wine were grown on vineyards adjacent to the winery. New rulings now stipulate the grapes can be grown anywhere in the county, on land owned by the vintner, or controlled by lease or other agreement.

Some producers, like Concannon, still adhere to the classic definition of Estate Bottled, and limit the term to wines made under personal supervision on a small estate. This is similar to the château and estate bottlings of Europe.

Special Labeling
Many wineries set aside batches of wine and give them a special label, as Concannon has done here. These wines usually cost more, and are superior to wines without the special designation. These terms have no legal meaning, and serve only to convey the vintner's judgment as to which wines he thinks are finer.

Producer
The name of this producer is clearly stated. Concannon is a family operation with 350 acres of vineyards. The winery has a hefty storage and fermenting capacity. Even when a wine comes from a specific vineyard, there is no way for the customer to know this unless there is a specific statement or description of that fact on either the front or back label. The word vineyard doesn't really mean anything. Often, a vineyard name may be used without any such vineyard even existing.

Vintage Dating

Putting a vintage date on a California wine has been a problem because of the strict Federal regulation requiring 100 percent of the wine to be of the year stated; the producer was required to keep records to prove it. Since wine evaporates while aging in barrels before bottling, the barrels must be replenished frequently. Most often, vintners are forced to "top" their wine with wines from a different year.

In 1972, the Federal regulation was amended to allow up to 5 percent of wine from another vintage to be added. Today, a vintage dating on a label means that at least 95 percent of the wine was made from grapes grown and crushed in that year.

The year 1969 on this label means simply that the wine was produced in that year—it is not necessarily of that vintage, unless so specified.

Alcoholic Content

All white table wines must have an alcohol content of 10 to 14 percent by volume. A red table wine must be 10.5 to 14 percent by volume. The law allows a 1½ percent tolerance, either way. If a table wine is made to exceed 14 percent, it must be so stated explicitly on the label. The taxes on such wines are considerably higher. Labels may omit an alcohol statement if they read "table wine" or "light wine," which means they do not exceed 14 percent.

FREEMARK ABBEY

1969
NAPA VALLEY

PINOT CHARDONNAY

Produced and Bottled by
FREEMARK ABBEY WINERY, ST. HELENA, CALIFORNIA

Alcohol 12½% by volume

Varietal Labeling

Because most California table wines are named after the grapes used to produce them, a Federal regulation requires that at least 51 percent of the named grape must be used if the wine is nonvintage. If the wine is vintage dated, then it must contain at least 51 percent of the named grape.

Produced and Bottled By

The vintner does not have to grow the grapes to earn this label designation. Under the new 1972 requirement, he must have fermented and finished at least 75 percent of the wine. Formerly, he also had to crush the grapes, but this is no longer a require-ment. Advanced technology now makes it possible to crush the grapes at the vineyard, following the harvest, and deliver the unfermented must to the winery.

Producer
On California labels the name of the producer, or bottler, is usually the most conspicuous item. It is important to know the reliable winemakers and the characteristics of their label markings.

The label must also give the town in which the winery is located. This, however, is not always as informative as it appears. A winery may open an office anywhere in the state and designate it as its headquarters, regardless of where the wine is made.

Appellation
A label is legally required to say where the wine was made. If less than 75 percent of the wine comes from a specific district, the wine must bear a place name with a broader designation such as North Coastal Counties, or simply, as in the case of this bottle, California. Designations of origin more specific than counties are not used in California. Any wine labeled with the name California — or any area of the state — must be made 100 percent from California grapes.

Wine Type
At one time, the term "mountain" indicated that the grapes used to produce the wine came from vineyards in mountainous regions. It is common knowledge that wines produced from mountain grapes are usually very expensive, for the yield of mountain grapes is much smaller than the yield of valley vineyards.

There appears to be no law governing the use of the term "mountain." Some wineries apply it to wines which are not as good as the rest of their line. The best bet is to find out which are the true mountain wineries, such as Woodside, and try their wines against those which are labeled "mountain." You will probably be surprised by the difference.

When a California wine is labeled simply "red," or has a generic name such as burgundy, claret, or chianti, the wine is the result of a blend of grapes. Some wineries describe the grapes used to blend the wine on the back label. Others do not.

Produced and Bottled By
This term requires the winery to have made at least 75 percent of the wine in the bottle — though, like Woodside, it may well have made all of it.

Another phrase, Made and bottled by, is often seen. This means much less than it would seem. The vintner must produce some of his wine — supposedly 10 percent — and blend or change it in some way. Federal law requires a minimum Bottled by, with the bottler's name and place of business. This designation tells the consumer that the wine was purchased from, or made by, another winery.

Vintage
This neck label indicates the wine in the bottle was made from grapes grown and fermented in the year stated. It is an assurance, also, that at least 95 percent of the named grape was used to produce the wine. If only the year appears on a label, without the word vintage, the consumer is assured that the wine was bottled in the stated year, but that the wine is not necessarily of that vintage.

Appellation
The Federal labeling regulation requires that 75 percent of the wine in the bottle must be produced from grapes grown in a district if it is stated on the label. In New York, Finger Lakes and New York State are the most common appellations named.

If more than 25 percent of the grapes used to make the wine come from somewhere else, a broader appellation is used. Because many New York wines contain more than 25 percent of California blending wines, the label appellation is often changed to read American. With the recent large plantings of French hybrid grapes in New York State, vintners are now able to supply their own neutral blending wines, rather than importing them. This protects their local appellations of origin, and even allows for an Estate Bottled designation, such as this bottle from Bully Hill, which indicates the vintner grew all his own grapes and fermented all the wine.

Name and address
All American wines must state the name and address of the bottler or packer on the label.

Alcoholic Content
The law requires that alcoholic content must be stated on the label of wines containing more than 14 percent alcohol by volume, the alcoholic content must be stated, or the label must be marked with the designation "dinner" wine (light wine or table wine).

Wine Type
Seyval Blanc is an Americanized varietal name given to the French hybrid Seyve-Villard 5276. The wine is rich and full flavored and reminiscent of Chardonnay. Many New York State wines are made from, or blended with, French hybrid grapes, the most popular being Baco Noir, Seibel, Maréchal Foch, Chelois, Chancellor, and Aurora.

To bear a varietal name, a wine must derive at least 51 percent of its volume from the grape whose name is used, and must have the flavor and aroma of that grape. Some varietal wines are made 100 percent from the grapes named; others include other grapes in their blends.

Many New York wine labels carry both a varietal and generic name to describe certain wines, a practice that attempts to guide the consumer to a style of wine he may prefer, even if he does not relate to the name of the principal grape stated. An example would be Baco Noir Burgundy, an attempt to convince the buyer that the wine in the bottle is a burgundy type. Because Baco Noir is the stated grape, the consumer may be assured that at least 51 percent of the grapes used in the wine are of that variety.

Produced and bottled by
The significance of this term is that the vintner crushed, fermented, matured, and bottled at least 75 percent of the wine in the bottle.

Many large wineries often exchange wines with one another to maintain balanced inventories, and regularly contract with other cellars to use their bulk wines. This practice allows for the use of the term Made and bottled by, which, as explained in the California labeling section, means less than it would appear.

The following definitions are recommended wine type specifications which have been developed by the Wine Institute Technical Advisory Committee for guidance of judges at wine-tasting competitions. They are the result of long and thoughtful discussions, but the terms are meaningless unless examined with a bottle of wine close at hand. For the neophyte wine drinker the recommendations will make no sense at all until he puts them all together with a wide range of wine-tasting experience.

Red Table Wines

Varietals

Barbera

A dry red table wine produced of Barbera grapes. In this type the heavier-bodied and darker-colored wines should be on an equal basis with the lighter-bodied and lighter-colored wines. In addition to the pronounced varietal aroma and flavor of the Barbera grape, these wines should possess a distinguishable high total acidity.

Cabernet Sauvignon

A dry red table wine produced of Cabernet Sauvignon grapes. In this type the heavier-bodied and darker-colored wines should be on an equal basis with the lighter-bodied and lighter-colored wines. It should be well balanced and aged. It should have a distinctive bottle bouquet.

Gamay

A dry red table wine produced of the Gamay grape. In this type the heavier-bodied and darker-colored wines should be on equal basis with the lighter-bodied and lighter-colored wines. The varietal aroma and flavor of the grape should be pronounced.

Grignolino

A dry red table wine produced of the Grignolino grape. The varietal flavor of the Grignolino grape should be pronounced. This wine type should be medium-bodied; the color varies from orange red to medium red. It should be aged sufficiently to produce the natural astringency to a palatable level.

Pinot Noir

A dry red table wine produced of Pinot Noir grapes. In this type the heavier-bodied and darker-colored wines should be on an equal basis with the lighter-bodied and lighter-colored wines. One of the main distinguishable characteristics is the relatively soft and smooth flavor. It should be well balanced and well aged. The varietal aroma and flavor of the Pinot Noir grape should be pronounced.

Red or Black Pinot

A dry red table wine type produced of Red Pinot grapes such as Pinot St. George, Pinot Meunier, and Pinot Pernand. The varietal aroma and flavor of the Pinot grape should be pronounced. In this type the heavier-bodied and darker-colored wines should be on an equal basis with the lighter-bodied and lighter-colored wines.

Zinfandel

A dry red table wine produced of Zinfandel grapes. In this type the heavier-bodied and darker-colored wines should be on an equal basis with the lighter-bodied and lighter-colored wines. It should be of moderate aging, well balanced, and should have the fruity aroma characteristic of the variety.

Generics

Burgundy

A dry table wine type called California burgundy should be medium to deep red in color and full-bodied. It should have balance and softness on the palate derived from proper aging.

Chianti

A dry red table wine type of medium red color, medium tartness, fruity and full-bodied. It should be moderately aged and well balanced.

Claret

The dry table wine called California claret should be light to medium red in color, tart, of light or medium body.

Red Table Wine

It is recommended that any red table wine containing not over 1.5 percent reducing sugar not specifically named in the foregoing recommendations be automatically judged in the class known as California Red Table Wine. It is recommended that wines with varietal or generic names entered into this class (for judging in exhibitions) be grouped together by name and that such groups be judged in an appropriate sequence. These wines should be judged on their general elements of quality rather than characteristics of any particular variety of grape unless they have a varietal label, in which case they will be judged on the appropriate varietal character. In this type the heavier-bodied and darker-colored wine should be on an equal basis with the lighter-bodied and lighter-colored wine. An amber color is objectionable.

Sweet Red Table Wine

The wines in this class should have the same characteristics as California red table wine with the exception that the reducing sugar should be above 1.5 percent.

White Table Wines

Varietals

Chardonnay

A dry white table wine produced from Pinot Chardonnay grapes possessing pronounced amount of varietal aroma and flavor of the Pinot Chardonnay grape. It should be medium- to full-bodied with medium acidity, pale to light golden in color, and have a good bottle bouquet.

Chenin Blanc (White Pinot)

A dry white table wine produced from Chenin Blanc (White Pinot, Pinot de la Loire) grapes. The flavor and aroma of the Chenin Blanc grape (White Pinot, Pinot de la Loire) should be pronounced. It should be tart, light-bodied, and have a good bottle bouquet.

Colombard

A dry white table wine produced from the French Colombard grapes. This wine should be pale to light golden in color, medium-bodied, fruity, and of medium acidity.

Folle Blanche

A dry white table wine produced from the Folle Blanche grapes. It should be light in color and body, tart, fruity, and fresh.

Grey Riesling

A dry white table wine produced from Grey Riesling grapes. It should be light straw to straw in color. It should have a distinguishable varietal aroma and flavor, be medium-bodied, and of medium acidity. It should have a good bottle bouquet.

Johannisberg (White) Riesling

A dry white table wine produced from White (Johannisberg) Riesling grapes. It should be light straw in color, preferably with a slight greenish tinge. It should have a distinguishable varietal aroma and flavor, be fruity, medium- to full-bodied, and rather tart. It should have a good bottle bouquet.

Light Sweet Muscat

A white table wine produced of Muscat grapes. The table wine called Light Sweet Muscat should have unmistakable Muscat aroma and flavor. It should have more than 6 percent reducing sugar. It should be medium- to full-bodied and well balanced. It should be light golden to golden in color.

Pinot Blanc

A dry white table wine produced from Pinot Blanc grapes. The flavor and aroma of the Pinot Blanc grapes should be pronounced. It should be moderately tart, medium-bodied, and have a good bottle bouquet.

Sauvignon Blanc

A white table wine produced of Sauvignon Blanc grapes. It should be straw to light golden in color. It should have a strong, easily distinguishable varietal aroma and flavor, medium acidity, and be full-bodied. It should have a good bottle bouquet. The reducing sugar should not be over 1.5 percent.

Sweet Sauvignon Blanc

The wine in this class should have the same characteristics as Sauvignon Blanc with the exception that the reducing sugar should be above 1.5 percent.

Sémillon

A white table wine produced of Sémillon grapes. It may have a color ranging from straw to gold. It should be soft and mellow and have a full body. It should have a strong, easily distinguishable varietal aroma and flavor. It should have a good bottle bouquet. The reducing sugar should not be over 1.5 percent.

Sweet Sémillon

The wine in this class should have the same characteristics as California Sémillon with the exception that the reducing sugar should be above 1.5 percent.

Sylvaner (Franken Riesling)

A dry white table wine produced from Sylvaner (Franken Riesling) grapes. It should be light straw in color, preferably with a slight greenish tinge. It should have a distinguishable varietal aroma and flavor, be fruity, medium-bodied, and of medium acidity. It should have good bottle bouquet.

Traminer (Gewürztraminer)

This wine should be straw to light golden in color. It should have easily distinguishable varietal aroma and flavor which is spicy and almost muscatlike. It should be of medium body and medium acidity and have a good bottle bouquet.

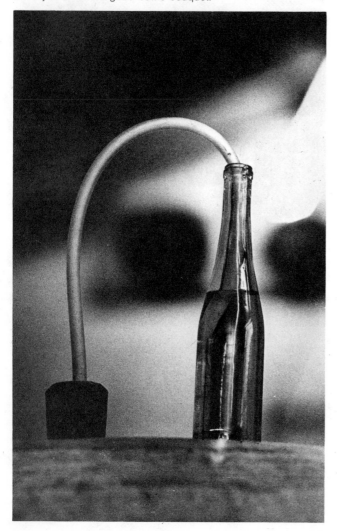

Generics

Chablis

The white table wine called California chablis should be light to medium straw in color. It should be light- to medium-bodied, of medium acidity, fruity, well balanced, and have a good bottle bouquet.

Riesling (Rhine)

The white table wine called California rhine or California riesling should be pale to medium straw in color. It should be medium-bodied, of medium acidity to tart, fresh and fruity, and have a good bottle bouquet.

Sauterne

The table wine type called California sauterne should be straw to light golden color, full-bodied without noticeable high acidity, and contain not over 1.5 percent reducing sugar. It should have balance and softness on the palate and a good bottle bouquet.

California Dry White Table Wine

It is recommended that any dry white table wine not specifically named in these specifications be automatically judged in a class to be known as California Dry White Table Wine. It is recommended that wines with varietal or generic names entered in this class be grouped together by name and that such groups be judged in an appropriate sequence. The wines should be judged on their general elements of quality rather than characteristics of any particular variety of grapes unless they have a varietal character. The color may range from pale straw to golden; they should be well balanced on the palate. The reducing sugar should be less than 1.0 percent.

Rosé Table Wines

Generics

Rosé

A dry table wine called rosé should be fruity, light, and tart. The color should be pink and should not have an amber tint. A noticeable Muscat aroma is undesirable in rosé.

Sweet Rosé

This rosé should have the same characteristics as rosé with the exception that the reducing sugar should be above 0.5 percent. A noticeable Muscat aroma is undesirable in sweet rosé.

Sparkling Wines

The Wine Institute states that the general specifications for sparkling wines, bottle-fermented or bulk process, are the same as for red and white still wines under 14 percent alcohol respectively. In addition, the sparkling wines must have been made naturally effervescent by a second fermentation within closed containers. Bottle and bulk-fermented champagne should be judged in two different classes.

Champagne

California champagne should be pale to straw color. It should have a good acidity and body. It should be fresh, fruity, well balanced, and show a distinctive bottle bouquet. It is recommended that champagne be rated in three groups according to sweetness, as follows:

Reducing Sugars in Percent

Group 1	0.0-1.5
Group 2	1.5-3.0
Group 3	Over 3.0

Champagne Rouge and Sparkling Burgundy

In this type the heavier-bodied and darker-colored wines should be on an equal basis with the lighter-bodied and lighter-colored wines. It should have a good acidity and be semisweet to sweet. Reducing sugar should be 1.5 percent or over. It should be fruity, smooth, and well balanced, and show distinctive bottle bouquet.

Cold Duck

A blend of approximately one-half California champagne and approximately one-half California sparkling burgundy. The color should be light red; an amber color is objectionable. It should be semisweet to sweet, having a reducing sugar of 1.5 percent or over. It may or may not have a recognizable labrusca flavor derived from *Vitis labrusca* grapes grown in California.

Pink Champagne

The color of this wine type should be pink and not have an amber tint. It should be fruity, fresh, light-bodied, tart, and well balanced. The reducing sugar should be 1.5 percent or over.

Sparkling Muscat

California sparkling Muscat should be pale to straw color, have good acidity and body. It should be fresh, fruity, well balanced, and have the unmistakable flavor and aroma of Muscat grapes. The reducing sugar should be 4 percent or over.

Dessert and Aperitif Wines

The wines called aperitif wines may range from light-flavored types to extremely strong, bitter types. The color may range from white, amber, or tawny to dark red. They may vary in sugar content from dry to sweet; they should be aromatic and well blended. A Muscat character is permissible.

Black Muscat

California Black Muscat should be medium to deep red, rich, fruity, and full-bodied, with a pronounced Muscat aroma and flavor derived from the Black Hamburg and Aleatico grapes. It should be fruity and show balance derived from proper aging.

Dry Sherry

This wine should be light straw to light amber in color, be nutty, and have a well-developed sherry character without any burnt taste. A flor sherry flavor and aroma is permissible. It should be light in body but mellow. Under California law, the reducing sugar should be lower than 2.5 percent.

Medium Sherry

This wine type should be light golden amber to medium golden amber in color, medium-bodied, nutty, and have a well-developed sherry character without any burnt taste. A flor sherry flavor and aroma is permissible. Under California law the sugar content should be between 2.5 and 4.0 percent.

Angelica

California angelica should be smooth, fruity in flavor, and full-bodied. The lighter colored wines should be on an equal basis with the dark amber wines. It should have moderate acidity.

Muscat

A white table wine produced of Muscat grapes. The table wine called Light Sweet Muscat should have unmistakable Muscat aroma and flavor. It should have more than 6 percent reducing sugar. It should be medium- to full-bodied and well balanced. It should be light golden to golden in color.

Muscat de Frontignan or Muscat Canelli

These wines should have the same characteristics as California muscatel and possess the pronounced rich, delicate Muscat character of the grape for which they are named. It should be fruity and show balance derived from proper aging.

Muscatel

California muscatel should be rich, fruity, and full-bodied with an unmistakable aroma and flavor of Muscat grapes. It may range in color from straw to amber and should have moderate acidity.

Port

California port should be medium to deep ruby red in color (amber color is objectionable). It should be rich, fruity, and well bodied, and have moderate acidity.

Sweet Sherry

This wine type should be medium to dark amber in color, full-bodied, rich and nutty, with a well-developed sherry character. It should be well balanced and smooth without any burnt taste. A flor sherry flavor and aroma is permissible. Under California law, the sugar content should be not less than 4 percent.

Tawny Port

California tawny port should be reddish brown and/or tawny color. It should be well matured, showing considerable aging.

Tokay

This is a blended wine. The amber-colored wines with a pinkish tint should be on an equal basis with the light red wines with an amber tint; a slight nutty sherry taste and light fruitiness is desirable. It should be mellow, well balanced, and have medium acidity. Light Muscat flavor and aroma are permissible in tokay.

White Port

California white port should be neutral in flavor, light straw to pale gold in color, smooth and medium- to full-bodied. It should be fresh and mellow.

Other Dessert Wines

Other than types listed: It is recommended that any California dessert wine not specifically named in the foregoing specifications be automatically judged in a class to be known as California Dessert Wine Other Than Types Listed. It is recommended that these wines with varietal or generic names entered into this class be grouped together by name and that the groups be judged in an appropriate sequence. This is a group which shall include only blended types or processed types; for example, marsala, other than types listed elsewhere but without flavors added. These wines may vary in color and general flavor characteristics.

California Dry Vermouth

The herb-flavored wine called California dry vermouth should be light in color. The sugar content should range from almost dry to not over 4 percent. The herb character should be well blended. While the herb flavor should be sufficient, not one single herb should be recognizable. Excessive bitterness is objectionable. Under California law the alcohol content must be above 15 percent by volume.

California Sweet Vermouth

The herb-flavored appetizer wine called California sweet vermouth should be from amber to dark amber in color. The herb character should be pronounced and well balanced. The wine should be full-bodied, well blended, smooth, with well-developed fragrance. Excessive bitterness is objectionable. A light Muscat flavor is permissible. Under California law, the alcohol content should be above 15 percent by volume.

TASTING NOTES

Wine: _____ Vintage: _____ Producer: _____

Date Acquired: _____ Purchase Price: _____ Date Served: _____

Comments: _____

_____

Wine: _____ Vintage: _____ Producer: _____

Date Acquired: _____ Purchase Price: _____ Date Served: _____

Comments: _____

_____

Wine: _____ Vintage: _____ Producer: _____

Date Acquired: _____ Purchase Price: _____ Date Served: _____

Comments: _____

_____

Wine: _____ Vintage: _____ Producer: _____

Date Acquired: _____ Purchase Price: _____ Date Served: _____

Comments: _____

_____

Wine: _____ Vintage: _____ Producer: _____

Date Acquired: _____ Purchase Price: _____ Date Served: _____

Comments: _____

_____

Wine: _____ Vintage: _____ Producer: _____

Date Acquired: _____ Purchase Price: _____ Date Served: _____

Comments: _____

_____

Wine: _____ Vintage: _____ Producer: _____

Date Acquired: _____ Purchase Price: _____ Date Served: _____

Comments: _____

_____

Wine: _____ Vintage: _____ Producer: _____

Date Acquired: _____ Purchase Price: _____ Date Served: _____

Comments: _____

_____

Wine: _____ Vintage: _____ Producer: _____

Date Acquired: _____ Purchase Price: _____ Date Served: _____

Comments: _____

_____

Wine: _____ Vintage: _____ Producer: _____

Date Acquired: _____ Purchase Price: _____ Date Served: _____

Comments: _____

_____

Wine: _____ Vintage: _____ Producer: _____

Date Acquired: _____ Purchase Price: _____ Date Served: _____

Comments: _____

_____

Wine: _____ Vintage: _____ Producer: _____

Date Acquired: _____ Purchase Price: _____ Date Served: _____

Comments: _____

_____

Wine: _____ Vintage: _____ Producer: _____

Date Acquired: _____ Purchase Price: _____ Date Served: _____

Comments: _____

_____

Wine: _____ Vintage: _____ Producer: _____

Date Acquired: _____ Purchase Price: _____ Date Served: _____

Comments: _____

_____

Wine: _____ Vintage: _____ Producer: _____

Date Acquired: _____ Purchase Price: _____ Date Served: _____

Comments: _____

_____

Wine: _____ Vintage: _____ Producer: _____

Date Acquired: _____ Purchase Price: _____ Date Served: _____

Comments: _____

_____

Wine: _____ Vintage: _____ Producer: _____

Date Acquired: _____ Purchase Price: _____ Date Served: _____

Comments: _____

_____

Wine: _____ Vintage: _____ Producer: _____

Date Acquired: _____ Purchase Price: _____ Date Served: _____

Comments: _____

_____

Wine: _____ Vintage: _____ Producer: _____

Date Acquired: _____ Purchase Price: _____ Date Served: _____

Comments: _____

_____

Wine: _____ Vintage: _____ Producer: _____

Date Acquired: _____ Purchase Price: _____ Date Served: _____

Comments: _____

_____

Nathan Chroman is a Beverly Hills, California, attorney who, for more than two decades, has made the study and tasting of wine more than an avocation. His credentials are impeccable: He writes a weekly wine column for the *Los Angeles Times;* he teaches a course in wine appreciation at UCLA Extension; he is chairman of the wine-judging committee for the Los Angeles County Fair; he selects and purchases the wine for the noted Los Angeles restaurant Scandia; and he is a contributing editor to *Wine World* magazine. He lives in West Los Angeles with his wife, Judie, and three daughters. *The Treasury of American Wines* is Mr. Chroman's first book.

The writing of a book about wine requires the benefit of research, information, and the bottles of others so numerous that one could fill a nebuchadnezzar brim full with acknowledgments and still not mention all concerned.

I sincerely acknowledge that my most precious informational and research source has been the grape, that is, wine itself. For it has been wine that has supplied the tasting experiences that are the basis of this book. Its contribution is incalculable, never ending, ever pleasure producing, and most of all truthful.

I wish to thank especially Darrel Corti, wine merchant, for his invaluable help in providing counsel for the manuscript and, in particular, information concerning some of California's smaller wineries. Another whose help was also invaluable is Dr. James F. Guymon, Professor of Enology, University of California, Department of Viticulture and Enology, whose palate is as great as his knowledge; I am thankful particularly for the number of corrections he recommended, which were gratefully accepted. Any mistakes in the book I acknowledge as my own; they cannot be attributed to either gentlemen, whose knowledge and company I have enjoyed over the years.

Heartfelt gratitude is due John Wiebusch, author, editor, and journalist, who helped me organize my thoughts, and to David Boss, who first envisioned this book and me as its author, and who literally pushed me into attempting it. Since wine-tasting lawyers do not ordinarily write, it took the extraordinary enthusiasm of David to get me to do it. I shall be forever grateful for his patience, direction, and companionship.

For encouraging me to write in the first place, I would like to thank Jeanne A. Voltz, former food editor of the Los Angeles Times, now food editor of Woman's Day magazine. She forced me to meet the weekly deadline of a wine column and, with considerable optimism, once told me, "One day you'll write a wine book."

Tasting experiences do not come easy. The opportunity to taste in fine surroundings with some of the world's finest food has been provided by my close friend Kenneth Hansen, restaurateur extraordinaire and proud owner of Scandia Restaurant of Los Angeles. Every Friday, for fifteen years, he has allowed—indeed encouraged—me to taste a glass of wine or two or three with him at luncheon, and much of this book is the sharing of those tasting experiences. No question, Kenneth's help may be the most important of all.

A special tribute goes to Harry G. Serlis of the California Wine Institute, as well as its efficient staff, whose assistance provided invaluable research material enabling me to rely on such important historical material as that of Herbert B. Leggett and Vincent P. Carosso. Technical Director Hugh Cook, Roy Taylor, Wine Consultant, and Larry Cahn were of especial help. In the same breath, a special thanks to Allen Arthur.

For providing me with the opportunity to teach the appreciation of wine, which I have enjoyed doing for over a decade through University Extension, University of California, Los Angeles, I must thank Robert Bartlett Haas, Director of Arts and Humanities of that worthy institution, and his assistant, Elizabeth M. Anderson. They have enabled me to teach, and it is through teaching that I have learned.

For assisting me in the tasting-learning process, I acknowledge the great opportunity to taste provided me by the Los Angeles County Fair Association, whose judgings I've had the privilege to head under the supervision of Phil Shepherd, Executive Secretary of the Fair, and my immediate superior, Earl Wilkenson.

Over the years, a tasting quartet has been of special help: Richard Foster of Ridge Vineyards, whose cellar always has one more interesting bottle for me to taste; Roy P. Brady, wine writer, who supplied both bottles and information of the first magnitude; and Dr. and Mrs. Bernard Rhodes, Oakland, California, whose gracious provision from their own cellar is only exceeded by their charm, their accuracy, and their honesty of palate.

It goes without saying that no book about American wines can be written without reference to, and understanding of, the expertise and wealth of information at the University of California, Department of Viticulture and Enology, Davis, California. I have enjoyed in particular the works of Dr. Maynard A. Amerine, Dr. Albert J. Winkler, Dr. Harold P. Olmo, Dr. Vernon Singleton, Dr. James Cook, Dr. Dinsmoor Webb, Dr. Maynard A. Joslyn, and Professor Harold Berg. Thanks as well to Dr. George Cooke of Agriculture Extension of that University for his enabling me to take special courses in wine and winemaking.

Nor could any book on American wines be written without the statistical and informational data of Philip Hiarings, Wines and Vines, its annual directory, and Charles H. Van Kriedt, California Wine Letter.

I could not have done without the books, pamphlets, and works of such acknowledged giants in wine writing as Philip Wagner, Frank Schoonmaker, Alexis Lichine, Dr. Konstantin Frank, John Melville, M. F. K. Fisher, Leon Adams, the late André Simon, Harry Waugh, Michael Broadbent, Morrison Wood, John Weaver, Robert Thompson, and Henry Rubin. Especial thanks to Dr. George "Jud" Hummer, whose medical wine information and palate is impeccable.

Over the years, I have enjoyed the company of many friends more than the wine they have supplied me, and they cannot go unmentioned. In no particular order I should like to acknowledge and thank the following: Marvin Zeidler, Greg Doerschlag, John Sola, Ty Jurras, Dr. Dale Hurley, Dr. George Linton, Narsai David, Robert Myerson, James Myerson, Allen Berlin, Dr. Terry Turkat, Fulton W. Haight, Joseph Harris, Marvin Moss, Dr. Leopold Tuchman, Joseph Rossi Walsh, Miklos Dora, Philippe Cottin, Robert Currie, Dr. Richard Alexander, Dr. Leonard Apt, Dr. Ben Ichinose, Dr. Robert Adamson, Dr. and Mrs. Stanley Burton, Joe Heitz, Jack Davies, Donn Chappellet, Brother Timothy, Richard C. Maddox, Grafton Tanquary, Jack A. Levin, Dr. Paul Scholten, Dr. Jack Tupper, John R. Martin, Dr. Arthur Dostrow, Dr. Richard Ritter, Dr. Burns Steele, Sam Stone, J. "Mike" Elwood, Richard Elwood, Joel Chroman, David Moss, James Meyler, Rick Jason, William W. Haines, Stoney Mayoc, Hershey Eisenberg, Paul Leserman, Dr. Albert Katz, Fred Boreman, Eugene Brown, James Barrett, John Dugan, Dr. Ronald Decker, Sebastian Cabot, Dr. Bernice Ennis, Rolfe Engen, Mr. and Mrs. Milton Eisle, Fred Holmes, Dr. Tobie Chroman, Robert Frank, the late Gallantin Powers, Lester Gruber, the late Silas Spitzer, Louis Gomberg, Rabbi Meyer Heller, Robert Haas, James Hanyen, A. C. McNally, Gregg Reynolds, Chef Gregoire Le Balch, Howard Huntington, S. F. Hallgarten, Hal Jurgensen, Rubin Lazar, Bernard de la Giradiere, John Stork, Richard Miller, Dr. Seth MacArthur, Ed Kressman, Wm. Lawson Martin, Henry Martin, Murray Neftin, Pierre Dourthe, Bruno Petoletti, Dr. Angew Pelligrini, Chef George Petersen, Glenn Ford, Willy Reuter, Congressman Thomas Rees, Maurice Sandahl, Dr. William Swanson, Robert Riddel, Richard Slavin, Peter Sichel, Leonard Shannon, Alex Kaluzny, Jerry Magnin, Robert Jany, Sid Greenberg, William Burkhart, William Shapiro, John Stahr, Stan Friedman, Kenneth Kew, Karl Petrowsky, Robert L. Balzer, John Movius, Raymond Andrieux, Jean Leon, Charles Kenis, Dr. Warren Cutting, Paul Marinkovich, James Van Renssalaer, the late Harold Richardson, the late Walt Petersen, Richard J. Collins, Ray Beindorf, Robert Cramer, Robert Bell, Hernando Courtwright, Dr. John Ragan, Jerome H. Rhodes, Richard Sherwin, Dr. Albert H. Lerner, Arne Terslin, Chef Mike Roy, Garth Hintz, Alex Perino, Judge Thomas Johnson, Mrs. Lois Dwan, Vittorio Sanguinetti, Eugene Donofrio, Irwin Daniels, Ray Silverman, George Starke, Mrs. Elizabeth Milius, Harold Edwards, Dr. Harry Leavitt, Don Sahlein, Jack Buchtel, Charles Elkins, Dr. Jack Weintraub, Jack Levin, Earl Nelson, the great trio Bennion, Crane, and Rosen, Dr. Leo A. Parker, James Norris, David Packer, Bud Berke, Robert Jany, Steve Mirassou, Jean Bourgeoise.

A most special acknowledgment to the late Robert Meyler, who shared with me the "old California rarities" of his cellar dating back to the 1890's. His knowledge and cellar were an inspiration and an education of grand cru proportions!

PHOTOGRAPHY CREDITS

David Boss
12, 19, 22-23, 34, 67a, b; 68-69, 87b, 88a, 89a, b; 114-115, 118-119, 172, 174-175, 177, 178, 181, 182-183, 186-187, 188, 189, 190-191, 192, 193, 194, 196, 198, 201, 213.

J. E. Cakebread
51, 61, 65, 66, 67a, 70-71, 73, 74b, 75, 76, 77a, b; 78-79, 82, 83, 84, 85, 87a, 90, 91, 92, 93, 94, 95, 97, 98, 99, 100b, 102, 103, 104, 105, 106, 107, 108, 109, 110, 111, 113, 120, 121, 122, 123, 124, 125, 126, 127a, 129, 130, 131, 132, 133a, 134c, 135, 136, 137, 138, 140, 141, 142, 143, 144, 145, 146, 147, 148, 149, 150b, 151, 152, 153, 154, 155, 156, 157, 158, 159, 160, 161,ʼ162, 163, 164, 165, 168, 202, 207, 208-209, 215, 218-219, 228, 244, 245a, 248a, 249b.

Stan Caplan Studio
Dust Jacket and all individual wine bottles.

Escalante and Johnston
Maps

J. Richard Forbes
5, 6, 7, 8, 9, 10-11, 30-31, 42, 43, 46, 47, 72, 77c, 80-81, 86, 88b, 96, 100a, 101, 116-117, 127b, 133b, 134a, b; 135-136, 150a, 166, 167, 169, 170-171,

196a, 205, 206, 212, 216, 217, 220-221, 224-225, 229, 232, 245b, 246, 247, 248b, 249a.

John E. Martin
184, 197, 199, 200.

Mision de Santo Tomas
196b.

Title Insurance Company
26, 33.

Martin Ray
139.

Seneca Foods Corp
185a, b.

Wine Institute
23 (Mission Grapes), 27, 28, 74a, 128.

Yale University
20.